Lecture Notes in Computer Science   13072

More information about this subseries at https://link.springer.com/bookseries/7411

Konstantinos Tserpes · Jörn Altmann ·
José Ángel Bañares · Orna Agmon Ben-Yehuda ·
Karim Djemame · Vlado Stankovski ·
Bruno Tuffin (Eds.)

Economics of Grids, Clouds, Systems, and Services

18th International Conference, GECON 2021
Virtual Event, September 21–23, 2021
Proceedings

 Springer

Editors
Konstantinos Tserpes ⓘ
Harokopio University
Athens, Greece

José Ángel Bañares ⓘ
University of Zaragoza
Zaragoza, Spain

Karim Djemame ⓘ
University of Leeds
Leeds, UK

Bruno Tuffin ⓘ
Inria Rennes - Bretagne Atlantique Research
Centre
Rennes, France

Jörn Altmann ⓘ
Seoul National University
Seoul, Korea (Republic of)

Orna Agmon Ben-Yehuda ⓘ
Caesarea Rothschild Institute
University of Haifa
Haifa, Israel

Vlado Stankovski ⓘ
University of Ljubljana
Ljubljana, Slovenia

ISSN 0302-9743   ISSN 1611-3349 (electronic)
Lecture Notes in Computer Science
ISBN 978-3-030-92915-2   ISBN 978-3-030-92916-9 (eBook)
https://doi.org/10.1007/978-3-030-92916-9

LNCS Sublibrary: SL5 – Computer Communication Networks and Telecommunications

This Springer imprint is published by the registered company Springer Nature Switzerland AG
The registered company address is: Gewerbestrasse 11, 6330 Cham, Switzerland

Preface

This volume constitutes the proceedings of the 18th International Conference on the Economics of Grids, Clouds, Systems, and Services (GECON 2021). GECON 2021 was held during September 21–23, 2021, virtually hosted by the Libera Università Maria SS. Assunta (LUMSA), Rome, Italy.

Every year since 2004, GECON has solicited novel work at the crossroads of economics and computer science with an aim to generate societal value through research. As such, the conference brings together an interdisciplinary community of scientists and practitioners with a strong mandate to maintain and cultivate the ties between them.

The objectives and content of the conference cannot be more relevant nowadays, considering the convergence between economics and digital technologies currently happening at full speed. One can safely state that computer science has become the vessel that enacts economies at all scales. Blockchains, artificial intelligence, the Internet of Things, cloud and edge computing, and whole classes of applications (e.g., fintech) bring about new ways to conduct business and move economies. GECON stands at the center of this convergence and fosters cross-fertilization of ideas and knowledge from both areas.

This year, we received 41 submissions in response to our call for papers. Each paper was peer-reviewed by at least four members of the international Program Committee (PC). Based on significance, novelty, and scientific quality, we selected seven full papers (17% acceptance rate), which are presented in this volume. Additionally, eight shorter work-in-progress papers, two extended abstracts presenting new idea papers, and five short work-in-progress papers presented in the workshop on "Trustworthy Services, Information Exchange and Content Handling in the Context of Blockchain" organized by Thanasis Papaioannou are included in the volume.

This volume has been structured following the seven sessions that comprised the conference program:

- Performance
- AI and Digital Economy
- Blockchains
- Clouds, Fogs
- Regulation, Compliance
- New Idea Papers
- Workshop on Trustworthy Services, Information Exchange and Content Handling in the Context of Blockchain

In addition to these topic sessions, this year's GECON featured three keynotes, evenly distributed in the program, and a poster session using Gather.town.

The keynote speaker on the first day was Rosa M. Badia from the Barcelona Supercomputer Center. Rosa's keynote "Dynamic and Intelligent Workflows with eFlows4HPC" presented the recently started project eFlows4HPC with the goal of providing workflow software stack and an additional set of services to enable the integration of HPC simulations and modeling with big data analytics and machine learning in scientific and industrial applications. The project will demonstrate its advances through three application pillars with high industrial and social relevance: manufacturing, climate, and urgent computing for natural hazards; these applications will help to prove how the realization of forthcoming efficient HPC and data-centric applications can be developed with new workflow technologies.

The keynote speaker on the second day was Nicolas Stier-Moses, Director at Facebook Core Data Science. His keynote "Pacing Mechanisms for Ad Auctions" presented the role that budgets play in real-world sequential auction markets such as those implemented by internet-based companies. To maximize the value provided to auction participants, spending is smoothed across auctions so budgets are used for the best opportunities. Motivated by pacing mechanisms used in practice by online ad auction platforms, he discussed smoothing procedures that ensure that campaign daily budgets are consistent with maximum bids. Reinterpreting this process as a game between bidders, Nicolas introduced the notion of pacing equilibrium, and has studied properties such as existence, uniqueness, complexity, and efficiency, both for the case of second and first price auctions. In addition, he connected these equilibria to more general notions of market equilibria, and studied how compact representations of a market lead to more efficient approaches to compute approximate equilibria.

On the third day, the keynote speaker Orr Dunkelman presented "How Not to Fight COVID19 Using Technology: An Illustrative Guide". The COVID-19 pandemic urged a great deal of emergency response. While many efforts were solely in the medical arena, e.g., developing vaccines and efficient treatments, there were also some technological efforts to reduce transmission or reduce the economic costs of the pandemic. Two of these solutions, namely digital contact tracing and vaccination passports (or in some cases, green passports for people who are considered "safe" to go around), are interesting not just from ethical perspectives but also from technological and legal viewpoints. In his talk, Orr presented these two solutions in depth, outlining how one can indeed use modern technology to reduce the case of infections in a pandemic. At the same time, he presented the impact of small design decisions on human rights, civil liberty, and trust in governments.

The conference also included a tutorial on "Energy Efficiency Methodologies in Cloud Computing", presented by Karim Djemane, and a panel on Law and Computer Science Challenges, chaired by Orna Agmon Ben-Yehuda with the participation of the panelists Niva Elkin-Koren of the Tel-Aviv University Faculty of Law and Supreeth Shastri of the University of Iowa. As law and computer science develop, they pose new challenges to each other. These challenges were expressed in questions addressed by the panelists such as, Where must computer scientists stretch their abilities to provide law with adequate solutions? What legal developments are required to deal with new computer science achievements?

Any conference is the fruit of the work of many people, and GECON is no exception. In particular, we wish to thank the authors, whose papers made up the body of the conference, and the members of the Program Committee and the reviewers, who devoted their time to review the papers on a tight schedule. We wish to thank the invited speakers, for bringing new viewpoints and inputs to the GECON community. Furthermore, we would like to thank Alfred Hofmann, Anna Kramer, and the whole team at Springer, which continues an established tradition of publishing GECON proceedings in its renowned LNCS series. Finally, we wish to thank the attendees, whose interest in the conference is the main driver for its organization.

September 2021

Jörn Altmann
José Ángel Bañares
Orna Agmon Ben-Yehuda
Karim Djemame
Vlado Stankovski
Bruno Tuffin
Konstantinos Tserpes

Organization

GECON 2021 was organized by the Libera Università Maria SS. Assunta (LUMSA), Rome, Italy. (https://www.lumsa.it/).

Executive Committee

Conference Chair

Maurizio Naldi   LUMSA, Italy

Conference Vice-chairs

Karim Djemame   University of Leeds, UK
Orna Agmon Ben-Yehuda   Caesarea Rothschild Institute, University of Haifa,
                                               Israel
Jörn Altmann   Seoul National University, South Korea
José Ángel Bañares   Zaragoza University, Spain
Bruno Tuffin   Inria, France
Vlado Stankovski   University of Ljubljana, Slovenia

Virtual Location Chair

Orna Agmon Ben-Yehuda   Caesarea Rothschild Institute, University of Haifa,
                                               Israel

Public Relations Chair

José Ángel Bañares   Zaragoza University, Spain

Proceedings Chair

Konstantinos Tserpes   Harokopio University of Athens, Greece

Program Chairs

Bruno Tuffin   Inria, France
Orna Agmon Ben-Yehuda   Caesarea Rothschild Institute, University of Haifa,
                                               Israel

Special Sessions and Tutorial Chair

Jörn Altmann   Seoul National University, South Korea

Poster Chair

Orna Agmon Ben-Yehuda   Caesarea Rothschild Institute, University of Haifa,
                             Israel

Workshop Organizer

Thanasis Papaioannou   Athens University of Economics and Business,
                             Greece

Program Committee

Aurilla Aurelie Arntzen	University of South-Eastern Norway, Norway
Unai Arronategui	University of Zaragoza, Spain
Ashraf Bany Mohamed	University of Jordan, Jordan
Stefano Bistarelli	Università degli Studi di Perugia, Italy
Rajkumar Buyya	University of Melbourne, Australia
María Emilia Cambronero	University of Castilla-La Mancha, Spain
Emanuele Carlini	ISTI-CNR, Italy
Jeremy Cohen	Imperial College London, UK
Massimo Coppola	ISTI-CNR, Italy
Daniele D'Agostino	IMATI-CNR, Italy
Patrizio Dazzi	ISTI-CNR, Italy
Alex Delis	University of Athens, Greece
Patricio Domingues	ESTG - Politécnico de Leiria, Portugal
Bernhard Egger	Seoul National University, South Korea
Sebastian Floerecke	University of Passau, Germany
Giancarlo Fortino	University of Calabria, Italy
Felix Freitag	Universitat Politècnica de Catalunya, Spain
Marc Frincu	Nottingham Trent University, UK
Daniel Grosu	Wayne State University, USA
Bahman Javadi	Western Sydney University, Australia
Songhee Kang	Software Policy and Research Institute, South Korea
Odej Kao	TU Berlin, Germany
Tobias Knoch	Erasmus MC, The Netherlands
Bastian Koller	HLRS - University of Stuttgart, Germany
Somayeh Koohborfardhaghighi	University of Amsterdam, The Netherlands
Harald Kornmayer	DHBW Mannheim, Germany
George Kousiouris	National Technical University of Athens, Greece
Dieter Kranzlmüller	Ludwig Maximilian University of Munich, Germany
Joerg Leukel	University of Hohenheim, Germany
Ivan Merelli	ITB-CNR, Italy
Roc Meseguer	Universitat Politècnica de Catalunya, Spain
Paolo Mori	IIT-CNR, Italy
Leandro Navarro	Universitat Politècnica de Catalunya, Spain
Marco Netto	IBM, Italy

Umara Noor	National University of Science and Technology, Pakistan
Alberto Nuñez	Complutense University of Madrid, Spain
Frank Pallas	TU Berlin, Germany
George Pallis	University of Cyprus, Cyprus
Rubem Pereira	Liverpool John Moores University, UK
Dana Petcu	West University of Timisoara, Romania
Ioan Petri	Cardiff University, UK
Congduc Pham	University of Pau, France
Zahid Rashid	Seoul National University, South Korea
Ivan Rodero	Rutgers University, USA
Rizos Sakellariou	University of Manchester, UK
Benjamin Satzger	Microsoft, USA
Lutz Schubert	University of Ulm, Germany
Jun Shen	University of Wollongong, Australia
Gheorghe Cosmin Silaghi	Babes-Bolyai University, Romania
Aleksander Slominski	IBM, USA
Burkhard Stiller	University of Zurich, Switzerland
Djamshid Sultanov	Seoul National University, South Korea
Stefan Tai	TU Berlin, Germany
Rafael Tolosana-Calasanz	University of Zaragoza, Spain
Konstantinos Tserpes	Harokopio University of Athens, Greece
Claudiu Vinte	Bucharest University of Economic Studies, Romania
Carl Waldspurger	Carl Waldspurger Consulting, USA
Ramin Yahyapour	University of Göttingen, Germany
Muhammad Zakarya	Abdul Wali Khan University Mardan, Pakistan
Dimitrios Zissis	University of the Aegean, Greece

Subreviewers

Luis Carlos Castillo Martinez	iXec, France
Anthony Simonet-Boulogne	iXec, France
Michalis Kasioulis	University of Cyprus, Cyprus
Francesco Betti Sorbelli	Università degli Studi di Perugia, Italy
Moysis Symeonidis	University of Cyprus, Cyprus
Matteo Mordacchini	IIT-CNR, Italy
Ivan Mercanti	Scuola IMT Alti Studi Lucca, Italy
Ioannis Savvidis	University of Cyprus, Cyprus
Luca Ferrucci	ISTI-CNR, Italy
Serkan Guldal	Adiyaman University, Turkey

Steering Committee

Karim Djemame   University of Leeds, UK
Jörn Altmann   Seoul National University, South Korea
Jose Ángel Bañares   Zaragoza University, Spain
Orna Agmon Ben-Yehuda Caesarea Rothschild Institute, University of Haifa,
                        Israel
Steven Miller   Singapore Management University, Singapore
Omer F. Rana   Cardiff University, UK
Gheorghe Cosmin Silaghi Babes-Bolyai University, Romania
Konstantinos Tserpes   Harokopio University of Athens, Greece
Maurizio Naldi   LUMSA, Italy

Contents

Workshop on Trustworthy Services, Information Exchange and Content Handling in the Context of Blockchain

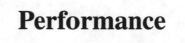

Performance

Workload Evaluation in Distributed Simulation of DESs

Paul Hodgetts, Hayk Kocharyan, Fidel Reviriego, Álvaro Santamaría,
Unai Arronategui$^{(\boxtimes)}$ ⓘ, José Ángel Bañares$^{(\boxtimes)}$ ⓘ, and José Manuel Colom$^{(\boxtimes)}$ ⓘ

Aragón Institute of Engineering Research (I3A), University of Zaragoza,
Zaragoza, Spain
{738701,757715,716678,756308,unai,banares,jm}@unizar.es

Abstract. Nowadays Discrete Event Systems (DESs) require complex and large models, for which distributed simulation engines become, in practice, the tools used to understand and analyse their behaviour. In this context, we have proposed a methodology based on Petri Nets (PNs) covering the phases from the modelling of the DES to the distributed simulation of the PN. The efficiency of the distributed simulation of these large-scale models is strongly dependent on the generation of initial partitions where the workload of the parts is well balanced among the individual simulation engines deployed. In the cloud the resources to support the simulation are provided in a flexible way using its own load balancing and migration mechanisms. Nevertheless, the distributed simulation of large DESs requires its own metrics to define the workload and mechanisms for load balancing. This divergence in concepts and mechanisms poses a significant difficulty in adopting the cloud for simulation, especially when computation and communication come at a cost. This paper revisits the basic principles of a distributed simulation of DESs models, and presents the first experimental results of a framework for simulating large scale timed PN models in a mini cluster as the necessary previous experimental work to large scale simulations on the cloud.

Keywords: Distributed simulation · Discrete-event systems · Timed Petri nets

1 Introduction

This paper revisits the principles of the discrete event system (DES) simulation, where the evolution from one modelled system's state to another is produced as a consequence of the appearance of a *discrete relevant fact* for the system, that is called *event*. The system's *actions* happen while the system is in a state. Actions can have associated information related with the state change that happens in an atomic manner, such as temporary duration, economic cost, or energy consumption [14]. Large scale DES models, which are not feasible to be simulated in a single execution unit, and the desire to speed up simulations by concurrently

© Springer Nature Switzerland AG 2021
K. Tserpes et al. (Eds.): GECON 2021, LNCS 13072, pp. 3–16, 2021.
https://doi.org/10.1007/978-3-030-92916-9_1

processing events in different processing units are at the heart of distributed DES simulations.

The discipline of distributed simulation of physical systems, where entities interact at discrete times, began with Chandy and Misra [6, 7] by the definition of *logical processes* (LP) that interact with asynchronous messages. Every physical process or entity is modelled by a LP, and entity interactions are modelled by asynchronous messages. LPs avoid global variables and the use of a global clock that will be a bottleneck for the scalability of the model. LPs must process events when it is safe, that is, complying with the local causality constraint [13]. Although the distributed simulation has been a promising discipline, it has not been able to move from academic to industrial or commercial sphere relying on the success of cloud computing. The cloud has shown to be an adequate executing platform for distributed simulation [18], but the complexity for estimating performance metrics and cost make difficult to use popularise distributed simulation in the cloud. The evolution of the discipline has intertwined the fundamental principles of distributed simulation with design decisions limited by the technical evolution.

We assume that the complexity of distributed simulation requires a previous experience with a local cluster, and that the use of the cloud is justified by the need to simulate large scale models. Large-scale models are impossible to analyse to generate initial partitions. A minimal infrastructure is required for generating the execution code, deploy the code in the cloud, and estimate the best partition of workload between nodes. Even if best model partition was achieved and deployed, small changes in the hardware configuration or the evolution of the simulation will produces large imbalances. Previous to the simulation at large scale, some metrics based on the experimentation for the load estimation, and the adequacy of the load to the node characteristics are essential.

This work reviews and places in the context of our PN-based methodology the fundamental principles of the distributed simulation discipline of DES. The efficiency of distributed simulation depends on the implementation of efficient simulation engines, the definition of data structures representing the workload and their dependencies, and the dynamic deployment of these workloads between the computational resources. The impossibility of analysing large models compels to monitor the simulation. Having adequate metrics to estimate how to distribute the workload between the nodes to obtain the best performance, and doing cost analysis before deploying a simulation in the cloud are essential aspects for the simulation in the cloud to be feasible.

The remainder of this paper is organised as follows: The first three sections briefly present the state of the art, putting our approach into context. Section 2 reviews the main principles at the basis of our work such as discrete event simulation, distributed simulation, our vision of partitions, and the mechanisms to support adaptive partitions at different levels of granularity. Section 3 introduces metrics for load estimation and to adequate the load to the computational and communications capacity of the node. Section 4 summarises works related with cost analysis of distributed simulations on the cloud. Section 5 presents tools for the deployment of simulations on a mini cluster with the objective to develop hybrid simulations on the cloud, and the first experimental results of our framework for simulating large scale timed Petri net models. Finally, in Sect. 6 we provide some final remarks.

2 Principles of Distributed Simulation

Classical distributed simulation of a model is carried out by means of a set of indivisible execution units named Logical Processes (LPs), each one devoted to a piece of the overall model. The execution of a LP depends on the events received from the other LPs of the set with which is related, and generates new events as a consequence of the state change produced by the processing of the incoming events.

In order to generate the set of LPs, the model is partitioned and each one of the disjoint parts is used to generate the code of LP, that it is not independent because the existing interactions with the other LPs of the set. However this methodology does not impose any **higher-level model**, see for example the component model defined by DEVS [20]. Observe, that the set of LPs in these approaches is stated before the simulation itself, requires some criteria to realise the partition of the model, and once the code of the LP is generated it cannot be reconfigured in runtime using the information of the starting model (dividing the LP in two or more LPs, or fusing several LPs in one single LP). It is said that in these approaches, the distributed simulation application is generated by compilation of the model into a set of LPs and the interactions among them by means of events.

The use of PNs as model of the system, contributes with a rich structural information of the system about the changes of state (transitions of the PN), the events that produce the enabling of changes (tokens arriving to the input places of transitions), and the new events produced after a change of state (tokens arriving to the output places of transitions after its occurrence). Therefore, in a first instance, this structural information can be used for the definition of LPs decomposing the structure in spatial subregions (subnets of the PN model) [10], or rising the level of abstraction by higher-level primitives such as resources, processes and communication channels [2]. This PN decomposition/partition can be used to generate the set of LP representing the partitioning of the model, therefore it must be done before simulation and after the elaboration of the original input PN model. However, these LPs don't need to end as a fixed code ready to be executed and forgetting the PN that aided to its definition.

Our proposal, after the initial partition of the model defining the LPs, maintain the visibility of the PN model (or the parts of the model in each LP) during the simulation phase. That is, a LP in the proposed approach is composed by a generic simulation engine of PNs specialised in playing the token game, and a data structure representing the piece of PN, and its current state, corresponding to the definition of the LP under consideration. It is said that in this approach, the distributed simulation application is composed of a set of identical simulation engines to play the token game (named Simbots), each one preloaded with the data structure and initial marking of the piece of PN that corresponds, and communicating with asynchronous messages that are the tokens interchanged by the occurrence of transitions. The execution of one of this LP, **execution model** [12], is not the execution of a code resulting from the compilation of the piece of PN model, but the interpreted execution of the PN model by the generic Simbot, which is essential for scaling simulations [20].

The translation of a PN based conceptual model to an efficient execution model of LPs is based on the mechanism of *Linear Enabling Function* (LEF) of a transition [3], and the network of LPs for the interchanging of events [1]. Semantic aspects of the conceptual model (the PN model) are separated from the executable model (the network of LPs) in order to prioritise efficiency, scalability and load balancing. This means that the simulation results will be reconstructed after the simulation from the conceptual model and the collection of the distributed traces. The main characteristics of this LEF-based execution code are that, 1) the model is not wired with the simulator, which enables load balancing, that is, the portability of the model to other simulators, 2) the representation of the event dependency network allows the propagation of events to only the affected parts of the execution model, which provides efficient interpreters, and facilitates the evolution of a dynamic *graph of LPs* since the migration of code carries the event network dependencies that can be used by interpreters to redefine neighbourhood relationships, and 3) The granularity of the code is not defined at compiled time, and it can used at different levels of abstraction.

In the following, for simplicity we will do reference to *LPs* as the simulation machine that executes a partition of the Petri net model, called SimBot, and provides the services to support the simulation as a process, that is, the execution code interpreter, and the synchronisation protocols.

3   Measurement and Estimation of Load and Performance Metrics

Different metrics can be used to estimate the LP's load. The field of distributed simulation has not the usual interpretation of load. For example, high rates of CPU utilisation in optimistic approaches can do useless work doing rollback most of the time.

A metric for fast estimation of the simulation load on a node can be based on the conceptual model using the number of entities, components, places or transitions in a PN. But we can have several elements without activity. A better approach is an indirect measure of the activity or the complexity of the model based in previous simulations. In a similar way that search algorithms, or rule based interpreters use the maximum and medium size of agendas to estimate the complexity of a problem, the number of scheduled events in a LP can be used to estimate the simulation load. However, a simple count of events in queues is related only with the model. This metric does not tell us how efficient the processor is in carrying out the simulation, taking into account other factors such as efficiency of the simulator or dependencies with other processes.

The usual metric to compare centralised DES simulators is the processing event rate (P), i.e., the number of events by unit of CPU time. In the case of distributed simulations, the slowest process imposes its simulation advanced rate to all processes. A complex combination of characteristics of the assigned partition model, the executing unit processing this partition, latency of communications, and dependency relationships with neighbouring processes define the load of this most *heavily loaded process*. The *simulation advance rate* is defined as the rate at which a process advances its simulation clock as a function of the amount of CPU time. This key concept was proposed in the context of optimistic simulations considering *effective work* the advance of simulation clock as opposed to lost work on a rollback [17]. Glazer and Tropper [15] defined the load of a process i, $Load_i$ as the CPU time it requires to advance its local simulation clock one unit, or the inverse of the simulation advance rate: $Load_i = \frac{CPU_i}{SA_i}$, where CPU_i, and SA_i, are the CPU allocation (in sec) and the simulated advance time of the LP (in simSec), respectively.

Next works reverted to a metric based only on the count of events, weighting in some way events in the queue as an estimate of future work. E. Deellman and B.K. Szymansky proposed in [8] to count the events in the future event list to determine the computational load of an LP in the future, instead of using the measure simulation advance rate, that is a measure of past performance. The metric was refined by weighting the number of events with the distance of events from the beginning of simulation. Other variant based on the same idea was proposed by Boukerche [4], who estimates load distinguishing the size of the buffer of null and real messages and weighting the addition of these sizes with a factor that is the result of experimental work.

A more comprehensive metric to evaluate distributed simulations considering the model and physical characteristics of the node (processing rate and communications) was proposed by Andras Varga et al. [19] for conservative simulations. In conservative simulations, a LP_i contains an incoming message FIFO queue for each neighbour LP. Each input queue Q_i has a timestamp field $T(Q_i)$ minimum time stamp. The LP can consume events from its own Future Event List (FUL) queue until time defined by lower bound time stamp (LBTS) $LBTS = min(T(Q_i))$ is reached. Andras Varga et al. take into account the latency of communications τ, the lookahead $LBTS$, and the simulation time advanced rate called by authors *relative speed*, R . Authors consider that null messages should reach the target LP before it runs out of work, and express it with the condition: $\tau < LBTS/R$. A more intuitive definition of this condition can be expressed as $\tau * P < LBTS * E$, where P is the event processing rate (events/sec), and E is the event density, that is, the number of precessed events per simulated second in (events/simSec) that can be calculated as $E = P/R$. This expression shows that the number of events the CPU can process during message transit $(\tau * P)$, which are dependent on CPU, network latency, and interpreter efficiency, must be less than the number of events to be processed by the LP until the next horizon time defined by the $LBTS$, which is model dependent.

Andras Varga et al. also define in [19] the coupling factor $\lambda = \frac{LTBS*E}{\tau*P}$. Values of $\lambda < 10$ are considered too small, that means that the load in the node is low and we will have low performance comparing with the centralised approach. To obtain good performances they consider values of $\lambda > 100$. This coupling factor metric can be considered a fitness function that allows us to estimate the adequacy of the load, which depends on the model (parameters $LBTS$ and E), to the processing unit (parameter P which depends on CPU processing rate and interpreter efficiency and τ, latency communications).

We can translate these metrics to our Simbot simulation machines based on LEF execution code. The *wall clock time* used in effective work, that is, in advancing the virtual clock, will depend on the time used in the execution code, in our case the time taken to interpret the PN LEF code. In conservative approaches, every LP can safely progress without interactions with other LPs until a safe temporal horizon. The advantage of use between optimistic and conservative approaches is neither conclusive, but the implementation of optimistic protocols introduce more complexity [11]. In fact, optimistic approaches trust the independent progress of LPs because an event is unlikely to come out or order. This unpredictability of optimistic approaches contrasts with conservative approaches, whose performance heavily depends on the definition of the lookahead, which is a model-dependent crucial parameter to introduce parallelism in the distributed simulation. In our case, the PN model allow to infer a precise *lookahead* parameter from the timed PN (TPN) structure at compilation time. The safe horizon time of simulation, i.e. the LBTS, is given by the minimum time stamp received by the neighbour LPs. If we consider a simulation step every interpretation of the model until the simulator reach the safe horizon time of simulation, we can estimate the load for the next step based on the LEF coded TPN interpreter and the Simbot distributed simulation manager presented in [1].

To estimate the future CPU allocation to interpret the model every simulation step, we consider that all events in the FUL until the safe simulation horizon are processed, and in the case they trigger new events, these are scheduled in the FUL. Therefore, the execution time depends on the number of events in the FUL whose time stamp is less than the LBTS, and the number of state changes that theses events produce during the execution time. This last estimation of new events produced during the simulation step is more complex. An event can produce several concurrent events in one state and not events in another state. To solve this problem, we can use the average size of the internal event list (**EVL**) used to execute the model. The EVL size provides a good estimation of the load in the same way the agenda size in search algorithms. In our case, the EVL is the list of *enabled transitions* used by the PN model interpreter. The product of the number of events in the FUL queue by the average number of events in the EVL divided by the interpreter event processing rate can be a simple estimation of wall clock time to interpret the PN during a simulation step. We can use brief centralized simulations to obtain a previous metric of event processing rates of resources.

Resuming the load of proposed by Glazer and Tropper [15], we propose as estimation of the future load of a LP_i during a simulation step q, $\widehat{Load}_{iq}$ as the inverse of the estimation of the future simulation advance rate:

$$\widehat{Load}_{iq} = \frac{\widehat{CPU}_{iq}}{LBTS_{iq}}$$

where $\widehat{CPU}_{iq}$, and LBS_{iq}, are the estimation of the CPU allocation estimation and lower bound time stamp of process LP_i respectively in the step q. Using the simplest estimation of $\widehat{CPU}_{iq}$, it results in the following load estimation:

$$\widehat{Load}_{iq} = \frac{\#events(LBS, FUL)_{iq} \times \overline{size(EVL)_i}}{P_{ip} \times LBTS_{iq}}$$

where $\#events(LBTS, FUL)_{iq}$ is the number of events in the FUL queue with time stamp less or equal the lower bound time stamp LBT in the q simulation step of the i process, $\overline{size(EVL)_i}$ is the average size of the enabled transition lists (EVL) in process i, and P_{ip} is the event processing rate of the LP_i in the current processor p. We can follow a similar approach to estimate the coupling factor in each simulation step, and use these estimations to define fitness functions to optimise distributed simulations and define load-balancing strategies.

4 Cost Analysis

To the best of our knowledge, few works have dealt with distributed DES simulation cost analysis. The work of K. Vanmechelen shows that running multiple LPs on Amazon high-end instance types provides a better trade-off between performance and cost. Although it can deliver higher cost-efficiency in individual simulations, the variance in performance observing lower-end instance types can have a significant negative impact on overall cost-efficiency [18]. This experimental work in the cloud confirms the importance of load balancing from an economical point of view, and the negative impact of resources performance variance.

A cost analysis of distributed DES simulations in a cloud was presented by G. D'Angelo in [9]. This work estimates the cost considering the Total Execution Cost (TEC) as the amount of time that is needed to complete a simulation run, which is composed of the Model Computation Cost (MCC) and the Communication Cost: ($TEC = MCC + CC$). In a distributed simulation the MCC is reduced with the use of nodes N, but there is a part of the model that can no be parallelised, and the CC is composed of the synchronization Cost (SC), the model interaction Cost (MIC), and some Middleware Management Cost (MMC). We don't consider MMC because it can be considered included in the rest of aspects and it is implementation dependent. Migration time for load balancing is also considered in the D'Angelo work, but we left this aspect out for simplicity. It results $TEC = \frac{MCC}{f(n)} + (SC + MIC)$, where $f(n) < N$ represents the fraction of the model that can not be parallelized. This function is also affected by the hardware heterogeneity.

The SC time represents the overhead of the synchronisation protocol to maintain causality constraints. The experimental work of K. Vanmechelen [18] shows that the relative performance of different synchronization protocols is retained on the cloud infrastructure using as reference the Ideal Simulation Protocol (ISP), introduced in [16]. ISP uses a trace of a previous simulation run to calculate the $LBTS$ and it determines if an LP can safely advance. In this way, before deploying to the cloud effort and spending time into tuning a parallel simulation for a new application, a smaller previous simulation can be executed using ISP to estimate the best possible speedup. And the comparison of speedups on different benchmarks on the private cloud using ISP can helps us separate the synchronisation time SC from the rest in the TEC.

The MIC is the time for delivering the interactions among the LPs. The MIC is composed of local and remote communications: $MIC = LCC + RCC$, with a strong impact of the ratio of between Local (LCC) and remote (RCC) in the total MIC. The objective of minimize remote communication guide the strategies for defining dynamic partitions and load-balancing.

If we consider an hybrid infrastructure, we can assume negligible the own infrastructure cost compared to that of the public cloud given the scale of the model. An hybrid simulation only will have sense if the coupling factor of all nodes (public and private) are similar. In a hybrid simulation we can distinguish the remote communication inside the cloud (RCC) and between the public and private cloud ($RCC\prime$). Data transfer cost between public and private cloud includes the cost per connection and duration, and the volume of data transferred. This cost can be considered negligible compared to the cost of using machines in the cloud. A first estimation of the cost of the simulation result: $Cost = cost_{pu} * (\frac{MCC}{f(n)} + SC + LCC + RCC + RCC\prime)$, where the $cost_{pu}$ is the cost of the private cloud machine instance by unit of time.

5   Experimental Work for Load Estimation in DES Distributed Simulation

Our experimental evaluation is based on two simulation models, which are shown in Fig. 1. The first model on the left is a pipelined wavefront array that performs a Matrix-Vector Multiplication problem in streaming fashion. We use this model to illustrate the LEF based efficiency of the interpreter. The interpretation of PNs heavily depends on the model size. Different approaches has been proposed to avoid the exponential growth of the simulation time depending on the size of the model. As will be seen in the experimental part, the execution time of an LEF interpreter grows linearly with the size of the model, facilitating the estimation of CPU time. The right model represents a synthetic PN that can be easily parametrised with the number of branches, which are chains of events

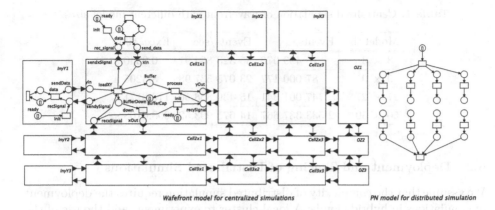

Wafefront model for centralized simulations   PN model for distributed simulation

Fig. 1. Models for simulation experimentation.

that can be executed in parallel without violating the causality constraint, and the number of transitions represents the simulation workload of each branch.

5.1 Efficient Scalable Centralized Simulation of DES Models

Java and C++ have been the most widely used languages for developing DES simulators [5]. Portability and a vast feature-rich library have made Java the most popular language for simulation. When efficiency is prioritised, the chosen option is C++ to improve performance. Rust, a language that is focused on safety and performance is establishing itself as an alternative to C++. Two versions of the Simbot has been implemented, one previous in Java, a more complete version taking advantage of available libraries, and another more basic in Rust, with improved performance and memory usage.

The Rust version has been implemented with version 1.52.1 of Rust compiler. Table 1 shows the execution of wavefront models with different number of cells 3×3, 9×9, 27×27 and 50×50. All transitions have a duration of a unit of time, and the simulated time for all experiments is 1,000,000 simSeconds. We will use the simSeconds as unit of simulated time to differentiate it from the execution time in seconds. The events column shows the number of fired transitions by simulation. The third column shows the P processing rate in events/sec, and finally the last column the total execution time. The results show that the simulation time grows linearly with the size of the model. These experiments has been executed in a PC with a Intel i5-4690 3.50 GHz processor, 32 GB of RAM and a Ubuntu 18.04 operating system with kernel version 5.4.0–70-generic.

The simulation time of the 9×9 wavefront in a Raspberry Pi 4 with 8 GB of RAM takes 28,95 s. The processing rate on the Raspberry Pi is approximately three times slower than on the PC.

Table 1. Centralized simulation of wavefront with different model sizes.

Model size	Events	Events/sec	Exec. time
3 × 3	16 499 976	35 328 834.91	0.9340 s
9 × 9	87 000 177	23 075 537.98	8.3205 s
27 × 27	747 001 341	15 430 858.56	110.8171 s
50 × 50	2 533 337 667	14 675 993.52	398.6108 s

5.2 Deployment and Tracing of Distributed Simulations

We assume that the complexity of distributed simulation requires the deployment of simulations in hybrid clouds: A local cluster to experiment, and the use of the cloud to simulate large scale models. We choose the Slurm Workload Manager as the main tool to make these simulations in a hybrid cloud as easy as possible. One node runs the Slurm controller and the other ones, called compute nodes, run the Slurm daemon, whose purpose is to run processes that are submitted from the controller. The requirements for starting a simulation is to have the simulator binary and the files needed for the simulation on every compute node. Once all this resources are located, a parallel job can be run using Slurm *srun* command.

To be useful the simulation is important to collect traces and observe the distributed behaviour. We have defined a distributed tracing system, based on Jaeger and OpenTelemetry, with three main considerations: purpose, syncing, and trace storage. The **purpose** is to capture as much useful information from the simulation as possible. A trail of simulation events should be easily tracked, both for analysis and debug purposes, all with minimally penalising the execution time and latency between nodes. An easy approach for this is to have an in-depth metrics system with a granular enable/disable setting upon execution and a per-node client solution.

The trace system must support the synchronization of its events timeline. This system should be able to traceback from present simulation time back to the desired point in form of a string of events. The result is a cascade of simulation timestamps and events, in a meaningful manner. This is lastly exposed in a Web UI from the server.

Finally, **trace storage** must be supported. When a simulation scales up, so it does the amount of information it can generate. Then, a simple logging system is not valid. Instead, the approach is to save traces in a logical and optimised system (considering Jaeger as opentelemetry compliant), backed with a log system only for warning and error traceback situations.

5.3 Speedup of Distributed Simulations

Table 2 shows the results obtained from the discrete event simulator implemented in Rust language running on a mini cluster of Raspberries Pi 4 with 8 GB of RAM, each one. The same PNs have been tested, with variations in depth and number of branches, for both versions of the simulator in order to draw conclusions as to which version is the ideal one in each case. The simulated time for these experiments is 10M SimSeconds.

Table 2. Distributed simulation versus centralized simulation with different loads by Simbot implemented in Rust.

SimBot simulator	#br.	trans/br.	Events	Nodes	Events/s	Exec. time
Centr.	2	10 000	19 998 003	1	7 522 936	2.658 s
Distr.	2	10 000	19 998 003	3	2 609 886	7.619 s
Centr.	2	100 000	19 999 803	1	7 529 029	2.656 s
Distr.	2	100 000	19 999 803	3	2 203 961	4.537 s
Centr.	7	10 000	69 988 013	1	4 407 922	17.79 s
Distr.	7	10 000	69 988 013	8	6 652 821	10.52 s

First two columns show lower load case of 2 branches with 10K transitions per branch, it is found that better results are obtained for the centralised simulator. However, when the depth is increased from 10K to 100K transitions per branch, an improvement is observed in the results of the distributed simulator, although they still do not overcome those of the centralised one. This means that, if the depth of the branches continues to be increased, the distributed one will be more suitable than the centralised simulator. Finally, the number of branches has been increased, trying to find a situation that is more suitable to the use of a distributed simulator. In this case, the real simulation time is less in the distributed version, which indicates that if the number of branches that run in parallel is increased, the simulation time of the centralised one substantially increases, and a distributed solution is more suitable. The sixth column shows the total number of events/second in the simulation. Observe, that the number of nodes is one by branch, and one additional node contains the PN part that synchronises all branches at the beginning and at the end. This Simbot contains a negligible number of transitions and is not considered for the processing rate in each branch. The number of events/second that we reach in the last case with 7 branches is approximately 6 652 821, which is near the centralised approach in the first row but executing a larger model.

To independently measure the efficiency of this distributed simulator in Rust, we have obtained parameters P, E and R. Together with the lookahead variables ($LBTS$, calculated in each simulation cycle) and communication latency between simulation nodes (τ), the coupling factor is obtained. Latency in previous experiments is around 350 μs. The coupling factor $\lambda = 13.52$ for experiments with 2 branches and 10K transitions by branch, and $\lambda = 117.49$ for 2 branches with 100k by branch. This means that in the first case, the Simbots runs out of work and the second case shows an excessive load by Simbot. The λ can be a useful to interpret results, but it is not enough to globally evaluate a partition.

In the last case of 7 branches, and 10K transitions by branch, with $\lambda = 17.25$, shows an appropriate size for distribution and the load partitions is adequate.

Table 3 shows similar results for the alternative implementation of the Simbots developed in Java. The Java version shows a slower rate of event processing per second P. Distributed simulations are executed in 8 nodes, one node by branch and one node for branch synchronisations.

Table 3. Distributed simulation versus centralised simulation with different loads by Simbot implemented in Java.

Version	Simulated time	#br.	Trans./branch	Events	Events/sec	Exec. time
Centr.	100k simSeconds	7	2k	699 413	596 515	1.173 s
Distr.	100k simSeconds	7	2k	699 413	403 521	1.734 s
Centr.	100k simSeconds	7	5k	699 773	632 243	1.107 s
Distr.	100k simSeconds	7	5k	699 773	554 145	1.263 s
Cent.	100k simSeconds	7	10k	699 893	613 455	1.141 s
Dist.	100k simSeconds	7	10k	699 893	819 608	0.854 s
Cent.	1M simSeconds	7	10k	6 998 813	817 306	8.564 s
Dist.	1M simSeconds	7	10k	6 998 813	1 612 394	4.341 s

6   Conclusions and Future Work

This paper has reviewed the model partition in disjoint LPs as the core of DES simulation. The classical LP methodology has been shown to require decomposing the conceptual model in a static graph of LP at compilation time. It can limit dynamic load balancing in execution. Our methodology based on PNs, which covers all phases from modelling to deployment and simulation, translates the PN based conceptual model to an efficient execution network model for the interchanging of events. The executable model is not wired to the simulator, which facilitates the evolution of dynamic partitions and load balancing.

We have also reviewed the metrics for evaluating and estimation of workload. These metrics has been adapted to the simulation algorithms that execute LEF PN execution code in a conservative simulation. We have shown how estimation metrics can be defined more precisely in function of the simulation interpreter and the PN model. Factors that will affect the simulation cost on hybrid infrastructures have been also presented.

Finally, the experimentation and deployment of services required in a mini cluster of Raspberries Pi has been presented as previous work to develop simulations on the cloud. The efficiency of distributed simulation depends on the efficient implementation of simulation engines. Our results shows that the centralised simulation time grows linearly with the size of the model. The experimentation also shows that the coupling factor metric can be a useful metric to interpret if Simbots are running out of work or with excessive load. However, it is not enough to globally evaluate if distributed simulation will improve centralised simulation.

Future work is focusing on the deployment of simulations in hybrid clouds, the implementation of load balancing mechanisms, and the use of metrics to define fitness functions for optimising partitions.

Acknowledgments. This work was co-financed by the Aragonese Government and the European Regional Development Fund "Construyendo Europa desde Aragón" (COSMOS research group); and by the Spanish program "Programa estatal del Generación de Conocimiento y Fortalecimiento Científico y Tecnológico del Sistema de I+D+i", project PGC2018-099815-B-100. We thank Carlos Gracia for assistance in designing and constructing the Raspberry Pi mini cluster.

References

1. Arronategui, U., Bañares, J.Á., Colom, J.M.: Towards an architecture proposal for federation of distributed DES simulators. In: Djemame, K., Altmann, J., Bañares, J.Á., Agmon Ben-Yehuda, O., Naldi, M. (eds.) GECON 2019. LNCS, vol. 11819, pp. 97–110. Springer, Cham (2019). https://doi.org/10.1007/978-3-030-36027-6_9
2. Arronategui, U., Bañares, J.Á., Colom, J.M.: A MDE approach for modelling and distributed simulation of health systems. In: Djemame, K., Altmann, J., Bañares, J.Á., Agmon Ben-Yehuda, O., Stankovski, V., Tuffin, B. (eds.) GECON 2020. LNCS, vol. 12441, pp. 89–103. Springer, Cham (2020). https://doi.org/10.1007/978-3-030-63058-4_9
3. Bañares, J.Á., Colom, J.M.: Model and simulation engines for distributed simulation of discrete event systems. In: Coppola, M., Carlini, E., D'Agostino, D., Altmann, J., Bañares, J.Á. (eds.) GECON 2018. LNCS, vol. 11113, pp. 77–91. Springer, Cham (2019). https://doi.org/10.1007/978-3-030-13342-9_7
4. Boukerche, A., Das, S.K.: Reducing null messages overhead through load balancing in conservative distributed simulation systems. J. Parall. Distrib. Comput. **64**(3), 330–344 (2004)
5. Byrne, J., et al.: A review of cloud computing simulation platforms and related environments. In: CLOSER17, Proceedings of the 7th International Conference on Cloud Computing and Services Science, pp. 679–691 (2017)
6. Chandy, K.M., Misra, J.: Asynchronous distributed simulation via a sequence of parallel computations. Commun. ACM **24**(4), 198–206 (1981)
7. Chandy, K., Misra, J.: Distributed simulation: a case study in design and verification of distributed programs. IEEE Trans. Softw. Eng. SE-**5**(5), 440–452 (1979)
8. Deelman, E., Szymanski, B.: Dynamic load balancing in parallel discrete event simulation for spatially explicit problems. In: Proceedings. Twelfth Workshop on Parallel and Distributed Simulation PADS 1998 (Cat. No.98TB100233), pp. 46–53 (1998)
9. D'Angelo, G.: The simulation model partitioning problem: an adaptive solution based on self-clustering. Simul. Model. Pract. Theor. **70**, 1–20 (2017)
10. Ferscha, A.: Parallel and distributed simulation of discrete event systems. In: Handbook of Parallel and Distributed Computing, pp. 1003–1041 (1995)
11. Ferscha, A., Johnson, J., Turner, S.J.: Distributed simulation performance data mining. Fut. Gene. Comput. Syst. **18**(1), 157–174 (2001), i. High Performance Numerical Methods and Applications. II. Performance Data Mining: Automated Diagnosis, Adaption, and Optimization

12. Fujimoto, R., Bock, C., Chen, W., Page, E., Panchal, J.H.: Research Challenges in Modeling and Simulation for Engineering Complex Systems, 1st edn. Springer, Cham (2017). https://doi.org/10.1007/978-3-319-58544-4
13. Fujimoto, R.M.: Parallel discrete event simulation. Commun. ACM **33**(10), 30–53 (1990)
14. Fujimoto, R.M.: Parallel and Distribution Simulation Systems. Wiley Series on Parallel and Distributed Computing, Wiley-Interscience, New York (2000)
15. Glazer, D., Tropper, C.: On process migration and load balancing in time warp. IEEE Trans. Parall. Distrib. Syst. **4**(3), 318–327 (1993)
16. Jha, V., Bagrodia, R.: A performance evaluation methodology for parallel simulation protocols. In: Proceedings of Symposium on Parallel and Distributed Tools, pp. 180–185 (1996)
17. Reiher, P.L., Jefferson, D.: Virtual time based dynamic load management in the time warp operating system. Trans. Soc. Comput. Simul. **7**, 103–111 (1990)
18. Vanmechelen, K., De Munck, S., Broeckhove, J.: Conservative distributed discrete-event simulation on the Amazon EC2 cloud: an evaluation of time synchronization protocol performance and cost efficiency. Simul. Model. Pract. Theory **34**, 126–143 (2013)
19. Varga, A., Sekercioglu, Y., Egan, G.: A practical efficiency criterion for the null message algorithm. In: Verbraeck, A., Hlupic, V. (eds.) Simulation in Industry: Proceedings of the 15th European Simulation Symposium (ESS 2003), pp. 81–92 (2003)
20. Zeigler, B.P., Muzy, A., Kofman, E.: Theory of Modeling and Simulation: Discrete Event and Iterative System Computational Foundations, 3rd edn. Academic Press, Inc., New York (2018)

Can VM Live Migration Improve Job Throughput? Evidence from a Real World Cluster Trace

Daon Park[iD], Hyunsoo Kim[iD], Youngsu Cho[iD], Changyeon Jo[iD],
and Bernhard Egger[✉][iD]

Seoul National University, Seoul, Republic of Korea
{daon,hyunsoo,youngsu,changyeon,bernhard}@csap.snu.ac.kr

Abstract. Cloud resource providers are putting more and more emphasis on efficiently management the resources of their data centers to achieve high utilization while minimizing energy consumption. Despite these efforts, an analysis of recent data center traces reveals that the utilization of CPU and memory resources has not improved significantly over the past decade. Resource overcommitment is a promising approach to improve resource utilization, because most workloads show a significant gap between their guaranteed and actually consumed resources. A wrong prediction of the actual usage, however, can lead to a severe performance degradation on overloaded nodes. Combining resource overcommitment with live migration of tasks can alleviate the situation, but its prohibitively high cost has so far prevented a wide adoption. Recent and rapid advancements in networking technology, however, are changing the status quo. With throughputs surpassing 100 Gb/s in 2021, even large tasks can be migrated within a few seconds. In light of these improvements, we believe it is time to rethink the application of resource overcommitment and live migration to improve data center resource utilization. Based on real-world cluster traces published by Google in 2019, we show that combining resource overcommitment with task live migration can reduce the mean task turnaround time by 16%, demonstrating that further research in this direction is both warranted and promising.

Keywords: Live migration · Data center · Virtualization · Load balancing

1 Introduction

Due to the huge benefits of flexibility and efficiency, many users and organizations have come to cloud computing to either use or service various products [14,18]. During this trend, virtual machines (VMs) have been the fundamental unit of cloud computing with the advantages of security, performance isolation, and ease of management [5]. Nowadays, the growing popularity of resource-intensive applications such as artificial intelligence (AI), machine learning (ML), and big data analytics demand larger VM instances to accommodate

© Springer Nature Switzerland AG 2021
K. Tserpes et al. (Eds.): GECON 2021, LNCS 13072, pp. 17–26, 2021.
https://doi.org/10.1007/978-3-030-92916-9_2

their workloads. There is a clear trend of increasing instance sizes to run resource-intensive applications; the median memory size of a VM in AWS EC2 catalog is 64 GB, and VMs with a memory size above 32 GB in Microsoft Azure see an increase from about 5% [3] to 10% [4] of all instances.

Despite the growing demand for computing resources, machines in the data centers still suffer from low resource utilization. The recently published cluster trace from Google [16] reveals that the average utilization of CPU and memory stagnated at the 60% level, indicating significant room for improvement. Other providers such Microsoft Azure [7] and Alibaba [9] report similarly low average resource utilization.

Under utilization is typically caused by tasks that reserve more resources than they actually use. Since tasks are scheduled onto a machine based on the requested resources, it is not easy to avoid under utilization if the total sum of requested resources are to fit within the node's capacity. To tackle this issue, resource overcommitment [8] became a promising solution to improve the resource utilization. However, the huge gap between the reservation and the actual usage makes seamless overcommitment challenging. An inaccurate prediction of resource usage causes a waste of resources when overestimated, or a performance degradation when underestimated. Since no prediction can be perfect every time, load balancing the key to achieve high utilization of nodes [12].

Live migration enables load balancing and is thus a promising solution to alleviate the problem of low resource utilization. A task is live migrated from one machine to another by copying its entire volatile state, i.e., its memory, from one machine to another and thus is a resource-intensive operation in itself. With typical virtual machine memory sizes reaching 64 GiB, however, migrating a task can take several minutes and is thus not typically used for load balancing.

Recent advancements in networking technology change this situation. With the arrival of Terabit Ethernet [15], even large tasks can be migrated within a few seconds, opening up new possibilities for resource overcommitment and load balancing. An interesting question in this context is by how much resource utilization can be improved in such environments. This paper explores this question by simulating the execution of a 2019 Google cluster trace in a data center cluster with an 100 Gb/s interconnection network.

The remainder of this paper is organized as follows: Sect. 2 discusses VM live migration and the 2019 Google cluster trace. Section 3 explains our simulator in detail, and Sect. 4 analyzes the experiments conducted with the simulator. Section 4.3 discusses related works, and Sect. 5 concludes this paper.

2   Background and Motivation

2.1   Cluster Scheduler and Scaling

The job of the cluster scheduler is to place incoming jobs on the cluster's nodes to improve throughput, turnaround time, and overall resource utilization. A job often comprises multiple tasks that each can be placed on different nodes. A node executes multiple tasks in parallel to maximize resource utilization and job throughput. Finding the proper balance when co-locating tasks is an important task of the cluster scheduler.

A major challenge in designing a cluster scheduler is accurately predicting the resource demands of each task. The mismatch between reservation and actual usage of resources makes it difficult to maximize the utilization of a cluster. For example, despite a task requesting 4 CPUs and 8 GiB of memory, the actual resources usage can be much lower than the requested amount of resources.

Task migration is an important tool to correct load mispredictions and allows rebalancing the load of each node. However, due to the high cost of migration, cluster schedulers try to minimize the number of migrated tasks. Instead, after assigning tasks, horizontal or vertical scaling or a combination of both [1,13] are used to achieve higher utilization. While these techniques can exploit slack caused by low average utilization, such scaling techniques are challenging to be applied during load spikes [2].

2.2   VM Live Migration

VM live migration is a useful technique that enables relocating a running VM to another node without a significant downtime. It is especially useful when a cluster has to change the placement of VMs for load balancing. With VM live migration, a task running on a heavily loaded node is migrated to a lightly loaded node to utilize resources better and improve overall task completion time.

A challenge with VM live migration for load balancing is reducing the total time of the migration itself. Migrating a VM requires sending a copy of the entire VM state to the destination node; for current VMs, this can take several minutes even with 10 Gb/s networks. A fluctuating resource usage of a task also makes applying VM live migration difficult. If migration takes too long to complete, the VM can be migrated at the wrong time, resulting in a waste of resources.

Due to its prohibitively high cost, in general, VM live migration is not used for load balancing purposes [7]. The rising popularity of fast networks, however, is bringing this cost down by several orders of magnitude. It is thus important to re-evaluate live migration as a load balancing tool. Currently, network performance doubles every few years; network throughputs of 100 Gb/s are now available for inter node data transfer [15]. Such fast network dramatically reduce the overall VM migration time and thereby make live migration for load balancing feasible [11]. Considering such technique employed in data centers, operators may need to rethink the use of VM live migration for load balancing.

2.3   Google Cluster Trace 2019

Google has published cluster traces of their warehouses in 2011 [17] and 2019 [16]. In this paper, we use the cluster trace published in 2019 for our analysis. The main content of the cluster trace is per-task resource usage over time. The trace includes 5-min averaged normalized CPU and memory usage with percentile values. By summing up the resource usage of tasks running on the same node, we can compute the total resource usages of each node over time. To analyze potential improvements in resource utilization, we simulate an overcommitted data center with and without live migration.

3   Cluster Simulation

To test the hypothesis of this work, we have implemented a cluster simulator. The simulator simulates a given number of heterogeneous physical machines for a number of tasks that are described in terms of their resource usage over time. In the following, the design and implementation of our simulator are explained in detail.

3.1   Simulation Parameters

The simulator is controlled with three main parameters. The *overcommit factor* determines by how much the resources of a physical node can be overcommitted. With an overcommit factor of 2, for example, the resources of a node can be reserved up to 200% of its actual capacity. The overcommit factor is a key parameter that significantly affects node utilization during the simulation. The *migration* parameter that controls whether tasks are allowed to be live migrated to other nodes for load balancing purposes. The *epochs* parameter, finally, sets the duration of the simulation in epochs. The number of simulated expochs should be sufficiently high to allow most tasks to terminate.

3.2   Tasks and Machines

Every task is associated with a resource reservation request and a resource utilization history. The resource reservation request defines how the amount of resources that the task reserves on a node. The resource utilization history of a task reflects the actual resource utilization of the task over time. Physical nodes are defined with a certain amount of resources. The sum of all co-located tasks' resource reservations on a node must not surpass the amount of resources multiplied by the overcommit factor. If the sum of the co-located tasks' actual resource utilization at a given point in time exceeds the physically available resources, the tasks experience a performance degradation (see below). All resources, resource requests, and resource utilizations are normalized to the largest amount of resources available in a single node.

3.3   Task Arrivals

We assume that all tasks are submitted at the beginning of the simulation (epoch 0). This is to have a large pool of schedulable jobs ready to get a better understanding the effect of live migration and resource overcommitment on the utilization of a data center. Simulations with task arrivals over time are left for future work.

3.4 Task Performance Degradation

As stated above, the sum of co-located tasks' resource reservations never exceeds the node's resource multiplied by the overcommit factor. It is, however, possible that the accumulated resource usage of all co-located tasks for a given epoch surpasses the physically available resources of the node. This situation is called *overload*. Since all resource metrics are normalized, *overload factor* is identical to the total of all co-located task's resource utilization. Whenever overload occurs, all co-located tasks on the overloaded node experience a performance degradation. The In this work, we slow down all co-located tasks equally by dividing the resource utilization by the overload factor. For example, if four co-located tasks request 50% of the physically available CPU resources on a node (an overload factor of 2), each task receives only $50/2 = 25\%$ CPU resources, effectively, halving their performance.

3.5 VM Live Migration Duration

For slower networks, the duration of live migration is an important metric since at least one full copy of a task's volatile state needs to be copied from the source to destination node. In dependence of the live migration algorithm, a significantly larger amount of data may get transferred [10]; this is especially true for algorithms based on pre-copy that iteratively send the modified data from the source to the destination node [6].

With network bandwidths approaching (or even exceeding) 100 Gb/s, live migration becomes "instant" for most practical purposes. A VM with 64 GiB of RAM, for example, can be migrated in less than 10 s even when assuming a duplication factor of 1.5 for pre-copy (i.e., copying 96 GiB of data). Since the sampling interval of Google's trace data with one sample per 5 min is significantly larger, we ignore the duration of live migration in this work.

3.6 Simulation Procedure

The simulator runs from epoch 0 to *epochs* as defined in the simulation parameters (Sect. 3.1). We only consider CPU and memory resources in this work; other resources such as network bandwidth are left for future work. At the start of each epoch, overcommitment and VM live migration are simulated as follows:

1. **Migration Candidate Selection.** In this first step, all nodes are checked for overload by summing up the current resource usage of each co-located task. The co-located tasks of a node are visited in random order. As soon as overload occurs for either the CPU or memory resource, the current and all following tasks are marked as migration candidates.
2. **VM live Migration.** In this step, the simulator tries to migrate all migration candidates to nodes with sufficient resources. The simulator tries to migrate each candidate task a node with idle resources; the order in which the nodes are visited is random. If no machine can host the task without getting overloaded, the task is not migrated and stays on its initial node.

3. **Task Scheduling.** After all migration candidates have been processed, the scheduler tries to place tasks from the job wait queue onto the cluster. Tasks in the wait queue are not reordered, i.e., task scheduling stops at the first task that cannot be mapped onto the cluster anymore.
4. **Proportional Scheduling.** In this last step, the performance of overloaded nodes is adjusted to simulate performance degradation. All co-located tasks on an overloaded node progress with the reciprocal of the overload factor for this epoch.

3.7   Implementation

The simulator is implemented in Python.

Table 1. Task completion and turnaround time in dependence of the over-commit factor.

	Completion time					Turnaround time				
	×1.0	×2.0	×2.5	×3.0	×3.5	×1.0	×2.0	×2.5	×3.0	×3.5
Median	7	8	9	12	14	38	10	11	13	15
Mean	39.4	40.6	43.1	46.2	50.4	2191.3	70.1	60.5	63.5	67
95%ile	77	82	89	98	109	9923	269	189	195	204
99%ile	645	647	698	658	742	11579	1284	980	965	981
Std. Dev.	250.5	250.9	252.4	251.8	255	3446.6	289.8	268.8	268.3	270.3

Table 2. Task completion and turnaround time depending on task live migration.

	Completion time		Turnaround time	
	W/o Migration	W/ Migration	W/o Migration	W/ Migration
Median	9	7	11	9
Mean	43.1	40.7	60.5	50.7
95%ile	89	87	189	145
99%ile	698	653	980	823
Std. Dev.	252.4	253.1	268.8	260

4   Evaluation

For the evaluation, we simulate 20 physical nodes and 400'000 tasks randomly selected from the 2019 Google Cluster Trace [16]. We first analyze how the over-commitment factor and task live migration affect the simulation in Sect. 4.1. Next, we investigate resource utilization over time with and without live migration in Sect. 4.2.

4.1 Task Completion and Turnaround Time

Table 1 shows the effects of different overcommit factors without task live migrations. The completion time denotes the time from then the task is scheduled to its completion. The turnaround time, on the other hand, reports the time from the task's submission time to its completion, i.e., includes the wait time between submission and the start of the execution. The results show that no overcommitment is best for tasks (as there is no performance degradation) but seriously harms the throughput of a data center. As the overcommit factor is raised, the data center's throughput increases significantly with a moderate increase in task completion time. We also observe that too much overcommitment starts to hurt data center performance but is still well above no overcommitment at an overcommit factor of 3.5.

Next, we analyze the effect of task migration on completion time and turnaround time. Table 2 shows the results for an overcommitment factor of 2.5 with and without task migration. We observe live migration that both completion time and turnaround time improve with live migration. The mean completion time is reduced by 5% while the mean turnaround time decreases by 16% compared to no task migration. While these numbers seem moderate, the benefits in terms of cost and energy savings are significant at warehouse-scale.

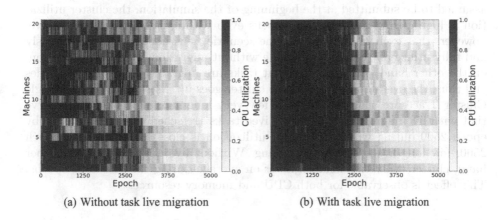

(a) Without task live migration   (b) With task live migration

Fig. 1. Node CPU utilization heatmap with and without task live migration.

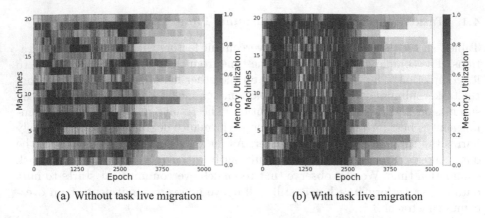

(a) Without task live migration   (b) With task live migration

Fig. 2. Node memory utilization heatmap with and without task live migration.

4.2   Resource Utilization

Cluster resource utilization and task throughput are visualized by Figs. 1 and 2. The figures show heatmaps of CPU and memory utilization for simulations with an overcommit factor of 2.5 with and without task migration. Since all tasks are assumed to be submitted at the beginning of the simulation, the cluster utilization is high during the first 2500 epochs even without migration. We observe, however, that even in such an extreme scenario, it is not easy to continuously and fully utilize all resources of a node without migration. With live migration, on the other hand, we clearly see that tasks are migrated to less-loaded nodes and thus, the overall utilization of the cluster goes up. Most tasks in the Google Cluster Trace are short-lived with a few very long running tasks. We observe that with live migration, most short-lived tasks are scheduled and complete by epoch 2500 during which the cluster utilization is close to 100%. After epoch 2500, few long-lived tasks keep running. Without live migration, on the other hand, cluster utilization is much lower on average during the first 2500 epochs. This effect is observable for both CPU and memory resource.

4.3   Discussion

The simulation in this work-in-progress paper are admittedly limited. Both the simulator itself, and the simulated scenario can be improved. Nevertheless, we believe that these initial results reveal the potential of live migration in fast networking environments. In future work, we plan to extend our simulator to include more realistic task scheduling and migration policies and also account for the overhead of live migration. This will require finer-grained resource usage statistics since the 5-min interval of the Google Cluster Trace does not allow exact modeling of performance degradation under overload or live migration scenarios.

5   Conclusion

In this paper, we have shown that new and faster network technologies allow for a renaissance of live migration for load balancing and, thus, better resource utilization in data centers. Using real-world task traces provided by Google, our simulations show that live migration has the potential to significantly improve overall resource utilization, task completion time, and task turnaround time. For future work, we plan to extend our simulator into a full-fledged cluster simulator to serve as a test bed for exploring new algorithms and policies for live migration, job placement, and overcommitment.

Acknowledgments. We thank the anonymous reviewers for their helpful feedback and suggestions. This work was supported by the Korean government (MSIT) through the National Research Foundation by grants 0536-20210093 and 21A20151113068 (BK21 Plus for Pioneers in Innovative Computing - Dept. of Computer Science and Engineering, SNU). ICT at Seoul National University provided research facilities for this study.

References

1. New AWS auto scaling - unified scaling for your cloud applications, May 2009. https://aws.amazon.com/blogs/aws/aws-auto-scaling-unified-scaling-for-your-cloud-applications/
2. Ari, I., Hong, B., Miller, E.L., Brandt, S.A., Long, D.D.: Managing flash crowds on the internet. In: 11th IEEE/ACM International Symposium on Modeling, Analysis and Simulation of Computer Telecommunications Systems. MASCOTS 2003, pp. 246–249. IEEE (2003)
3. Azure: Azure public dataset - trace analysis.ipynb, October 2017. https://github.com/Azure/AzurePublicDataset/blob/master/analysis/Azure
4. Azure: Azure 2019 public dataset v2 - trace analysis.ipynb, July 2019. https://github.com/Azure/AzurePublicDataset/blob/master/analysis/Azure
5. Beloglazov, A., Buyya, R.: Managing overloaded hosts for dynamic consolidation of virtual machines in cloud data centers under quality of service constraints. IEEE Trans. Parallel Distrib. Syst. **24**(7), 1366–1379 (2012)
6. Clark, C., et al.: Live migration of virtual machines. In: Proceedings of the 2nd Conference on Symposium on Networked Systems Design and Implementation-Volume 2, pp. 273–286 (2005)
7. Cortez, E., Bonde, A., Muzio, A., Russinovich, M., Fontoura, M., Bianchini, R.: Resource central: Understanding and predicting workloads for improved resource management in large cloud platforms. In: Proceedings of the 26th Symposium on Operating Systems Principles, pp. 153–167 (2017)
8. Ghosh, R., Naik, V.K.: Biting off safely more than you can chew: predictive analytics for resource over-commit in IAAS cloud. In: 2012 IEEE Fifth International Conference on Cloud Computing, pp. 25–32. IEEE (2012)
9. Guo, J., Chang, Z., Wang, S., Ding, H., Feng, Y., Mao, L., Bao, Y.: Who limits the resource efficiency of my datacenter: an analysis of Alibaba datacenter traces. In: 2019 IEEE/ACM 27th International Symposium on Quality of Service (IWQoS), pp. 1–10. IEEE (2019)

10. Jo, C., Cho, Y., Egger, B.: A machine learning approach to live migration modeling. In: ACM Symposium on Cloud Computing. SoCC 2017, September 2017
11. Jo, C., Kim, H., Egger, B.: Instant virtual machine live migration. In: Djemame, K., Altmann, J., Bañares, J.Á., Agmon Ben-Yehuda, O., Stankovski, V., Tuffin, B. (eds.) GECON 2020. LNCS, vol. 12441, pp. 155–170. Springer, Cham (2020). https://doi.org/10.1007/978-3-030-63058-4_14
12. Kansal, N.J., Chana, I.: Cloud load balancing techniques: a step towards green computing. IJCSI Int. J. Comput. Sci. Issues **9**(1), 238–246 (2012)
13. Rzadca, K., et al.: Autopilot: workload autoscaling at google. In: Proceedings of the Fifteenth European Conference on Computer Systems, pp. 1–16 (2020)
14. Subramanian, N., Jeyaraj, A.: Recent security challenges in cloud computing. Comput. Electr. Eng. **71**, 28–42 (2018)
15. Technology, L.: Terabit ethernet: The new hot trend in data centers, March 2020. https://www.lanner-america.com/blog/terabit-ethernet-new-hot-trend-data-centers/
16. Tirmazi, M., et al.: Borg: the next generation. In: Proceedings of the Fifteenth European Conference on Computer Systems, pp. 1–14 (2020)
17. Verma, A., Pedrosa, L., Korupolu, M., Oppenheimer, D., Tune, E., Wilkes, J.: Large-scale cluster management at google with Borg. In: Proceedings of the Tenth European Conference on Computer Systems, pp. 1–17 (2015)
18. Zhang, X., et al.: Energy-aware virtual machine allocation for cloud with resource reservation. J. Syst. Softw. **147**, 147–161 (2019)

Last Mile Delivery by Drone: a Technoeconomic Approach

Evgenia Skoufi, Evangelia Filiopoulou[✉], Angelos Skoufis,
and Christos Michalakelis

Department of Informatics and Telematics, Harokopio University,
Omirou 9, PS 17778 Athens, Greece
evangelf@hua.gr
https://dit.hua.gr

Abstract. As consumers progressively turn to e-commerce for all their shopping needs, on time delivery is of major importance. Logistics companies struggle to find strategies that improve efficiency and reduce costs. Drone-based distribution is an alternative for last mile delivery, gaining popularity, as it can provide reliable and safe services. In this paper the severe challenges of last mile delivery are discussed and a techno economic analysis is presented, introducing and describing a drone distribution model. In addition the drone distribution model is compared with the classic two-wheeled motorcycle distribution model, highlighting the fundamental contribution drones can have in the supply chain.

Keywords: Last mile delivery · Drone · Capital expenses · Operating expenses · Techno-economic analysis

1   Introduction

Last mile delivery refers to the last step of the delivery process when a parcel is moved from a transportation hub to its final destination, which usually, is a personal residence or retail store. Growth in Last Mile Delivery (LMD) had been strong for a number of years. Then came the COVID-19 pandemic and has created a spike in demand for delivery. The LMD market is constantly growing and is predicted that will record a Compound Annual Growth Rate (CAGR) of over 14% during 2020–2024 [1]. Therefore, it is not surprising that major Logistics providers, such as UPS, FedEx and XPO Logistics offer last mile delivery services to small and large retailers.

A large challenge when delivering products is the time frame upon which the product will be delivered. Several proposed strategies have studied the complex problem of packages distribution in last mile logistics chain. Based on literature the last mile delivery can be successful by combining drone with truck [1], or by using electric vehicles that are considered feasible solutions in reducing the carbon footprint [11]. In addition, introduction of known distribution algorithms that resolve delivery problems such as the Vehicle Routing Problem with Time

© Springer Nature Switzerland AG 2021
K. Tserpes et al. (Eds.): GECON 2021, LNCS 13072, pp. 27–35, 2021.
https://doi.org/10.1007/978-3-030-92916-9_3

Windows (VRPTW) and the classic version of Vehicle Routing Problem (VRP) are evolved by proposing a transport model and achieving the goal of successful deliveries [5, 8, 10, 12].

Companies need to explore and adopt innovative technologies to enhance their LMD services. Into this context, businesses can gain a competitive edge by adopting drones for last mile delivery optimization. A delivery drone is an autonomous vehicle that transports packages, food or other products.

Drone technology is a rapidly evolving research area, focusing on the technical improvement of air crafts, their operation through a combination of technologies, including computer vision, artificial intelligence and other similar aspects [17]. However, so far the contribution to the literature, related the techno-economic assessment of the drone technology is relatively limited, despite the fact that the economic standpoint of a corresponding investment of paramount importance. Established commercial companies and transportation service companies integrate their distribution systems services by using drones. Amazon, Google, UPS and DHL are some of these companies developing pilot drone projects for the last mile delivery of their products [17].

Towards this direction a techno-economic analysis is introduced, examining the employment of drones in the LMD service. The analysis introduces a case study that compares and evaluates the drone and the traditional motorcycle-based delivery approaches. In addition, the work performed in this paper and the derived results can also serve as a valuable input for potential investors and provide a roadmap to the drone technology business.

The rest of the paper is organized as follows: Sect. 2 introduces the case study, where a motorcycle and a drone last mile delivery service are compared. Section 3 discusses the results and finally Sect. 4 presents the conclusions, the limitations of the paper, together with future research.

2   Last Mile Delivery-Case Study

In the proposed scenario, a hypothetical local courier distribution center handles the last mile delivery services, named HuaLmd. The proposed case study is initially implemented by a motorcycle-based last mile delivery model and then a drone last mile delivery model is adopted. The scenario of using an electric motorcycle was initially considered, but this technology has not been adopted by Greek distribution companies yet.

Capital Expenses (Capex) and Operating Expenses (Opex) are estimated for each individual model. Capex correspond to the money an organization or corporate entity spends, in order to buy, maintain, or improve its fixed assets, such as buildings, vehicles, equipment [9] where as Opex are the ongoing costs for running a product, business, or system [14]. The following delivery details describe the specifications of each delivery model:

- Transport box dimensions.
- Parcel characteristics, such as the dimensions and the weight of the parcel. Without loss of generality, an average parcel was chosen.

- Delivery Points: The end point where the user receives the parcel.
- Package Delivery: In the current work each delivery consists of only one parcel.
- Estimated Time: The time required from the departure of the parcel from the distribution center to its final recipient.
- Completed Routes: Number of successful deliveries in a prearranged time frame.

2.1 Last Mile Delivery by Motorcycle

The delivery details for the LMD motorcycle model are based on data collected by courier companies [3,15,16] and are presented in Table 1. A Greek urban area was chosen for the implementation of the model (Egaleo, Greece). In Egaleo the longest delivery route is 6 km while the shortest route is set to zero (0). Therefore, the average distance equals to 3 km.

Table 1. Motorcycle LMD details.

Transport box dimensions	$L0, 57\,cm \times W0, 52\,cm \times H0, 54\,cm$
Parcel dimensions and weight	$L0.20\,cm \times W0.10\,cm \times H0.05\,cm$ and 1,5 kg
Delivery points	48
Delivery packages	48
Completed routes	2
Estimated time	8 h

In the motorcycle distribution model, the Capex includes the cost of purchasing the motorcycle (2200.00€) which is an average price of a motorcycle model for deliveries and the shipping box (170.00€). Thus the estimated total amount equals to 2370.00€. The operating expenses of this case are presented in Table 2.

Table 2. Total operating expenditure cost of motorcycle on an annual basis.

Salary	9100.00€
Fuel consumption	1576.80€
Vehicle tax fees	22.00€
Insurance premiums	190.00€
Motorcycle maintenance costs	450.00€
Total	11338.80€

2.2 Last Mile Delivery by Drone

The delivery details for the LMD drone model are based on drone specifications. The specific drone [13] can fly in moderate weather conditions with temperatures between −10 °C and 40 °C. The climate of Greece is Mediterranean with low possibility of rain and snow, thus drone can fly without weather many interruptions. For comparative reasons the characteristics of the transport box and parcel are similar to the corresponding characteristics of motorcycle model. The details of the drone model are presented in Table 3.

Table 3. Drone LMD details.

Transport box dimensions	$L0,57\,cm \times W0,52\,cm \times H0,54\,cm$
Parcel dimensions and Weight	$L0.20\,cm \times W0.10\,cm \times H0.05\,cm$ and 1,5 kg
Delivery points	61
Delivery packages	61
Completed routes	61
Estimated time	8 h
Flight time [13]	32 min

For comparative reasons, the selected urban area where the last mile delivery takes place remains the same. The longest distance that drone will need to cover from the starting point (HuaLmd's distribution center) is 1.93 km, The shortest route is set to zero as in the motorcycle delivery model. Thus, the average distance is defined almost at 1 km. Based on drone's specifications [13] the autonomy of the drone with a load of 1,5 kg is 32 min, thus the drone is capable of four completed flights with a full charge. Aiming to avoid delivery interruption due to battery recharging, four DJI TB48S flight batteries and the corresponding DJI hex charger model are purchased [7]. The required time for a full charge is set at 110 min [13]. After four completed routes the first battery will be replaced by the second fully charged and the first one will begin charging. Then having completed four more flights, the second battery will be replaced by the third one while the second will also begin charging.

In the drone distribution model, the drone purchase considers to be the main capital cost (4.300,00€) [13]. As mentioned above, the company purchases four back-up batteries (768,00€), thus the distribution will not be interrupted by the re-charging of the battery. Finally, for charging simultaneously up to four batteries a specific charger was bought (333,00€). Capital expenditure of drone case study equals to 5401,00€.

The operating expenses of this model includes the cost for purchasing routing platform software [13] and power consumption cost during batteries charging. Finally, insurance premiums[4] and maintenance cost service are taken into account. The insurance covers compensation for personal injury, material damage to third parties, replacement of the drone, ground navigation system coverage and payload coverage. The maintenance cost includes occasional changes of spare parts like propellers of the drone. In addition, the operator of the routing platform is one of the existing employees of the company. The depreciation period of the drone is 3 years while the depreciation period of batteries is 4 years, so the batteries are not replaced prior to the deprecation of the drone. Table 4 presents the operating costs.

Table 4. Total operating expenditure cost of drone on an annual basis.

Routing platform software	6.360,00€
Electricity consumption	1211,80€
Insurance premiums	300,00€
Maintenance cost	190,00€
Total	8061,80€

In order to set the best possible prices for the last mile service provided by HuaLmd, the following framework is formed:

- The company already owns a fleet of motorcycles for the distribution. In the existing fleet a drone is added in order to cover the needs of its customers that arising during the day.
- Motorcycle driver completes two routes within an 8-hour period. The first route refers to orders that have been placed the previous days, whereas the second route includes deliveries from same day orders.
- The success of drone LMD service is related to the lead time, which is limited to 10 min per order. Lead time is the time from the moment the customer places an order to the moment it is ready for delivery.
- The arrival of orders follows a Poisson distribution, with mean value and standard deviation, deriving from the available courier data. Poisson distribution is a discrete distribution that measures the probability of a given number of events happening in a specified time period [2].
- The distributions serviced by drone, will execute the same day orders. Services with a short lead time delivery will be offered with additional charge.
- In the motorcycle distribution model, orders are grouped twice a day and the loading is scheduled every four hours at the distribution center.
- In motorcycle scenario 50% of the deliveries have lead time same day delivery and the remaining 50% of deliveries have lead time next day deliveries.
- In drone model, the number of delivered packets are estimated by Poisson distribution based on the lead time. Therefore, drone carries out 65% of deliveries within 8 h, 25% of deliveries within 4 h and 10% of deliveries within 1 h.

Pricing is based on the lead time and it is derived from the average market prices [3,15,16]. Therefore, HuaLmd offers next day delivery at 6.00€ and same day deliveries at 13.00€. Regarding the drone distribution service, the proposed pricing scheme includes three different prices for the same day deliveries based on the lead time of the delivery, in particular the shorter the lead-time implies the higher the price. More specific, the price for 8, 4 and 1 h lead time equals to 13€, 18€ and 35€ respectively.

2.3 Application Scenario

The techno-economic analysis presents the investment process of the case study for the following three years. Delivery service pricing, initial cost investment and the monthly operating expenses are taken into account through the analysis. Furthermore, the most important assessment indices, the Net Present Value is calculated [30]. NPV is the sum of the present values of incoming and outgoing cash flows over a period of time, as presented in Eq. 1.

$$NPV = \sum_{t=0}^{n} \frac{R_t}{(1+i)^t} \tag{1}$$

where R_t represents net cash flow at time t, i denotes discount rate and t defines time of the cash flow [6].

Motorcycle Last Mile Delivery Scenario. In the current scenario the two-wheeled motorcycle, based on lead time, the 50% of the deliveries are served the same day and the remaining 50% are delivered the next day. Based on the above assumption, Table 5 presents the parameters that are taken into account for the calculation of the NPV. By setting the annual discount rate to 10%, the calculated NPV for the first three years of operation is: 270088,37€.

Table 5. NPV parameters.

Lead time	Price per delivery	Deliveries	Revenue/year
Next day	6€	8760	52.5606€
Same day	13€	8760	113.880€

Drone Scenario. In the drone scenario, the drone serve orders of the same day. The number of delivered packets are estimated by Poisson distribution based on the lead time. Therefore, drone carries out 65% of deliveries within 8 h, 25% of deliveries within 4 h and 10% of deliveries within 1 h. Table 6 presents the overall number of deliveries. Taking into account the Capex and Opex, the calculated NPV for the first three years equals to 62.1180,05€.

Table 6. NPV parameters.

Lead time	Rate of deliveries packets	Revenue/year
8 h	65%	189800.00€
4 h	25%	98550.00€
1 h	10%	76650.00€

3   Results and Discussion

In both models, the motorcycle and drone purchase constitute the main factor of the Capex, since the cost of acquiring the appropriate transportation mean contributes up to 93% and 80% of the total capital cost, respectively. As shown in Fig. 1, the total Capex of the drone model is twice the cost of the motorcycle model. The annualized Capex for motorcycle and drone equipment is depreciated over 8 and 4 years respectively.

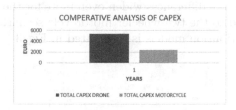

Fig. 1. Comparative analysis of motorcycle and drone Capex.

The average depreciation period of a motorcycle, provided that it is used only for product distribution, is estimated and equals to 8 years, and the annual rate equals to 13%. Regarding the drone distribution model, the average depreciation period is estimated and equals to 4 years and the annual rate is set at 25%. Drones' depreciation estimations are based on data derived by distribution models in Canada, Australia and new Zealand where drone delivery service is already applied [18].

In the motorcycle distribution model, the driver's salary and the annual consumed fuel contribute highly to the operating costs. These two individual costs represent the 94% of the total operation expenses. In the drone distribution model the software platform that replaces the driver of the motorcycle contributes up to 82% of total expenses.

Electricity consumption follows with an estimated contribution up to 16% in the Opex. Even though the cost for drone purchase is twice as much as the motorcycle purchase, the corresponding annual operating costs of the motorcycle are 1.5 times higher than the drone and is equal to 3577.00€. The project is scheduled to be carried out for the following three years, therefore, the difference at the end of the three year is equal to 10731,00€. Figure 2 presents a comparative illustration between motorcycle and drone Opex.

Summarizing the two different models, it is evident that the drone last mile deliver service is more profitable than the classic two-wheeled motorcycle delivery. Comparing motorcycle and drone-based scenario an increase in the number of the deliveries is highlighted. Replacing the motorcycle by a drone, 13 more deliveries are made per day. The growth rate is 27%. The growth of services in combination with the new price in the price list, increase revenues in the realistic scenario with a drone by 117% compared to the scenario of motorcycle. Over

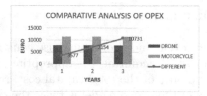

Fig. 2. Comparative analysis of motorcycle and drone operating expenses.

the three-year period, the differences widen even more for the drone distribution scenario, as compared to the two-wheeler motorcycle scenario. The comparison between the two distribution models is illustrated in Fig. 3

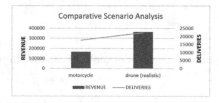

Fig. 3. Comparative scenario analysis

4   Conclusions

The proposed techno-economic analysis focused on the last mile delivery, thus a case study was introduced that proposed HuaLmd, a hypothetical established distribution company, which added a drone to its of already owned fleet of motorcycles.

According to the results, it is evident that the required Capex for the drone adoption for the last mile delivery service is rather high, however the corresponding annual operating costs of the motorcycle are 1.5 times higher than the drone costs. The results indicate that the drone approach is more profitable than the classic two-wheeled motorcycle distribution service, maintaining a substantially higher level of revenues.

The current techno-economic analysis is subject to some limitations. Initially, HuaLmd is assumed to be active in the Greek market for several years, therefore it has already a pool of customers who will try the drone delivery. The offered pricing list service was also based on popular transportation companies of the Greek market. The application cost of the drone distribution model in a startup transportation company with a limited clientele is expected to be higher. Thus, a techno-economic analysis based on a startup company would be an interesting future research direction. In addition, a comparison between a drone and an electric car or motor-cycle distribution model would be challenging.

References

1. Bamburry, D.: Drones: designed for product delivery. Des. Manag. Rev. **26**(1), 40–48 (2015)
2. Consul, P.C., Jain, G.C.: A generalization of the Poisson distribution. Technometrics **15**(4), 791–799 (1973)
3. Courier, E. https://www.elta-courier.gr/portaporta
4. Drone, I.: Drone insurance. https://www.drones-insurance.gr
5. Ehmke, J.F., Mattfeld, D.C.: Vehicle routing for attended home delivery in city logistics. Procedia-Soc. Behav. Sci. **39**, 622–632 (2012)
6. Elmaghraby, S.E., Herroelen, W.S.: The scheduling of activities to maximize the net present value of projects. Eur. J. Oper. Res. **49**(1), 35–49 (1990)
7. Flytrex. https://flytrex.com
8. Goodman, R.W.: Whatever you call it, just don't think of last-mile logistics, last. Glob. Logist. Suppl. Chain Strat. **9**(12) (2005)
9. Kitjacharoenchai, P., Min, B.C., Lee, S.: Two echelon vehicle routing problem with drones in last mile delivery. Int. J. Prod. Econ. **225**, 107598 (2020)
10. Köhler, C., Ehmke, J.F., Campbell, A.M.: Flexible time window management for attended home deliveries. Omega **91**, 102023 (2020)
11. Manerba, D., Mansini, R., Zanotti, R.: Attended home delivery: reducing last-mile environmental impact by changing customer habits. IFAC-PapersOnLine **51**(5), 55–60 (2018)
12. Murray, C.C., Chu, A.G.: The flying sidekick traveling salesman problem: optimization of drone-assisted parcel delivery. Transp. Res. Part C Emerg. Technol. **54**, 86–109 (2015)
13. Digital Platform. https://www.dji.com/gr/matrice600-pro/info
14. Di Puglia Pugliese, L., Guerriero, F.: Last-Mile deliveries by using drones and classical vehicles. In: Sforza, A., Sterle, C. (eds.) ODS 2017. SPMS, vol. 217, pp. 557–565. Springer, Cham (2017). https://doi.org/10.1007/978-3-319-67308-0_56
15. Speedex. http://www.speedex.gr/
16. taxydromiki. https://www.taxydromiki.com/
17. Verbrugge, S., et al.: Methodology and input availability parameters for calculating OPEX and capex costs for realistic network scenarios. J. Opt. Netw. **5**(6), 509–520 (2006)
18. Yoo, H.D., Chankov, S.M.: Drone-delivery using autonomous mobility: an innovative approach to future last-mile delivery problems. In: 2018 IEEE International Conference on Industrial Engineering and Engineering Management (IEEM), pp. 1216–1220. IEEE (2018)

AI and Digital Economy

AI Technologies and Motives for AI Adoption by Countries and Firms: A Systematic Literature Review

Rene Kabalisa[✉] and Jörn Altmann[✉]

Technology Management, Economics and Policy Program,
Seoul National University, Seoul, Korea
cfmrene@snu.ac.kr, jorn.altmann@acm.org

Abstract. In this era of digital revolution, artificial intelligence stands to be one of the emerging technologies to revolutionize the way we live, work, or communicate. While everyone is fighting to lead in this technology, their readiness differs and adoption challenges arise in many sectors. These competitions also result in various economic impacts on countries, firms, and individuals. This paper uses a systematic literature review to analyze the existing economic impact of AI adoption and the technology used. Overall, this paper presents clear evidence that AI adoption has a large effect on an economy. Findings of this research help researchers and practitioners to identify important economic impacts of adopting AI, identify directions for future research, and set policies that need to be put in place.

Keywords: Systematic literature review · Artificial Intelligence · Adoption · Economic impact · AI technology

1   Introduction

Countries, firms, and even individuals are economically impacted by technological change. Their decision to adopt a certain technology and its effective use can be crucial to their success. Artificial intelligence (AI) is considered as one of the most time changing technologies in this era of the 4th industrial revolution. Rao and Verweij projected in 2017 that by 2030 the global GDP will grow by 15.7 trillion US dollars [1].

Artificial intelligence is one of the computer science branches, in which machines can work and respond like humans [3]. In this paper, we consider AI as a combination of technologies that allow machines to act at a high level and enable humans to increase their capabilities in different activities.

Countries are racing in adopting AI technologies. Chen et al. expect that the adoption of AI can directly increase countries' GDP [4]. The adoption of AI in different sectors is expected to make countries become leaders in those sectors, hence increasing that country's economy and hegemony. In 2017, according

K. Tserpes et al. (Eds.): GECON 2021, LNCS 13072, pp. 39–51, 2021.
https://doi.org/10.1007/978-3-030-92916-9_4

to the Chinese State Council's development plan, China made AI a "new and important" driver of their economy, they expected to become global leaders by 2020, which they have achieved with the AI Chinese industry able to generate around $59 billion US Dollars annually [4]. Similarly, other countries have formulated strategic policies related to the adoption and diffusion of AI. Examples are South Korea, Canada, Russia, Philippines, and India.

Not only have countries recognized the importance of AI, but firms also adjusted their business strategies by adopting AI. For example, Google was the pioneer when it formulated the first AI policy followed by Apple. In China, big companies such as Baidu, Tencent, and Alibaba have responded positively by investing in startups that have interest in AI. In that context, small firms chose to adopt AI in search of new investments.

According to the McKinsey Global Institute report released in 2018, more than 70% of firms will adopt AI in their businesses by the year 2030. It also predicts that the global economic output production will grow by 16%. In terms of AI market share structure, the latest report by Allied Market research forecasts that the global artificial intelligence market size is expected to reach $169,411.8 million by 2025 with a growth rate of 55.6%. The prediction also identifies segments of AI that would lead the market such as machine learning, natural language processing, image processing, and speech recognition.

Furthermore, the large-scale adoption of AI not only generates economic growth to countries and firms but also affects individuals that use that technology every day. So many social implications are being witnessed. Many people are losing their jobs mainly due to the use of AI for automation. In the article about the effect of artificial intelligence on China's labor market, Zhou [8] estimates between 201 and 333 million jobs replaced by either automation or use of robots by 2049. He also highlights that benefits on individuals will be relatively high compared to the time before AI adoption. For example, considering the acceleration of the aging population, elderly people will be able to physically work with less energy due to the use of AI-controlled robot support. To investigate this cost and benefits in more detail, a review of existing literature would be very helpful.

Therefore, the main objective of this systematic literature review is to investigate the economic impact of AI adoption with respect to identifying the industries impacted, the motivation for adoption, and the AI technology used. The Objective of the research can be expressed in detail with help of the following three research questions (RQ):

RQ1 What AI technologies impact the most?

RQ2 What motivates countries, firms, or individuals to adopt AI?

RQ3 What are the industries in which the impact of AI adoption is mostly observed?

Subsequent sections of this paper are organized as follows. Section 2 presents the background. Section 3 presents the methodology used, including the details on the systematic literature review protocol. Section 4 presents the analysis and the findings of the review. Section 5 discusses the findings and draws directions for future research. Finally, the conclusion wraps up the key points of the review.

2   Background

In this paper, AI is considered as any type of learning-based technology that is able to increase human performance or replace humans in executing some of their everyday tasks by exhibiting some degree of intelligence or autonomy, if, at the end, they gain a positive economic benefit. AI can be integrated into voice assistants, facial recognition, or embedded in special hardware devices like robots, drones, or Internet of things. Chatbots are AI systems that use natural language processing techniques to conduct a conversation via text or audio. It allows recognizing voices and understanding what is said and being able to respond accordingly. Autonomous machines are defined as a machine that can perform different tasks with no human interventions.

Machine learning is an AI subset that focuses on learning algorithms for machines. It allows machines to learn about new data with no human intervention.

AI is a busy word that is interchangeably used with other terms and words, in this article. The following technical terms will come up very often: automation, mechanization, virtual personal assistance, machine vision, deep learning, NLP, platforms [28], and machine learning.

3   Methodology

To conduct the systematic literature review (SLR), this paper adapts the methodology by Webster and Watson [12]. The methodology is explained in the paper "Webster, J., & Watson, R. T. (2002). Analyzing the past to prepare for the future: Writing a literature review". The Webster and Watson Systematic literature review model identifies relevant literature in a certain field, in order to identify what theories, concepts, and developments are currently discussed in that field. It also helps identifying possible gaps with the aim of developing new theories and new research proposals. Many authors tackling emerging issues on topics such as AI, IoT, Big Data, and Drones use the Webster and Watson model.

Below are the methodological steps that we follow, while conducting this research:

- Step 1: Define topic,
- Step 2: Formulate research questions,
- Step 3: Identify keywords,
- Step 4: Identify search terms,
- Step 5: Identify search in specific databases,
- Step 7: Set selection criteria (i.e., publication types, dates, and languages) and quality assessment criteria,
- Step 8: Collect articles, then use EndNote to organize them,
- Step 9: Reduce the number of articles by applying set of selection criteria, screening,
- Step 10: Fill the data extraction form with the selected papers,
- Step 11: Analyze and document data.

3.1   Review Protocol

The review protocol stores detailed information about the steps applied while searching, selecting, including, and assessing articles to be reviewed in this study. It includes information about:

Research Questions and Keywords: After finishing setting up the topic and the research questions, as laid out in the introduction, keywords are identified that are synonymous to the words used in the research questions.

Search Terms: A manual search was conduced using the terms *"artificial intelligence AND adoption"*, *"artificial intelligence AND adoption AND economic impact"*, *"artificial intelligence AND adoption AND benefit".*, in order to check the list of terms used.

Databases: The selection of databases comprises the three most frequently used databases by researchers in the technology area. They are *Scopus, Web of Science, and Science Direct.*

Inclusion Criteria: In order to clearly describe the relevant articles that answers our research questions, we developed a set of inclusion criteria:

- Inclusion criterion 1: As publication date of the research articles, the years between 2000 and 2021 should be selected.
- Inclusion criterion 2: As publication languages, only research articles written in English or French should be selected.
- Inclusion criterion 3: Among the studies obtained, only research articles published in journal articles, conferences proceedings, and early access journals should be selected.
- Inclusion criterion 4: In order to assure quality, articles that comprise an analysis of data and a discussion of results should be selected.
- Inclusion criterion 5: Studies that address the domains of automation, artificial intelligence, and economics should be selected.

Search Queries: Search queries were performed in the three electronic databases using the three search terms. The number of articles obtained after performing the search queries are:

Selection Process: The initial search using the search queries produced a total of 627 articles. After applying the predefined selection criteria (i.e., inclusion criteria), 63 articles were recorded related to automation, AI, and economy. Those 63 articles were read, in order to decide whether those articles are relevance to the research topic and the research questions. Then, the quality of the research articles has been checked, resulting in 30 articles that are used for the systematic literature research.

4   Analysis of Results

This section describes the results obtained from our analysis of the selected research articles, organized into a descriptive analysis and findings that answer our research questions (Table 1).

Table 1. Summary of collected articles.

Search queries	Electronic databases	Records
Artificial intelligence AND adoption	Science Direct	16
	Web of Science	19
	Scopus	449
Artificial intelligence AND adoption AND economic impact	Science Direct	7
	Web of Science	14
	Scopus	2
Artificial intelligence AND benefit	Science Direct	24
	Web of Science	24
	Scopus	72
Total		627

4.1 Descriptive Analysis

Our findings are based on the results presented in the 30 articles selected. All 30 selected articles were peer-reviewed articles in scientific publications or conference proceedings. Among those 30 articles, 15 were from Web of Science and the other 15 from Scopus. None of our reviewed articles is from Science Direct.

Even though we searched for papers published in year 2000 onwards, those that addressed our research questions started from year 2018. As no other paper could be found that was published before 2018, it can be stated that the economic impact of AI adoption is still a new topic of research. Moreover, most of the research papers (i.e., 12 of 30 research papers) were published in 2020. As this research was conducted in early June 2021, the number of research papers might increase until the end of the year 2021.

The distribution of selected papers considering countries, in which the AI was adopted, indicates that most research papers on AI adoption focus on emerging and developing countries. Countries like India, China, South-Africa, and Philippines have many research articles on AI adoption.

Regarding the areas of AI adoption, most selected research articles show that AI was adopted in the private sector, followed by a combination of private and public institutions.

Several research methods have been used by research articles selected in our review. Most research articles use surveys though. One of the findings is that most research on AI adoption in countries and firms tend to address practical issues by using surveys. They focus on conceptual framework or policies on how to better adopt and diffuse the use of AI.

4.2 Economic Impact of AI Adoption

This section presents the findings with respect to the research questions. The findings address (RQ1) the different types of AI technologies that impact the most (Subsect. 4.2.1), (RQ2) the motives of countries and firms for adopting AI (Subsect. 4.2.2), and (RQ3) the industries, in which the economic impact of AI adoption is mostly observed, (Subsect. 4.2.3).

4.2.1 Technologies Adopted

Figure 1 shows the types of technologies adopted together with AI, according to the reviewed research articles. Although many selected articles only mention AI adoption to reach their goals, some articles are more concrete by mentioning adoptions of combinations of AI with other related technologies. For example, they are highlighted as AI & automation, AI & robots, AI with satellites and drones, AI & cloud computing & IoT & blockchain & big data, automation through robots, as well as Big Data powered with AI.

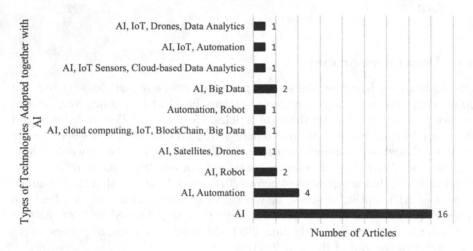

Fig. 1. Distribution of types of technologies adopted from the selected articles.

The AI mentioned in most articles are algorithms and software (e.g., deep learning), which are able to investigate behaviors and support big data analysis. Furthermore, AI robots were also mentioned. It was defined as a combination of machines with software, which is able to act like humans or which is able to be controlled remotely. An example given was electronic vending machines. AI and automation were also mentioned in few articles. It has been identified for cost reduction as well as production growth, but was mentioned mostly in combination with the retail and construction industry.

4.2.2 Motives for AI Adoption

The findings from reviewed articles reveal what motivate countries and firms have when adopting AI. The exhaustive list of 13 categories of motives for AI adoption are summarized in Table 2. The most mentioned motivation for AI adoption was to catch up with AI trends and technologies. This motives was given in 10 articles

[9, 14, 18, 21, 23, 25, 29, 39, 41, 43]. Our interpretation is that most articles focused on emerging economies (e.g., China, India, South Africa, and Philippines). These nations are racing to achieve global innovation advantage in AI, in order to catch up with the global leaders (e.g., United States of America, Korea, or Israel) by boosting competitiveness and increasing productivity. The second explanation is that these countries do not want to be left behind in this technology. Support for this is that there are also a few articles with the "catch up" motive that end with designing and formulating "AI policy implementation plans". Examples for that have been articles on India, China, as well as Philippines.

Another major motive that should be highlighted is *Pressure to Change*. The articles [15, 16] address this motive in the context of SMEs in Australia and the wine industry in France. Australian startups and SMEs have a lot of pressure, in order to change the way they serve their clients. Similar issues were identified in the case of the wine industry in France.

The motive *"Positioning as a Leader"* in AI was also mentioned often in the selected studies. Atwal et al. [4] highlight how the French wine industry, which is currently the global leader, has to adopt AI if it wants to keep its position. As China is competing for global hegemony with the USA in AI [4], it needs to demonstrate leadership. Germany, which is the leader in oil and gas drilling, wants to keep its position as a leader [18] with the help of AI. South Africa that wants to keep its banking sector dominating the African economy [36] by using AI. Similarly, Romania [43] and India [9] want to become leaders in the automobile and health sector with the help of AI.

The motive *"Competition"* was one of the main motives of AI adoption as well. Nations as well as firms' competitiveness depend on the capacity to innovate [30, 35]. In this case, many countries and companies chose to adopt AI, increase R&D funds, or to develop AI policies, in order to be able to compete with other rivals on the global market. In detail, articles were found, which stated the main reason for adopting AI to be: *pressure to competition* [17]; *competitiveness* [9, 20, 29, 39, 44]; *competition* [4, 23, 37, 41]; *sustain global competitiveness* [32]; *increase competitiveness* [33]; *maintain competitiveness advantages* [36]; and *get competitiveness advantages* [43].

Another motivation for AI adoption, which is related to the private sector, is *productivity*. India plans to *increase productivity* in agriculture and health sector [33], the EU *attain productivity growth* [24], Greece wants to *increase productivity efficiency* in the transport sector [31], and China envisages to *increase productivity and economic growth* in almost all sectors [8].

With respect to the motive *Country Plan*, which is about aligning AI adoption with a country's goals [44], India is a good example. Although India is still far away from AI adoption and diffusion, it aims to *attain technological maturity*, according to the article of Krishna [32]. For this, the article proposed an AI framework and policy plan for India for almost all sectors of the economy.

Other motives, which are mentioned in the selected articles, are either focused on a single economic aspect or are very general. The motives that were mentioned are *Cost* [36, 38], *Customer Acquisition* [37], *Profit Maximization* [37], *Saving Money* [27], *Employment Opportunity* [24], and the general motive *Economic Benefits* [19, 20, 26, 27]. Table 2, summarizes the motives for adopting AI.

Table 2. Overview of motivation for AI adoption.

Number	Category of motive for adopting AI	Sub-motives
1	Catching up	Catching up with the AI trend (Bello et al. 2019; Alrashedi & Abbod 2020; Chatterjee 2020; Concepcion et al. 2019; Fouda 2020; Hammer & Karmakar 2021; Rosales et al. 2020; Somjai et al. 2020; Srivastava 2018; Turlacu et al. 2018)
2	Pressure to change	Pressure to change (Alsheibani et al. 2019); external pressure and organizational readiness (Atwal et al. 2021)
3	Positioning as a leader	Positioning as a leader in AI (Atwal et al. 2021); leader (Bello et al. 2019); be the leader in AI (Chen et al. 2021); maintain economic advantages advantages over other countries (Mamela et al. 2020); market positioning (Srivastava 2018); position itself in global market (Turlacu et al. 2018)
4	Competition	Pressure to competition (Bab et al. 2021); competitiveness (Casalino et al. 2020; Hammer & Karmakar 2021; Rosales et al. 2020; Srivastava 2018; Tyson & Sauers 2021); competition (Chen et al. 2021); Concepcion et al. 2019; Nam et al. 2020; Somjai et al. 2020); sustain global competitiveness (Krishna 2018); increase competitiveness (Lakshmi 2020); maintain competitiveness advantages (Mamela et al. 2020); get competitiveness advantages (Turlacu et al. 2018)
5	Productivity	Increase productivity (Lakshmi 2020; Ernst et al. 2019); attain productivity growth (Ernst et al. 2019); increase productivity efficiency (Kopsacheilis et al. 2020); increase productivity and economic growth (Zhou et al. 2020)
6	Economic benefits	Perceived economic benefits that come with adoption of new technologies in business (Bilgeri et al. 2018; Casalino et al. 2020; Gavrilova & Gurvitsh-Suits 2020; Gomes et al. 2020)
7	Country plan	Align with country's goals and objectives (Tyson & Sauers 2021); attain technological maturity (Krishna 2018)
8	Cost	Manage workforce by reducing cost (Pan et al. 2021; Mamela et al. 2020, Lakshmi 2020)
9	Customer acquisition	Gain customers and market positioning (Nam et al. 2020)
10	Profit maximization	Profit maximization through reducing cost (Lakshmi 2020)
11	Saving money	Saving operational expenses (Gomes et al. 2020)
12	Employment opportunity	Obtain employment opportunities and impact on jobs (Ernst et al. 2019)

4.2.3 Industries that are Economically Impacted by AI Adoption

A number of economic impacts of AI adoption were identified in industries. The selected articles covered a wide variety of industry sectors and organizational aspects of firms, in which AI was adopted: governance, SMEs, beverage & wine, automobile, oil & gas drilling, automotive, chemistry, firms organizational structure, government, telecom, manufacturing, high tech, agriculture, industrial production, manufacturing, education, transport, distribution, agriculture, accounting, hydrology (dam), transport, healthcare, banking, and tourism. It shows that AI will have an impact in all aspects of our economy.

Several targeted aspects of firms included: increasing performance, cost reduction, increasing sales, competitiveness, production growth, value creation, reducing resources in organizational structure, increasing productivity, and increasing GDP. These aspects are general objectives of a firm [40].

By adopting AI, articles stated that the performance was increased. In some countries after implementing AI policies, their positions on the global markets rose. Examples are China and India. In the case of firms, many firms increased productivity, saved costs and time after adopting AI. Some mentioned improving operating efficiency and solving many optimization problems.

5   Discussion and Conclusion

In this paper, a systematic review of existing literature from 2000 to 2021 on the economic impact of AI adoption by countries and firms has been presented. We carried out a systematic literature review identifying relevant research articles that answered our research questions from Scopus, Web of Science, and Science Direct databases, eventually resulting in 627 papers. After applying selection criteria, 63 papers were considered for cross-reading and quality checking. After this process, 30 articles remained for our final review.

All research articles in our sample were published in the last four years. Most research papers in our sample focus on emerging and developing countries and also show that the majority of the AI adoption happened in firms. This paper also identified different technologies that were adopted in combination with AI, those are 1) AI & automation, 2) AI & robots, 3) AI with satellites and drones, 4) AI & cloud computing, 5) automation & robots, and 6) big data powered with AI.

Referring to research questions, this paper identifies the motives of AI adoption. The most repeated motives were catch up, pressure to change, positioning as a leader, competition, increase productivity, reduce cost, other perceived economic benefits, attain technological maturity, align with the country's goals, market positioning, and saving operational expenses.

We were expecting cases of papers about AI adoption by certain individuals. Many jobs will be carried out by machines, software's, or robots, in this sense AI adoption can affect workers. We couldn't find any specific article explaining which jobs would be lost or which new job opportunities were created by the AI adoption and how it impacted certain individuals.

Most cases were either AI adoption by countries or firms. A number of economic impacts were also identified, including increasing performance, cost reduction, increased sales, competitiveness, production growth, value creation, reduced resources in organizational structure, increased productivity, and increased GDP. This confirms that AI is a technology that can be adopted across different sectors of the economy. Deep and more research on economic adoption of AI in different industries (financial, government, ...) are proposed for future research. Our review couldn't find articles related to the economic impact of AI adoption on individuals. The economic impact of AI adoption by individuals mostly on employment or any cases where AI can make individuals' life simpler or relaxed is proposed for future studies. Which jobs are to be lost as well as which industry to be affected by AI adoption and which industry is to produce new jobs will be good research questions. Also, research on AI best practices is needed, most of our research is from countries where the AI index is low, further research about the economic impact on countries with higher AI index is recommended.

Furthermore, research on economic factors that led to the adoption of AI as well as economic factors that challenges the Adoption of AI is proposed for future studies. Today, it is hard to measure the positive effect of AI adoption or the negative effect of AI adoption. We would like to propose a kind of performance measure for AI adoption for future studies.

Finally, we will provide tools and technologies used for the adoption and diffusion of AI which can benefit individuals looking for new skills and new jobs opportunities.

Acknowledgements. This research was supported by the BK21 FOUR (Fostering Outstanding Universities for Research) funded by the Ministry of Education (MOE, Korea) and National Research Foundation of Korea (NRF). This work was also supported by the National Research Foundation of Korea (NRF) grant (No. NRF-2019R1F1A1058487) funded by the Ministry of Science and ICT (MSIT) of Korea.

References

1. Jan, S.T., Ishakian, V., Muthusamy, V.: AI trust in business processes: the need for process-aware explanations. In: Proceedings of the AAAI Conference on Artificial Intelligence, vol. 34, pp. 13403–13404 (2020)
2. Brown, N., Sandholm, T.: Superhuman AI for heads-up no-limit poker: Libratus beats top professionals. Science **359**, 418–424 (2018). https://doi.org/10.1126/science.aao1733
3. Miller, S.: Computer Scientist Coined 'Artificial Intelligence'. WS (2011)
4. Chen, H., Li, L., Chen, Y.: Explore success factors that impact artificial intelligence adoption on telecom industry in China. J. Manag. Anal. **8**, 36–68 (2021)
5. Dutton, T.: An overview of national AI strategies. Politics+ AI (2018)
6. Hall, O.P., Virtue, J.: Artificial intelligence techniques enhance business forecasts: computer-based analysis increases accuracy. Graziadio Bus. Rev. **5**, 4–8 (2002)
7. Simon, J.P.: Artificial intelligence: scope, players, markets and geography. Digital Policy, Regulation and Governance (2019)

8. Zhou, G., Chu, G., Li, L., Meng, L.: The effect of artificial intelligence on China's labor market. China Econ. J. **13**, 24–41 (2020)
9. Srivastava, S.K.: Artificial Intelligence: way forward for India. JISTEM-J. Inf. Syst. Technol. Manage. **15**, 4–20 (2018)
10. Bughin, J., Seong, J., Manyika, J., Chui, M., Joshi, R.: Notes from the AI frontier: modeling the impact of AI on the world economy. McKinsey Global Institute (2018)
11. Frey, C.B., Osborne, M.A.: The future of employment: how susceptible are jobs to computerisation? Technol. Forecast. Soc. Chang. **114**, 254–280 (2017)
12. Webster, J., Watson, R.T.: Analyzing the past to prepare for the future: writing a literature review. MIS Q. **26**, xiii–xxiii (2002)
13. Wiles, J.: Action plan for HR as artificial intelligence spreads. Gartner report (2018)
14. Alrashedi, A., Abbod, M.: The effect of using artificial intelligence on performance of appraisal system: a case study for University of Jeddah Staff in Saudi Arabia. In: Arai, K., Kapoor, S., Bhatia, R. (eds.) IntelliSys 2020. AISC, vol. 1250, pp. 145–154. Springer, Cham (2021). https://doi.org/10.1007/978-3-030-55180-3_11
15. Alsheibani, S.A., Cheung, D., Messom, D.: Factors inhibiting the adoption of artificial intelligence at organizational-level: a preliminary investigation (2019)
16. Atwal, G., Bryson, D., Williams, A.: An exploratory study of the adoption of artificial intelligence in Burgundy's wine industry. Strateg. Chang. **30**, 299–306 (2021)
17. Bag, S., Pretorius, J.H.C., Gupta, S., Dwivedi, Y.K.: Role of institutional pressures and resources in the adoption of big data analytics powered artificial intelligence, sustainable manufacturing practices and circular economy capabilities. Technol. Forecast. Soc. Chang. **163**, 120420 (2021)
18. Bello, O., Teodoriu, C., Oluwafemi, O., Olayiwola, O.: Successful Geothermal Operation Management: Technology Adoption of Oil and Gas Drilling Rig Systems
19. Bilgeri, D., Fleisch, E., Wortmann, F.: How the IoT affects multibusiness industrial companies: IoT organizational archetypes (2018)
20. Casalino, N., Saso, T., Borin, B., Massella, E., Lancioni, F.: Digital competences for civil servants and digital ecosystems for more effective working processes in public organizations. In: Agrifoglio, R., Lamboglia, R., Mancini, D., Ricciardi, F. (eds.) Digital Business Transformation. LNISO, vol. 38, pp. 315–326. Springer, Cham (2020). https://doi.org/10.1007/978-3-030-47355-6_21
21. Chatterjee, S.: AI strategy of India: policy framework, adoption challenges and actions for government. Transforming Government: People, Process and Policy (2020)
22. Chung, H.: Adoption and development of the fourth industrial revolution technology: features and determinants. Sustainability **13**, 871 (2021)
23. Concepcion, R.S., Bedruz, R.A.R., Culaba, A.B., Dadios, E.P., Pascua, A.R.A.R.: The technology adoption and governance of artificial intelligence in the Philippines. In: 2019 IEEE 11th International Conference on Humanoid, Nanotechnology, Information Technology, Communication and Control, Environment, and Management (HNICEM), pp. 1–10. IEEE (2019)
24. Ernst, E., Merola, R., Samaan, D.: Economics of artificial intelligence: implications for the future of work. IZA J. Labor Policy **9**, 1–35 (2019)
25. Fouda, T.: Impact of the fourth industrial revolution on the development of scientific research in the field of agricultural engineering in Egypt and Arab World. Scientific Papers Series-Management, Economic Engineering in Agriculture and Rural Development, vol. 20, pp. 253–258 (2020)

26. Avrilova, V., Gurvitsh-Suits, N.A.: Contemporary innovation challenges-future of adoption artificial intelligence: case of Estonia. Eur. Integr. Stud. **14**, 217–225 (2020)
27. Gomes, M.G., et al.: Economic, environmental and social gains of the implementation of artificial intelligence at dam operations toward Industry 4.0 principles. Sustainability **12**, 3604 (2020)
28. Haile, N., Altmann, J.: Evaluating investments in portability and interoperability between software service platforms. Futur. Gener. Comput. Syst. **78**, 224–241 (2018). https://doi.org/10.1016/j.future.2017.04.040
29. Hammer, A., Karmakar, S.: Automation, AI and the future of work in India. Empl. Relat. Int. J. **43**, 1327–1341 (2021)
30. Kim, K., Altmann, J.: Platform provider roles in innovation in software service ecosystems. IEEE Trans. Eng. Manage., 1–10 (2020). https://doi.org/10.1109/tem.2019.2949023
31. Kopsacheilis, A., Nikolaidou, A., Georgiadis, G., Politis, I., Papaioannou, P.: Investigating the prospect of adopting artificial intelligence techniques from transport operators in Greece. In: Nathanail, E.G., Adamos, G., Karakikes, I. (eds.) CSUM 2020. AISC, vol. 1278, pp. 1097–1106. Springer, Cham (2021). https://doi.org/10.1007/978-3-030-61075-3_105
32. Lakshmi, V.: Exploring autonomous vehicle technology - a case study for the Indian automotive industry (2018)
33. Lakshmi, V., Bahli, B.: Understanding the robotization landscape transformation: a centering resonance analysis. J. Innov. Knowl. **5**, 59–67 (2020)
34. Lee, C.S., Tajudeen, F.P.: Impact of artificial intelligence on accounting: evidence from Malaysian organizations. Asian J. Bus. Account. **13**, 214–222 (2020)
35. Lee, W., Yoon, J., Altmann, J., Lee, J.-D.: Model for identifying firm's product innovation dynamics: applied to the case of the Korean mobile phone industry. Technol. Anal. Strateg. Manag. **33**, 335–348 (2020). https://doi.org/10.1080/09537325.2020.1813271
36. Mamela, T.L., Sukdeo, N., Mukwakungu, S.C.: The integration of AI on workforce performance for a South African Banking Institution. In: 2020 International Conference on Artificial Intelligence, Big Data, Computing and Data Communication Systems (icABCD), pp. 1–8. IEEE (2020)
37. Nam, K., Dutt, C.S., Chathoth, P., Daghfous, A., Khan, M.S.: The adoption of artificial intelligence and robotics in the hotel industry: prospects and challenges. Electron. Mark. **31**, 1–22 (2020)
38. Pan, Y., Froese, F., Liu, N., Hu, Y., Ye, M.: The adoption of artificial intelligence in employee recruitment: the influence of contextual factors. Int. J. Hum. Resour. Manag. **25**, 1–23 (2021)
39. Rosales, M.A., Jo-ann, V.M., Palconit, M.G.B., Culaba, A.B., Dadios, E.P.: Artificial intelligence: the technology adoption and impact in the Philippines. In: 2020 IEEE 12th International Conference on Humanoid, Nanotechnology, Information Technology, Communication and Control, Environment, and Management (HNICEM), pp. 1–6. IEEE (2020)
40. Shim, D., Kim, J.G., Altmann, J.: Strategic management of R&D and marketing integration for multi-dimensional success of new product developments: an empirical investigation in the Korean ICT industry. Asian J. Technol. Innov. **24**, 293–316 (2016). https://doi.org/10.1080/19761597.2016.1253023
41. Somjai, S., Jermsittiparsert, K., Chankoson, T.: Determining the initial and subsequent impact of artificial intelligence adoption on economy: a macroeconomic survey from ASEAN. J. Intell. Fuzzy Syst. **39**, 1–16 (2020)

42. Szalavetz, A.: Artificial intelligence-based development strategy in dependent market economies-any room amidst big power rivalry? Cent. Eur. Bus. Rev. **8**, 40–54 (2019)
43. Chivu, R.G., Orzan, M., Turlacu, L.M., Radu, A.V.: Alternative evaluation methods in university education. eLearn. Softw. Educ. **4**, 7–12 (2018)
44. Tyson, M.M., Sauers, N.J.: School leaders' adoption and implementation of artificial intelligence. J. Educ. Admin. **59**, 229–234 (2021)
45. Markram, H.: The human brain project. Sci. Am. **306**, 50–55 (2012)

Reinforcement Learning for Modeling and Capturing the Effect of Partner Selection Strategies on the Emergence of Cooperation

Somayeh Koohborfardhaghighi[1]([✉]) and Eric Pauwels[2]

[1] School of Economics and Business, University of Amsterdam, Amsterdam, The Netherlands
s.koohborfardhaghighi@uva.nl
[2] Centrum Wiskunde & Informatica (CWI), Amsterdam, The Netherlands
eric.pauwels@cwi.nl

Abstract. In this research we study the statistical mechanics of cooperation through a simple case of aspiration-driven dynamics in structured populations with mixed strategies. Comparing to the existing literature, we define a pool of possible behaviors for the agents based on the bandits learning algorithms and we highlight settings of the Iterated Prisoner's Dilemma Game which may have positive influence on the emergence of cooperation from the aspect of both the entire population and the individual players. We present the level of cooperation and its variation in terms of the median (M) and the interquartile range (IQ) in accordance to the observed topological characteristics of the network structures and partner selection strategies. Our experimental results show that regardless of the underlying network structures, it is difficult to maintain a fully cooperative society in the shade of Random and Epsilon Greedy partner selection strategies. The reported Median values are the lowest and the changes in the IQRs do not follow a sharp increase or decrease in both strategies. Contrary to this, it will even take a shorter time to see a fully cooperative population though UCB, Epsilon First and Epsilon Decreasing strategies. Our observation with respect to different network structures also shows that, considering a certain level of heterogeneity both in terms of distance to others as well as clustering coefficient is more conductive in the spread of cooperative behavior among a networked population.

Keywords: Iterated prisoner's dilemma · Cooperation · Reinforcement learning · Network structure · Network measures · Agent-based modeling and simulation · Bandits learning algorithms

1 Introduction

An important part of understanding cooperative behavior of humans is to investigate what motivates it, how it grows within a population, and which conditions stop it from happening. Kimmo Eriksson in [1] defines the evolution of cooperation as a hard problem. Such a definition cannot be beyond our imagination, considering the complexity of human

© Springer Nature Switzerland AG 2021
K. Tserpes et al. (Eds.): GECON 2021, LNCS 13072, pp. 52–65, 2021.
https://doi.org/10.1007/978-3-030-92916-9_5

behavior, individual variation with respect to cooperative inclinations, the expected outcome out of cooperation, change of rules, strategies to deal with non-cooperative individuals, spatial proximity or social arrangements, operational rules within institutions, capability to switch partners, coalition partnerships, noises, infinite or unknown length collaborations, memory of interactions, and possible effects of other existing parameters. Hence, a large body of literature has grown up showing how the emergence of cooperation can be measured using a variety of very different parameters, including those mentioned above. Some even used the combination of the parameters which make the inter-comparison of the studies so difficult.

The first step to reproduce the cooperative behavior of humans through artificial agents is to incorporate explicit agent motivations that are chosen to favor cooperative responses. In this regard, variety of models based on imitation dynamics and aspiration-driven dynamics have been proposed in the literature [4]. Imitation dynamics have been considered for scenarios in which individuals imitate the strategy of a more successful partner [5–7] and it has been widely studied in the literature (i.e., with both mixed strategies and structured populations) [5–10]. An Aspiration based model depicts how aspirations on an individual level could affect the evolution of cooperation. It can be considered as a form of self-learning or self-testing model in which based on aspiration, an artificial agent could adjust its strategy persistence level during the game. That is to say, agents hold to their played strategies longer if it brings them a satisfactory payoff, otherwise they will switch to other alternative choices. Aspiration-based dynamics require less information about an agent's strategic environment comparing to the imitation dynamics so it has a simpler setup comparing to imitation-based models. The findings of several studies in the literature [11–13] show that an appropriately tuned aspiration value may be seen as a universally applicable promoter of cooperation.

The second step in the creation of an artificially cooperative society is to look into the characteristic of the agents' social interactions. At the macro level, variety of network structures can be utilized to introduce a level of social connectedness among the individuals. Through such network structures the social system will be able to apply a certain level of control on its members. For instance, it can restrict or promote the level of interactions within the individuals. Even within the introduced boundary of social connectedness, individuals still can follow different strategies for selecting or filtering the interacting partners. Findings of several conducted studies elaborate on the importance of modeling the capability of an individual to freely choose his/her interacting partners [14, 15]. Knowing that the choices of an artificial agent for selecting the partners are limited to the designed network structures, the agent still needs to decide who is going to be the "neighbor of choice". Due to the underlying network structure, a self-learning agent has certain choices in selecting partners with uncertain outcomes. The question here is how should the agent act to maximize the quality of its outcomes over many trials? One can easily imagine that each neighbor the agent chooses as a partner has a different payoff associated with it, therefore, a successful cooperation requires good exploration abilities and strategies. We need to figure out an algorithm that explores enough of our search space (in this case selecting the right partner) so that the agent can exploit the best actions. When it comes to modeling an agent's ability to explore its environment, various exploration strategies have been proposed. For instance, the literature shows the promising results of reinforcement learning algorithms (such as Q-learning agents) in which the interaction between an agent and an environment is modeled as a Markov decision process [14, 16]. Also, variety of actor-critic architectures such as TD3 and SAC [17, 18] have been presented to incorporate an entropy measure of the policy into the reward to encourage exploration. We can also find examples of evolutionary algorithms (EAs) which are based on Heuristic search procedures [19]. Bandit algorithms such as ε-greedy [20], ε-first or ε-decreasing [21], Exponential-weight algorithm for Exploration and Exploitation (EXP3) [22] and Upper-Confidence Bound algorithms (UCB) [23, 24] are also being used in a lot of research projects [25] but they have typically received little attention as partner selection strategies in the context of the evolution of cooperation.

In this research, by taking into account the network structures, individual differences in partner selection strategies and self-learning process we aim to investigate the emergence of cooperation through a numerical simulation and Iterated Prisoner's Dilemma Game. We study the statistical mechanics of cooperation through a simple case of aspiration-driven dynamics in structured populations with mixed strategies. We define a pool of possible behaviors for the agents based on the bandits learning algorithms and we highlight settings of the game which may have positive influence on the emergence of cooperation from the aspect of both the entire population and the individual players. We present the levels of cooperation and its variation in terms of the median (M) and the interquartile range (IQ) in accordance to the observed topological properties of the network structures and partner selection strategies. To the best of our knowledge no study has explored the emergence of cooperation from simultaneous use of three different perspectives (i.e., Aspiration-based learning, network structure, bandits learning algorithms) in social dilemmas such as Iterated Prisoner's Dilemma Game. The rest of this paper is organized as follows: In Sect. 2, we formulate our methodology and experimental setup. This is followed by an explanation of the statistical estimates and experimental results in Sect. 3. A summary of our findings has been presented in the conclusion section of the paper which is presented in Sect. 4.

2 Methodology and Experimental Setup

The main objective of this research is to shed light on the potential mechanisms that promote the emergence of cooperation among networked individuals. For this purpose, we performed a social dilemma experiment to examine whether different partner selection strategies help in improving the overall level of cooperation among individuals arranged in variety of network structures (i.e., network of contacts). We divided the experiment into six separate trials. In the control treatment, agents play a traditional PD game which is characterized with the payoff matrix $\begin{pmatrix} 3 & 0 \\ 4 & 1 \end{pmatrix}$. In one round of the simulation, each agent interacts with another random agent in its neighborhood. Our framework follows an aspiration-driven dynamic, therefore, the aspiration value of agents determines the acceptable desired outcome out of the played game. The propensity of cooperation for each agent will be updated during the simulation according to the pseudo code presented in the next section.

In order to measure the effectiveness of partner selection strategies relative to the control treatment, we setup another 5 separate trials in which the agents follow the same setup assigned to the control group (depicted in Table 1). In contrast to the control treatment, the agents in other trials follow certain partner selection strategies in the hope that such behaviors lead to a better outcome for them. Suppose the agent has a set of K neighbors labeled by the integers {1, 2,.….., K}. The agent can then play a game where, in each round, it chooses an action (a partner to play), and it observes the resulting payout. Over many rounds, the agent might explore the neighbors by trying some at random. Finally, the agent plays the neighboring partners that seem to pay off well more frequently so that in the long run this action maximize the agent's total winnings.

Technically, we can describe the problem as developing a model iteratively such that it will converge towards the true value of selecting each partner.

$$Q_t(k) = E[R_n|Ps_n = k] \qquad (1)$$

Where $Q_t(k)$ is the estimated, expected reward Rn, when the partner selection strategy (Ps) select neighbor k at step n. The partner selection strategies which we chose for our analysis are mainly "Random", "Epsilon-greedy", "Epsilon-first", "Epsilon-decreasing", and "UBC" which their formal descriptions and their formulations are presented below.

- Random selection of partners: The most obvious method for an agent to choose a partner is to select them uniformly at random. We consider this strategy as the base of comparison for other algorithms.
- Epsilon-greedy approach: Through this approach, at each time step, the agent selects a partner from its neighborhood which it thinks will maximize its utility.

$$Ps_n = \max_{k}(Q_n(k)) \qquad (2)$$

In order to avoid exploiting the maximum reward by an agent, this approach introduces a parameter called "Epsilon" which controls the level of exploitation and exploration activities of our agents. This probability ensures that the agent keeps trying other options as well.

- Epsilon-decreasing approach: In this approach, Epsilon decays over time because, the need for exploration decreases over time. Selecting random agents becomes increasingly inefficient because eventually agents gather complete information about the surrounding neighbors over time.
- Epsilon-first: At the beginning of the simulation, the agents pick their partners at random for a certain amount of time, and afterward purely exploits their neighborhoods. There are two variables which are related to this strategy (Time-frame and Epsilon).
- Upper Confidence Bound Algorithm: This algorithm selects the neighbor with the highest UCB. The first term $\overline{X}_{t,k}$ corresponds to the mean observed reward out of the interaction with a neighbor k at current time t, and n_k is the number of times this neighbor has been chosen so far.

$$\overline{X}_{t,k} + \frac{\sqrt{2log(t)}}{n_k} \qquad (3)$$

Table 1 also shows our simulation parameters and finally, we setup networks of our agents to play 5000 rounds of the Prisoner's Dilemma game. The impact of such topological characteristics on the evolution of cooperation is particularly critical and this has been discussed by a great number of authors in the literature. For example, the authors in [29] showed that a static network structure (homogeneity) can stabilize human cooperation. They suggested that regularity in the network structure can contribute to cooperation. However, complex social systems within human societies may follow network structures which are not homogeneous in terms of connectivity patterns. This issue appeared as a new direction for scientific research with an emerging consensus that networks that exhibit heterogeneity in their connectivity patterns are more conducive to the spread of cooperative behaviors [30]. In order to show the effect of underlying network structure on the emergence of cooperation, agents in our simulation are connected to each other through networks with different topological characteristics (depicted in Table 2). More specifically, the connectivity patterns followed the "Random" (ER), "Scale Free" (BA), "Geometric" (GEOM), "Spatially Clustered" (SCM), "Grid", "Bipartite" (Bip) and three "Small World" (SW0.1, SW0.03, SW0.3) networks with different rewiring probabilities.

Table 1. Simulation parameters.

Parameter	Description
Aspiration value ∈ [2–4]	This parameter determines the acceptable desired outcome out of the played game for agents
Initial propensity value ∈ [0.2, 0.3, 0.5, 0.8]	It defines the percentage of the population which has higher chance of cooperation with others at the beginning of the simulation. The initial value will be the same at the beginning of the simulation for all agents but will be updated in time
P_step = 0.1	This parameter depicts the amount of changes in the propensity of cooperation in case of a successful or unsuccessful experience during the game played in each round of simulation
Partner selection strategies	This parameter defines how agents decide to pick their partner
	• Random (N = 100)
	• ε-first (N = 100, ε =70, Timeframe = 500)
	• ε-decreasing (N = 100)
	• ε-greedy (N = 100)
	• UCB (N = 100)
Simulation time = 5000	This is the maximum value, the simulation run time will be lower in case we reach a fully cooperative or defective population sooner than that

Table 2. Underlying network structures among agents and their topological characteristics (CC = Clustering Coefficients, AVL = Average Shortest Path Length). Networks from left to right (BA, SW0.03, SW0.1, SW0.3, Bip, GEOM, SCM, GRID, ElliR)

	AVL	CC	Density	Diameter
BA	3	0.48	0.04	5
SW0.03	7.64	0.45	0.04	18
SW0.1	6	0.42	0.04	12
SW0.3	3.63	0.12	0.04	7
Bip	3.6	0	0.04	8
GEOM	4.63	0.19	0.04	10
SCM	8.27	0.45	0.04	20
Grid	5.05	0	0.04	10
ER	3.4	0.05	0.04	7

3 Statistical Estimates and Experimental Results

3.1 Effects of the Initial Propensity Value and Aspiration Values on a Sample Run

In this part of our analysis, we aim to isolate the effects of network structure and partner selection strategies and focus our attention on two important parameters of our model which are mainly Initial Propensity Value and Initial Aspiration Value. In order to clarify the points we wish to raise in this section, at first we need to justify what could be good values for these two parameters. Initial Propensity Value defines the percentage of the population which has higher chance of cooperation with others at the beginning of the simulation. The value of this parameter can be picked from a hypothetical rang such as [0.2, 0.3, 0.5, 0.8]. For example, a value of 0.3 means that there is a higher chance that around 30% of the population follows the cooperative strategy (appeared as green color agents in Table 2) at the beginning of the simulation. This value will be fixed at the first step of the simulation, however, since the Initial Propensity Value will be updated for the agents during the simulation, this percentage varies as time goes by. The following Pseudo code shows the process of the updates. The payoff matrix of the prisoner's dilemma game also shows that the generated outcome out of the game can be 0, 1, 3 and 4. Therefore, it is possible to set the aspiration value of agents to any of those values. Obviously if we set a larger value (e.g., 0.5, 0.8) as the Initial Propensity Value in our model, at the beginning of the game a large population of individuals will follow a cooperative strategy, and later on the dynamics of the game rule this pattern. Setting this parameter to a smaller value make more sense because if agents learn to cooperate in our model this percentage ultimately should go up. Since, the combination of Aspiration Values with Initial Propensity Values may result in interesting patterns during the evolution of cooperation, we decided to perform a sensitivity analysis on these two parameters.

Pseudo code 1: Process of the Updating the Propensity of Cooperation

```
IF   Cooperate = TRUE
          IF        (Utility > Aspiration_Value)
                         propensity_of_coop = propensity_of_coop + propensity_step
          ELSEIF  (Utility < Aspiration_Value)
                         propensity_of_coop = propensity_of_coop - propensity_step
          ELSE
                         propensity-of-coop= propensity-of-coop
ELSE
          IF        (Utility > Aspiration_Value)
                         propensity_of_coop = propensity_of_coop - propensity_step
          ELSEIF  (Utility < Aspiration_Value)
                         propensity_of_coop = propensity_of_coop + propensity_step
          ELSE
                         propensity_of_coop = propensity_of_coop
```

Our first observation was that despite setting different initial propensity values to agents, in the long run (we set the Aspiration Values to 3 and we run our simulation for 10000 ticks with random partner selection strategy) the percentage of agents that follow the cooperative (CC) strategy has been stabilized. That means in such a setting we can expect to observe the emergence of mutual cooperation among the population in the long run (almost 48%). In addition to that, since the cooperation survives, the defective strategy will not be a dominant strategy in the population.

Another interesting observation was related to the effect of the assigned propensity values. The result showed that with a higher propensity value we can expect to observe a higher pick for the level of mutual cooperation. Our initial expectation was that a lower propensity values pushes the population towards a non-cooperative regime. However, agents within our model successfully learned from their interactions and reinforce the strategies which produce them a better outcome. It obviously led to an increase in the percentage of mutual CC strategies. This trend continues until the level of CC strategy stabilizes itself around 48%. We observed that aspiration values around 2 and 3 produce a higher percentage of mutual cooperation among the population. The level of mutual cooperation reaches its peak at 90%, and has been stabilized again around 45%. Larger Aspiration values (e.g., 4), left us with a population which has less tendency for mutual cooperation (almost 10%). Our observed behavior is consistent with the results reported in the previous findings in [26, 27]. Since, we aim to analyze the emergence of cooperation, similar to previous studies we decided to set the Aspiration Value and Initial Propensity Value to 2 and 0.3 respectively during the rest of our analysis.

3.2 Effects of Partner Selection Strategies

In the second part of our experiments, we look into the joint effect of the network structure and the partner selection strategies on the evolution of cooperation. We setup networks of our agents (9 networks) in which they play 5000 rounds of the game for each partner selection strategy (5 strategies). Therefore, in total we have had 45 experiments and 45 observations about different patterns for the emergence of cooperation. The simulation stops if we observe a fully cooperative or defective society. Our initial observation was that, the level of cooperation follows different patterns with respect to the both underlying network topologies and partner selection strategies.

In order to show that the observed levels of cooperation differ with respect to the introduced partner selection strategies, we performed a pairwise two-tailed Welch's t-test across the experiments, which does not assume equal population variance among the observations. The results of the test showed that the p-value was very small (0.000) and we therefore, rejected the null-hypothesis (H0). This outcome verifies, with statistical significance, that the distribution of the rate of cooperation differs with respect to the introduced partner selection strategies. As we depicted in Fig. 1, Random and Epsilon Greedy partner selection strategies produce fluctuations in the level of cooperation (i.e., it is depicted as the harmonic mean) and they could not help the society in being fully cooperative as the simulation time goes by. Contrary to this, regardless of the underlying network structure, it will take shorter time to see a cooperative population though UCB and Epsilon First strategies.

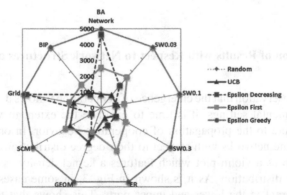

Fig. 1. Maintaining different level of cooperation through time (5000 simulation steps). It will take shorter time for UCB and Epsilon First strategies to produce a cooperative population.

We also followed the methodology presented in [31] to measure the dispersion in our observations. We reported the level of cooperation and its variation in terms of the median and the interquartile range and the results of our analysis are shown in Fig. 2. As we can see in Fig. 2(A), the reported Median values are higher in top performing partner selection strategies (i.e., UCB, Epsilon First and Epsilon Decreasing). We observe that the difference between UCB's median values are less than the Epsilon First and Epsilon Decreasing partner selection strategies. That is to say, regardless of the underlying network structure, agents were able to reach a high level of cooperation among each other. Having said that, as it is shown in Fig. 2(B), IQR values for Epsilon First and Epsilon Decreasing partner selection strategies show larger dispersion in the level of cooperation especially for certain network structures (i.e., SW0.1 for Epsilon First or SCM for Epsilon Decreasing). On the contrary, the reported Median values are the lowest and are almost identical in Random and Epsilon Greedy partner selection strategies. In fact, in the presence of Random partner selection strategy, the maximum and minimum Median values are reached through SCM and Grid network topologies. Also, the changes in the IQRs do not follow a sharp increase or decrease in both strategies.

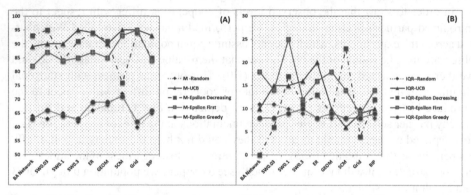

Fig. 2. (A) Median (B) The interquartile range (IQR) as a measure of variability or dispersion.

3.3 Interpretation of Results with Respect to Network Structures and Network Measures

After having the observation that the emergence of cooperation follows different patterns within our experimental settings, it is time to examine the extent to which network properties contribute to the propagation of cooperative behavior. In order to do this, first we compare the networks with respect to their degree distributions. We plot each degree distribution as a violin plot which features a kernel density estimation of the underlying degree distribution. As it is shown in Fig. 3, in some cases the shapes of the plots are different in the lower and upper parts. This shows that the distribution of the node degrees is not equal among different networks. In addition to that, higher density is observed around the mean values of the violin plots. The presence of a small number of nodes with large degrees are noticeable in the case of BA network which leads to having the largest asymmetric observation among the shape of the violin plots. Since, the node degree in Grid Network is equal to 4 for all the nodes, its violin plot is presented as a horizontal line. Similarly, SCM and all the Small World networks (i.e., presented with SW) also show certain degree of symmetry in their connectivity patterns. Paying attention to the distribution of degrees of connectivity is important in the sense that nodes with a degree greater (or less) than the average degree are expected to have more (or fewer) interactions than the others. We should also mention that the ranges in the frequency of interactions not just differ based on the type of network but also with respect to different partner selection strategies. To provide a detailed explanation for this result, we also looked into the frequency of interactions within each network with respect to the partner selection strategies of the network members. We observed that regardless of the underlying network topology, Random and Epsilon Greedy strategies always produce the higher frequency of interactions.

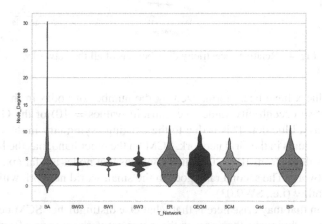

Fig. 3. Underlying degree distribution of all networks.

We reported in Fig. 2A that by following these two strategies agents were not able to see themselves in a fully cooperative society. Our findings here confirm that higher frequency of interactions does not necessary translate into the promotion of cooperative behavior. Contrary to this, UCB limits the number of interactions with only those who might have a better chance of doing cooperation which promotes the emergence of cooperation even in shorter time. Another interesting observation was that, one combination out of all the combinations of network topologies and partner selection strategies stands out and that is related to the case of SCM network. In this specific case, UCB delivers the lowest frequency of interactions. Therefore, we aimed to investigate the topological characteristics of this network further in details to justify our findings.

As it is depicted in Table 2, SCM is a network with three distinctive features, a high clustering coefficient, large average shortest path length and a very large diameter. A large average shortest path length accompanies by a very large diameter in SCM network is a good indicator that there is a considerable distance among the nodes in SCM network. Therefore, we decided to plot the Relative Eccentricity Distributions of all networks. Figure 4 shows the relative eccentricity distributions of all the networks in our simulation.

The eccentricity of a node v is defined as the length of a longest shortest path from the node v to any other node [28]. The relative eccentricity distribution lists for each

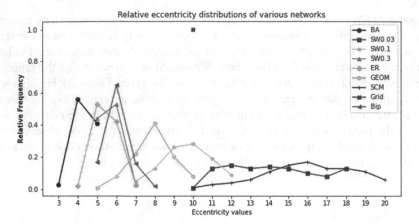

Fig. 4. Relative eccentricity distributions of all the networks.

eccentricity value x have been normalized by the number of nodes in the network. In Fig. 4, the relative eccentricity values (eccentricity values = 10) of the Grid network have appeared as a blue dot. This is due to the existing asymmetry in the connectivity patterns of individuals in the Grid network. SCM on the other hand, has the largest range of eccentricity values (from 10 to 20) which confirms that nodes are far apart from each other in this network. The second rank goes to the small world network with the lowest rewiring probability (i.e., SW0.03).

One question that may arise here is that what else distinguishes SCM network from SW0.03 network. Obviously, the nodes in these two networks are apart from each other but SCM still performs better. Therefore, we decided to look into the association between the common features of the two networks which are the distribution of the clustering coefficient and closeness centrality of the individuals within each network. The results have been shown in Fig. 5. In this figure, the distributions of the closeness of central-ity values are shown by violin plots while the clustering coefficients values are shown through box plots. As it is clearly shown, what distinguishes the SCM from the small network (i.e., SW0.03) is the variety in the observed values for the clustering coefficient of individuals. That is to say, in case of SW0.03, we are dealing with a kind of homoge-neous population in terms of the degree of connectivity, similar patterns of connection with a large distance between individuals. However, the box plot of the clustering values in SCM network shows a form of heterogeneity in the population structure. Therefore, we can conclude that considering such heterogeneity at both levels (i.e., in terms of distance to others as well as clustering coefficient) is more conducive to the spread of cooperative behavior among a networked population.

4   Conclusion

There is no doubt that promoting cooperative behaviors and its maintenance are of great importance for complex human societies. While at the micro level, the interactions of individuals within a structured population can follow a cooperative or non-cooperative

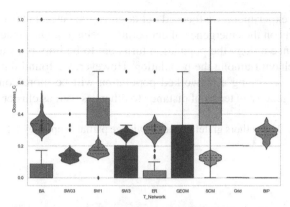

Fig. 5. Association between the distribution of the clustering coefficient (box plots) and closeness centrality (violin plots) of the individuals within different networks.

pattern, at the macro level, the evolution of cooperation can contribute to economic as well as social benefits or losses. Therefore, any system owner (or its management team) has a particular interest in prevailing and stabilizing cooperation among the individuals rather than encouraging them to compete with one another. Despite recognizing the broad importance of the evolution of cooperation in the literature, a general framework is needed to see how the existence of such forces impact the evolution of cooperation. Therefore, in this research, we argued that there is a feedback loop between forces which are happening at both micro and macro levels [32–34]. That is to say, different combinations of individual choices at the micro levels and intentionally designed inter-organizational networks at the macro level may lead to different levels of cooperation. In order to simplify the problem at hand we presented a simplified evolutionary version of the Prisoner's dilemma game through which each group of networked individuals could follow different partner selection strategies. Within our framework the aspiration value depicted the acceptable desired outcome out of the game played by individuals. Individuals also followed five different partner selections strategies which were mainly "Random", "Epsilon-greedy", "Epsilon-first", "Epsilon-decreasing", and "UBC". Individuals were connected to each other through different network structures with different topological characteristics. More specifically, the connectivity patters followed the "Random", "Small World", "Scale Free", "Geometric", "Spatially Clustered", "Grid" and "Bipartite" networks. Through this connectivity feature, we introduced and varied the level of social connectedness among the individuals which could potentially influence their level of interactions with others.

The results of our analysis verified with statistical significance that the distribution of the level of cooperation differs with respect to the introduced partner selection strategies and network structures. We observed that regardless of the underlying network structures in the presence of the Random or Epsilon-greedy partner selection strategies, the level of cooperation is significantly lower than other top performing strategies such as UCB, Epsilon First or Epsilon Decreasing. Expanding on this idea, such winning strategies led to a rapid increase in the evolution of cooperation among networked individuals. In the second part of our experiment, we focused our attention on certain network characteristics and their effects on the emergence of cooperative behavior. On a macroscopic level, considerable distance among the population turns out to be important for maintaining the cooperative behavior among the population. However, we found out that spread of cooperative behavior among a networked population will be more conductive in the presence of heterogeneity in terms of distance to others as well as clustering coefficient.

Acknowledgments. The authors gratefully acknowledge partial support by NL-NWO ESI-Bida project 647.003.001.

References

1. Eriksson, K., Strimling, P.: The hard problem of cooperation. PLoS ONE **77**(2), e40325 (2012)
2. Axelrod, R., Hamilton, W.D.: The evolution of cooperation. Science **211**(4489), 1390–1396 (1981)
3. Flood, M.M.: Some experimental game. Manage. Sci. **5**(1), 5–26 (1958)
4. Du, J., Wu, B., Altrock, P.M., Wang, L.: Aspiration dynamics of multi-player games in finite populations. J. R. Soc. Interface **11**(94), 20140077 (2014)
5. Gintis, H.: Game Theory Evolving: A Problem-Centered Introduction to Modeling Strategic Interaction, 2nd edn, REV - Revised, Princeton University Press, Princeton (2009)
6. Traulsen, A., Claussen, J.C., Hauert, C.: Coevolutionary dynamics: from finite to infinite populations. Phys. Rev. Lett. **95**(23), 238701 (2005)
7. Wu, B., Altrock, P.M., Wang, L., Traulsen, A.: Universality of weak selection. Phys. Rev. E **82**(4), 046106 (2010)
8. Szabó, G., Fáth, G.: Evolutionary games on graphs. Phys. Rep. **446**(4), 97–216 (2007)
9. Fudenberg, D., Imhof, L.A.: Imitation processes with small mutations. J. Econ. Theory **131**(1), 251–262 (2006)
10. Chen, X,. Wang, L.: Promotion of cooperation induced by appropriate payoff aspirations in a small-world networked game. Phys. Rev. E Stat. Nonlinear Soft Matter Phys. **77**(1) Pt 2, 17103 (2008)
11. Perc, M., Wang, Z.: heterogeneous aspirations promote cooperation in the prisoner's dilemma game. PLoS ONE **5**(12), e15117 (2010)
12. Zhang, L., Huang, C., Li, H., Dai, Q.: Aspiration-dependent strategy persistence promotes cooperation in spatial prisoner's dilemma game. EPL **126**(1), 18001 (2019)
13. Liu, Y., Chen, X., Wang, L., Li, B., Zhang, W., Wang, H.: Aspiration-based learning promotes cooperation in spatial prisoners dilemma games. EPL (Europhys. Lett.) **94**(6), 60002 (2011)
14. Anastassacos, N., Hailes, S., Musolesi, M.: Partner Selection for the emergence of cooperation in multi-agent systems using reinforcement learning. Proc. AAAI Conf. Artif. Intell. **34**(05), 7047–7054 (2020)
15. Santos, F.C., Santos, M.D., Pacheco, J.M.: Social diversity promotes the emergence of cooperation in public goods games. Nature **454**(7201), 213–216 (2008)
16. Zheng, H., Jiang, J., Wei, P., Long, G., Zhang, C.: Competitive and cooperative heterogeneous deep reinforcement learning. In: An, B., Yorke-Smith, N., El Fallah Seghrouchni, A., Sukthankar, G. (eds.) Proceedings of the 19th International Conference on Autonomous Agents and Multi-agent Systems (AAMAS 2020), 9–13 May 2020, pp. 1656–1664. Auckland, New Zealand (2020)

17. Fujimoto, S., Hoof, H.V., Meger, D.: Addressing function approximation error in actor-critic methods. arXiv:1802.09477 [cs, stat] (2018)
18. Haarnoja, T., Zhou, A., Abbeel, P., Levine, S.: Soft actor-critic: off-policy maximum entropy deep reinforcement learning with a stochastic actor. arXiv:1801.01290 [cs, stat] (2018)
19. Lüders, B., Schläger, M., Korach, A., Risi, S.: Continual and one-shot learning through neural networks with dynamic external memory. In: Squillero, G., Sim, K. (eds.) EvoApplications 2017. LNCS, vol. 10199, pp. 886–901. Springer, Cham (2017). https://doi.org/10.1007/978-3-319-55849-3_57
20. Watkins, C.J.C.H.: Learning from Delayed Rewards. University of Cambridge, Cambridge (1989)
21. Caelen, O., Bontempi, G.: Improving the exploration strategy in bandit algorithms. In: Maniezzo, V., Battiti, R., Watson, J.-P. (eds.) LION 2007. LNCS, vol. 5313, pp. 56–68. Springer, Heidelberg (2008). https://doi.org/10.1007/978-3-540-92695-5_5
22. Auer, P., Cesa-Bianchi, N., Freund, Y., Schapire, R.E.: The nonstochastic multiarmed bandit problem. SIAM J. Comput. 32(1), 48–77 (2002)
23. Auer, P.: Using confidence bounds for exploitation-exploration trade-offs. J. Mach. Learn. Res. 3, 397–422 (2003)
24. Chu, W., Li, L., Reyzin, L., Schapire, R.: Contextual bandits with linear payoff functions. In: Proceedings of the Fourteenth International Conference on Artificial Intelligence and Statistics, pp. 208–214 (2011)
25. Lin, B., Bouneffouf, D., Cecchi, G.: Online learning in iterated prisoner's dilemma to mimic human behavior. arXiv:2006.06580 [cs, q-bio] (2020)
26. Sutton, R.S., Barto, A.G.: Reinforcement Learning: An Introduction, p. 342. MIT Press, Cambridge (1998)
27. Ezaki, T., Horita, Y., Takezawa, M., Masuda, N.: Reinforcement learning explains conditional .cooperation and its moody cousin. PLoS Comput. Biol. 12(7), e1005034 (2016)
28. Takes, F.W., Kosters, W.A.: Computing the eccentricity distribution of large graphs. Algorithms 6(1), 100–118 (2013)
29. Rand, D.G., Nowak, M.A., Fowler, J.H., Christakis, N.A.: Static network structure can stabilize human cooperation. Proc. Natl. Acad. Sci. 111(48), 17093 (2014)
30. Maciejewski, W., Fu, F., Hauert, C.: Evolutionary game dynamics in populations with heterogenous structures. PLoS Comput. Biol. 10(4), e1003567 (2014)
31. Ge, X., Li, H., Li, L.: Effects of centrality and heterogeneity on evolutionary games. In: Pan, J.-S., Lin, J.C.-W., Sui, B., Tseng, S.-P. (eds.) ICGEC 2018. AISC, vol. 834, pp. 51–63. Springer, Singapore (2019). https://doi.org/10.1007/978-981-13-5841-8_6
32. Koohborfardhaghighi, S., Altmann, J.: How structural changes in complex networks impact organizational learning performance (No. 2014111). Seoul National University; Technology Management, Economics, and Policy Program (2014)
33. Koohborfardhaghighi, S., Romero, J.P., Maliphol, S., Liu, Y., Altmann, J.: How bounded rationality of individuals in social interactions impacts evolutionary dynamics of cooperation. In: Proceedings of the International Conference on Web Intelligence, pp. 381–388 (2017)
34. Koohborfardhaghighi, S., Altmann, J.: How variability in individual patterns of behavior changes the structural properties of networks. In: Ślęzak, D., Schaefer, G., Vuong, S.T., Kim, Y.-S. (eds.) AMT 2014. LNCS, vol. 8610, pp. 49–60. Springer, Cham (2014). https://doi.org/10.1007/978-3-319-09912-5_5

Architecture for Orchestrating Containers in Cloud Federations

Yodit Gebrealif[1]([✉]) [iD], Mohammed Mubarkoot[1] [iD], Jörn Altmann[1]([✉]) [iD],
and Bernhard Egger[2] [iD]

[1] Technology Management, Economics and Policy Program, Seoul, South Korea
mubarkoot@snu.ac.kr, jorn.altmann@acm.org
[2] Department of Computer Science and Engineering,
Seoul National University, Seoul, South Korea
bernhard@csap.snu.ac.kr

Abstract. Containerization technology helps achieving not only better portability and interoperability but also better performance and efficiency on various cloud computing arrangements. Such technology is expected to empower cloud federations by enhancing portability and scalability across the federation. In this paper, we propose an architecture by adding two subcomponents to the NIST reference architecture for identifying resources and managing container orchestration in cloud federation environments. The architecture adds two subcomponents to the NIST reference architecture. The proposed two new sub-components enable resource identification and container orchestration across cloud federation members. These names of the two subcomponents are the Resource Identifier and the Container Orchestrator, respectively. The Resource Identifier component identifies the appropriate federated member for allocating tasks based on previous experience and current status. The Container Orchestrator facilitates the management and orchestration of containers at the federation level. We also identified several techniques, which can be used for resource identification. Among those, linear regression technique is selected for resource provisioning and identification of federation members. Further, these techniques are also expected to learn from log files from previous executions and prioritize resources based on the current resource status and previous experience.

Keywords: Container orchestration · Distributed cloud federation · Artificial Intelligence (AI) · Resource identification · Linear regression technique

1 Introduction

Cloud federations extend the use of cloud resources beyond a provider's resources and enhance collaboration between cloud service providers (CSP) based on a service level agreement (SLA) [1, 2]. This helps addressing issues related to scalability, interoperability, and maximization of resource utilization [3]. Implementation arrangements of cloud federations can include centralized and peer-to-peer models. In all arrangements, the

K. Tserpes et al. (Eds.): GECON 2021, LNCS 13072, pp. 66–75, 2021.
https://doi.org/10.1007/978-3-030-92916-9_6

federation manager (FM) is the key component that handles such collaboration between federation members [1, 4].

One of the key challenges that cloud federation aims at addressing is the scalability of resources. A certain CSP might experience a lack of resources, while, at the same time, other CSPs possess extra resources that are not fully utilized [5, 6]. We believe that orchestrating resources between CSPs can be a game-changer in cloud federations. Among resource orchestration frameworks that exist in the market (Table 1), only the MiCADO framework [7] deals with container orchestration. However, MiCADO only targets multi-cloud environments and not cloud federations. The main difference between a multi-cloud and a federated cloud is that the latter is collaborative in nature, while, in a multi-cloud, the relationships between the CSPs are independent [1]. Other differences also include service composition and user-provider relationship [8].

Containerization technology can efficiently enhance scalability, security, and governance of orchestrated resources [7]. Containers are resource-efficient units, since they require minimum resources to run. A container image encapsulates all requirements and dependencies of an application into a packaged unit [4, 7, 8]. This makes them highly scalable and portable [7]. While managing containers is usually the task of the container orchestrator (e.g., Kubernetes and Docker Swarm [7]), these orchestrators work within the resources of a CSP and cannot extend their functionality to other CSPs. As a result, this restricts the full utilization of containerization technology at the federation level. Furthermore, implementing container orchestration at the federation level has an impact on improving the portability and scalability of applications. Moreover, enhancing that with machine learning capabilities can efficiently optimize resource identification and prioritization. In this paper, we propose an architecture that utilizes containerization technology for cloud federations and allows resource identification and container orchestrating across a federation.

The remainder of this paper is structured as follows: Sect. 2 introduces the existing state of art cloud resource orchestration frameworks. Section 3 presents the overall proposed architecture, and Sect. 4 discusses the new components and how they work in detail. Finally, Sect. 5 presents the conclusion and future work.

2 State-of-the-Art

There are many resource orchestration frameworks in the market (Table 1). While most of these frameworks target multi-cloud environments, only MiCADO [7] deals with container orchestration, though only within the context of multi-cloud environments.

Table 1. Cloud resource orchestrators available in the market, based on [7].

Name	Description
Heat	Heat launches multiple composite cloud applications in the form of text files (via templates) that are treated like a code
Cloudify	Cloudify provides integrated infrastructure with Ansible, Kubernetes, AWS Cloud Formation, Azure ARM, and Terraform
Brooklyn	This framework for cloud orchestration allows deployment and management of applications via declarative blueprints
Startos	Startos of polyglot PaaS provides a platform for developing, testing, and running applications on all major cloud infrastructures
Alien4-Cloud	This web-based platform accelerates the design of application infrastructures and enables reusability by providing a blueprint catalog and components
CloudFormation	CloudFormation is part of the AWS infrastructure and provides a blueprint of an application that helps to design, model, and set up infrastructure using JSON encoded templates
Cloudiator	This multi-user-capable web-based service allows the description of application and deployment on different public and private clouds
Roboconf	Roboconf is a platform and a tool to deploy and manage elastic cloud applications using deployment, probes, automatic reactions, and reconfigurations
INDIGO	This data and computing platform targets scientific communities and provides an e-infrastructure with cloud frameworks, applications, and tools for clouds and grids
MiCADO	MiCADO is a multi-cloud orchestration and auto-scaling framework for application clusters of Docker containers run on Kubernetes

3   Proposed Architecture

3.1   Requirements for a Cloud Federation Architecture

To utilize containerization technology in cloud federations, the management of containers requires to:

- Have control over container clusters deployed on different CSPs. It is required, in order to support the orchestration lifecycle of containers (i.e., create, deploy, update, scale and terminate) and enhance monitoring.
- Regularly monitor container instances running across different CSPs. It is needed to check their health status and take necessary actions (e.g., replace failed instances).
- Have elastic resource provisioning so that the load and usage of resources can efficiently be managed and calculated.
- Have a component that allows secure management of customers' instances running across the federation.

Fulfilling these requirements enables a provider-agnostic and successful orchestration of containers across a federation and a clear picture to customers on where their containers are running. Moreover, it facilitates managing, monitoring, and billing of container clusters and instances running across the federation. Based on the reviewed literature, the NIST reference architecture is well suited to apply container orchestration for achieving system portability [4]. Given this, applying container technology enhances portability, scalability, efficiency, and service resiliency in cloud federations [9].

3.2 Overall Architecture

The National Institute of Standards and Technology (NIST) defines four components in a cloud federation reference architecture (Fig. 1). These are the Federation Broker, the Federation Operator (FO), the Federation Audit, and the Federation Carrier component [4]. The FO includes six subcomponents namely the Membership Manager, the Policy Manager, the Resource Manager, the Monitoring & Reporting component, the Accounting & Billing component, and the Portability & Interoperability component. These subcomponents are in charge of specific tasks in the federation; the interested reader is referred to NIST Cloud Federation Reference Architecture [4] for a detailed explanation of each subcomponent. In this paper, we adapted the NIST architecture for a centralized (i.e., central broker) arrangement. We further assume that each CSP has a Resource Manager (RM) interface, through which the current status of the CSP's resources can be sent to the central broker.

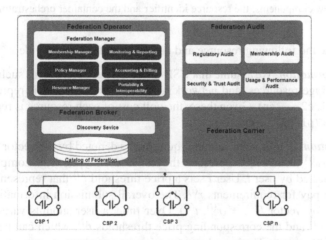

Fig. 1. NIST cloud federation reference architecture [4]

To meet our objective and requirements, we propose two new components to the NIST architecture: the Resource Identifier and the Container Orchestrator.

3.3 New Sub-components

Resource Identifier (RI). The purpose of this subcomponent is to identify resources and enhance the RM's activity (Fig. 2) through the application of various techniques.

The most widely used techniques for resource provisioning are neural networks, linear regression, and support vector machines [10]. Zhang et al. [11] use machine learning techniques to analyze a multi-dimensional cloud resource allocation problem and conclude that the linear allocation algorithm achieves the best performance in their experiment. Therefore and as a starting point, we also propose the linear regression technique for the Resource Identifier component.

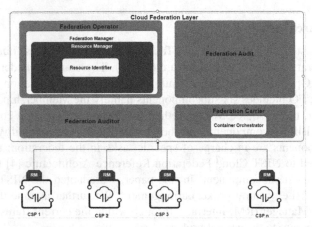

Fig. 2. The proposed cloud federation architecture, which is based on the NIST architecture, includes two new components: the resource identifier and the container orchestrator.

We assume the following resource and user information are provided:

Resource Information. We assume that CSPs offer n types of resources such as compute resources, storage resources, and network resources. The capacity is represented as a vector C = (c1, c2, ..., cn). Given these, the unit cost of each resource is represented in the vector P = (p1, p2, ..., pn).

User Information. A user i can submit requirements denoted by the vector $r^{(i)} = (r_1^{(i)}, r_2^{(i)}, r_3^{(i)}, ..., r_n^{(i)})$, where $r_s^{(i)}$ represents the resources of type s (e.g., compute, storage, network) requested by user i. User i sets a price threshold $t^{(i)}$ that represents the user's willingness to pay for requirements $r^{(i)}$. The overall submission information of user i is represented by vector $R^{(i)} = (r^{(i)}, t^{(i)})$. Over time, a user submits various resource requirements $r^{(i)}$ and the corresponding price thresholds $t^{(i)}$, which can be considered in a hypothesis function. The hypothesis function is given by:

$$h_\beta(t^{(i)}) = \beta_0 + \beta_1 r_1^{(i)} + \beta_2 r_2^{(i)} + ... + \beta_n r_n^{(i)} \tag{1}$$

Where β_1, β_2, ..., β_n stand for the predicted unit price of n types of resources requested by the user i, and β_0 is the prediction noise. The variable $h_\beta(t(i))$ can be understood as a price expression of the resources required by user i. This hypothesis function predicts the unit willingness-to-pay β_i for each requested resource by user i according to the price t(i) that the user was willing to pay.

Based on the resource information and the user information, the aim is to determine the appropriate CSPs for handling the required resources requested. The RI component is initialized when the client's request for extra resources is received along with the price that the client is willing to pay. Then, the RI component contacts all CSPs for their current resource status. Once the status of CSPs is identified, the list of available CSPs will be filtered. If the forwarded list is empty, which means, there is no available CSP currently, then the message about the unavailability of all CSPs will be sent to the requester. But if the list is not empty, then the log file, which contains historical information of requested resources, proposed price by a customer, and information on allocated CSP for that request will be extracted from the database. Then, the log files will be checked, in order to check whether the same request has been fulfilled before. Once identified, the CSP information, which was chosen previously for a similar request, will be forwarded to filter the list based on the geographically nearest location. This step is conducted to save computational power. But if a similar request could not be found in the log file database, then the component uses Eq. 1 to compute and predict whether the user of the requesting CSP would accept the available resources of the CSPs. This is the case, if the price of the available resources of the CSPs is lower than the estimated price. After the unit price is predicted and a list of CSPs, which can deliver their service based on the price, are identified. Then, the geographically nearest CSP from the list is selected. Finally, the resource identifier returns the selected CSP information and updates its log file. Figure 3 presents the detailed step-by-step activity of the RI component.

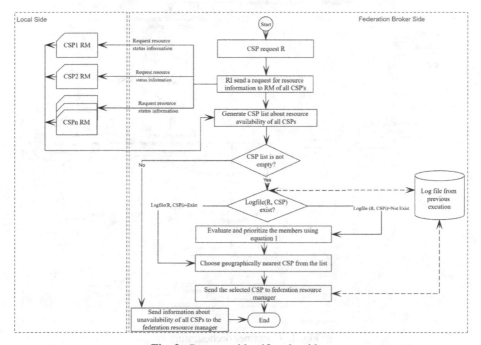

Fig. 3. Resource identifier algorithm.

Container Orchestrator. This subcomponent is proposed as part of the Federation Carrier component. It facilitates the orchestration of containers across the federation. Whenever the federation orchestrator receives a request, for example, for regular cloud computing, containers are managed and controlled by the orchestrator (e.g., Docker Swarm, Kubernetes). However, since cloud federation deals with completely independent entities, managing container clusters and updating master nodes that typically lead to rebuilding the container image, can be challenging from many aspects. To overcome such problems, the federation container orchestrator takes full control of container clusters deployed across federation members and manages all their lifecycle. In other words, creating, deploying, scaling, and terminating containers across the federation is the responsibility of the container orchestrator.

The container orchestrator is initialized by a request from a CSP along with a container's token. The token is used to uniquely identify each container image. Once the request is received, this component checks whether or not the image exists in the repository. If so, the container orchestrator pulls a copy of the container image from the container repository. If not, it accesses the container image from the requester CSP. Once the container image has been received either from the CSP or from the repository, communication can be established with the CSP, which is selected by the resource identifier for deploying the container. Figure 4 visualizes the operation of the container orchestrator component.

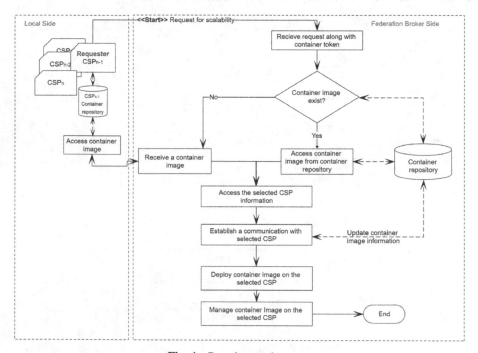

Fig. 4. Container orchestrator.

4   Discussion

Cloud federation provides an inexpensive way of maximizing resource utilization through increased resource flexibility, scalability, and efficient service delivery. Optimizing resource identification and taking advantage of containerization technology in the resource management of a federated environment can add more benefits to cloud clients and CSPs. On top of these benefits are: (i) the resource identification technique matches the customers' needed resources within the budget they can afford. As a result, customers save time and effort as they do not have to hassle looking up and comparing prices for the resources they need; (ii) The containerization technology maximizes the efficiency of resources, as containers require less system resources compared to virtual machines and, more importantly, they are highly portable regardless of where they are deployed; (iii) The combination of resource identification and container orchestration across federation accelerates deployment and production cycles. This work aims at achieving that by proposing a component for resource identification and a component for container orchestration in cloud federations.

Regarding resource identification, Tsakalidou et al. [10] found that the most widely used techniques for resource provisioning are neural networks, linear regression, and support vector machines. Linear regression, in particular, is found to achieve better performance compared to other techniques. Therefore, the linear regression technique is chosen over other techniques for our purpose. The Linear regression technique enhances resource identification of the cloud federation based on previously generated provisioning logs, tracing and monitoring information, and the currently available resources of the federation members [7]. In this regard, the continuous provisioning of resources by federation members can be leveraged to create a self-optimizing resource identification mechanism. This can help optimizing resource provisioning by federation members and improve their accuracy for future requests. As a result, this continuous optimization of resource identification and provisioning enhances the overall quality of service on one hand and helps spot potential improvements of federation members on the other hand. Moreover, it can help drive better resource allocation decisions and orchestrate resources in the federation with minimum cost and more efficiency. Therefore, the resource identifier plays an important role not only in choosing where to orchestrate resources efficiently but also in addressing possible improvements of the whole federation.

Regarding the second component, container orchestration solves the problem of compatibility and portability of applications that are already implemented in other cloud arrangements [7]. The proposed architecture includes the container orchestrator, which is a sub-component of the distribution manager, is responsible for orchestrating containers across federation members. While existing container orchestrator's work at the provider level, the proposed one manages container clusters at the federation level. At a high level, this gives the federation an advantage of maximizing the use of resources in an efficient way. At a low level, this adds more flexibility and portability support for an application. An additional benefit is that it allows automated management of applications, and therefore, reduces the overhead needed to manage the entire lifecycle of containers deployed across a federation. As container orchestration in the federation has not been proposed in cloud federation, this sub-component could give additional benefits for federated clouds with respect to scalability, flexibility, and portability.

5 Conclusion and Future Work

In this article, we presented a container orchestration architecture in a centralized (i.e., cloud broker) federation environment. The proposed architecture allows the resource manager to prioritize the selection among federated CSPs based on logs and tracing information generated from continuous provisioning of resources, enabling self-optimizing decisions.

By enhancing the NIST reference architecture, we added two subcomponents called Resource Identifier and Container Orchestrator. These two subcomponents track the available resources in the federated cloud and use this information to prioritize and decide on which federation members shall run the container. By taking advantage of containerization technology, these sub-components allow managing and orchestrating containers across federation members and, as a result, enhance portability and scalability of applications in federated environments. For future work, a proper simulation tool will be selected to analyze and evaluate the proposed architecture by implementing the linear regression technique for resource identification.

Acknowledgments. This research was supported by the BK21 FOUR (Fostering Outstanding Universities for Research) funded by the Ministry of Education (MOE, Korea) and National Research Foundation of Korea (NRF). This work was also supported by the National Research Foundation of Korea (NRF) grant (No. NRF-2019R1F1A1058487) funded by the Ministry of Science and ICT (MSIT) of Korea.

References

1. Aryal, R.G., Marshall, J., Altmann, J.: Architecture and business logic specification for dynamic cloud federations. In: Djemame, K., Altmann, J., Bañares, J.Á., Agmon Ben-Yehuda, O., Naldi, M. (eds.) GECON 2019. LNCS, vol. 11819, pp. 83–96. Springer, Cham (2019). https://doi.org/10.1007/978-3-030-36027-6_8
2. Cho, Y., Jo, C., Kim, H., Egger, B.: Towards economical live migration in data centers. In: Djemame, K., Altmann, J., Bañares, J.Á., Agmon Ben-Yehuda, O., Stankovski, V., Tuffin, B. (eds.) GECON 2020. LNCS, vol. 12441, pp. 173–188. Springer, Cham (2020). https://doi.org/10.1007/978-3-030-63058-4_15
3. Kurze, T., Klems, M., Bermbach, D., Lenk, A., Tai, S., Kunze, M.: Cloud federation. In: Computing, p. 7 (2011). https://www.researchgate.net/publication/312280049_Cloud_federation. Accessed 23 Mar 2021
4. Lee, C.A., Bohn, R.B., Michel, M.: The NIST Cloud Federation Reference Architecture (2020). https://nvlpubs.nist.gov/nistpubs/SpecialPublications/NIST.SP.500-332.pdf
5. Aryal, R.G., Altmann, J.: Fairness in revenue sharing for stable cloud federations. In: Pham, C., Altmann, J., Bañares, J.Á. (eds.) GECON 2017. LNCS, vol. 10537, pp. 219–232. Springer, Cham (2017). https://doi.org/10.1007/978-3-319-68066-8_17
6. Aryal, R.G., Altmann, J.: Dynamic application deployment in federations of clouds and edge resources using a multiobjective optimization AI algorithm. In: 2018 3rd International Conference Fog Mobile Edge Computing. FMEC 2018, pp. 147–154 (2018). https://doi.org/10.1109/FMEC.2018.8364057

7. Tomarchio, O., Calcaterra, D., Modica, G.D.: Cloud resource orchestration in the multi-cloud landscape: a systematic review of existing frameworks. J. Cloud Comput. **9**(1), 1–24 (2020). https://doi.org/10.1186/s13677-020-00194-7
8. Ahmed, U., Raza, I., Hussain, S.A.: Trust evaluation in cross-cloud federation: survey and requirement analysis. ACM Comput. Surv. **52**(1), 1–37 (2019). https://doi.org/10.1145/329 2499
9. Kim, D., Muhammad, H., Kim, E., Helal, S., Lee, C.: TOSCA-based and federation-aware cloud orchestration for Kubernetes container platform. Appl. Sci. **9**(1), 1–14 (2019). https://doi.org/10.3390/app9010191
10. Tsakalidou, V.N., Mitsou, P., Papakostas, G.A.: Machine learning for cloud resources management -- An overview, January 2021. http://arxiv.org/abs/2101.11984. Accessed 25 May 2021
11. Zhang, J., Xie, N., Zhang, X., Yue, K., Li, W., Kumar, D.: Machine learning based resource allocation of cloud computing in auction. Comput. Mater. Contin. **56**(1), 123–135 (2018). https://doi.org/10.3970/cmc.2018.03728

Blockchains

SaCI: A Blockchain-Based Cyber Insurance Approach for the Deployment and Management of a Contract Coverage

Muriel Franco[✉], Noah Berni, Eder Scheid, Christian Killer,
Bruno Rodrigues, and Burkhard Stiller

Communication Systems Group CSG, Department of Informatics IfI,
University of Zürich UZH, Binzmühlestrasse 14, 8050 Zürich, Switzerland
{franco,scheid,killer,rodrigues,stiller}@ifi.uzh.ch, noah.berni@uzh.ch

Abstract. The cyber insurance market is still in its infancy but growing fast. Novel models and standards for this particular insurance market are essential due to the use of modern IT (Information Technology) and since insurance providers need to create suitable models for customers.

In this work, a refreshing approach SaCI for the deployment and management of contract coverage is introduced. SaCI translates relevant information of a cyber insurance contract to Smart Contracts (SC) running on the Blockchain (BC). Thus, SaCI *(i)* allows for recording agreements in an immutable way, *(ii)* simplifies interactions between stakeholders (e.g., customers and insurers), and *(iii)* ensures a trustworthy and transparent process during the life-cycle of the contract. A case study is provided to show evidence of the feasibility of the approach, which is backed by a cost analysis and discussion regarding especially the application of BCs.

Keywords: Cyber insurance · Cybersecurity economics · Blockchain · Smart Contract (SC)

1 Introduction

Cybersecurity stands as one of the key investment pillars for companies applying IT (Information Technology) to gain competitiveness in the market due to the continuously increase in the number of cyberattacks on IT systems over the past years. Predictions state that cybercrime will cost the world 10.5 trillion US\$ annually by 2025, up from 3 trillion US\$ in 2015, which represents the most significant transfer of economic wealth in history [9]. In this sense, to reduce the impact of successful attacks and to enable companies to recover faster and with less costs, different cybersecurity investment strategies have been investigated [14], in which one of the most prominent strategies includes cyber insurance coverage models [12]. Although the cyber insurance market is fast-paced and is under strong development [6,7], cyber insurance approaches still have room to advance from a rarely used risk transfer tool to a critical requirement for companies risk management.

© Springer Nature Switzerland AG 2021
K. Tserpes et al. (Eds.): GECON 2021, LNCS 13072, pp. 79–92, 2021.
https://doi.org/10.1007/978-3-030-92916-9_7

Currently, different cyber insurance approaches are explored by companies, effectively expanding the market, either *(a)* introducing new business models and mechanisms to gain advantages or *(b)* improving their insurance services by using new technologies. However, critical open challenges for a cyber insurance adoption exist, *e.g.*, the information asymmetry that has to be considered during the contract's design and the customer's eligibility for coverage [1]. Thus, different cyber insurance approaches have been proposed and new paradigms have been applied in such a context [16]. One such a new paradigm that is a relevant catalyst in the insurance market is the Blockchain (BC). BCs allow for the implementation of Smart Contracts (SC) to remove intermediaries, automate the deployment and management of insurance contracts, and support novel insurance models [4]. Due to the automation of SCs and the immutability of the BC, BC-based cyber insurance models can provide a trustworthy and immutable agreement between cyber insurers and customers; thus, both stakeholders can profit from the benefits introduced by the BC.

This paper introduces a BC-based approach for the creation, deployment, and management of a cyber insurance contract. SaCI correlates relevant customers' aspects and cyber insurance companies' (*i.e.*, insurers) requirements, such as business information, contract constraints, and security aspects, to create an SC that describes and manages the agreement between customers and insurers. Based on this, both stakeholders can interact with the SC to proceed with coverage requests, contract updates, and premium payments. SaCI ensures a trustworthy record of the contract coverage and all changes along time; thus, not only *(i)* providing automation of the process, but also *(ii)* acting as a referee or proof in case of disputes (*e.g.*, customers requesting payment for a loss due to a cyberattack that the insurer has denied payment for). Further, if funds are available and contractual requirements are satisfied, SaCI automatically transfer funds between stakeholder to execute payments, such as those related to premiums paid and loss coverage due to a cyberattack.

The remainder of this paper is organized as follows: Background and related work are reviewed in Sect. 2. While Sect. 3 introduces SaCI and details of the implementation, Sect. 4 discusses the feasibility of SaCI and presents a suitable case study subject to a cost evaluation. Finally, Sect. 5 summarizes the paper and outlines future work.

2   Background and Related Work

A cyber insurance is a specific product of an insurance company, which is commercially offered to cover damage caused by cyber-incidents, direct or indirect impacts caused by cyberattacks. A cyber insurance is offered for companies, governments, or individuals, who want to reduce or share financial risks of an attack and which shall cover costs for recovering from an incident [7]. Typically, the process of cyber insurance contract creation involves three main steps: *(i)* Risk identification, which is based on the identification of assets that can be affected by different threats [14], *(ii)* Risk analysis, which determines the likelihood of a threat and also its impact, and *(iii)* Contract establishment with a focus on coverage specifications and premium definition. With the increase of cyberattacks and their actual impacts, the cyber insurance market also has to evolve to handle different aspects, such as incomplete, asymmetric, or even insufficient data for pricing premiums and coverage, lack of regulations and standards, and the gap between cybersecurity and risk transfer [5].

According to a study conducted in South Korea [10], companies with high incomes, high education, and insurance contracts are more likely to "pay extra" for insurance policies using BCs and SCs. Thus, a strategic development of insurance products using BCs targeting these customers can increase the number of policyholders, which can, in turn, increase premium revenues. Thus, the application of BCs can provide efficiency and trust in the entire process, while insurers become innovators in their relation to customers.

In this context, [2] introduces a conceptual framework for cybersecurity investments and cyber insurance decisions. The framework advocates the use of SCs for cyber insurance coverage and premium management as one of its key pillars. A case study focuses on the maritime sector and shows evidence of the framework's applicability. However, no implementation details are provided at all. [17] provides a model for determining insurance premiums based on the Stackelberg Game to improve the time efficiency of BC applications. A BC-based crowdsourcing system was developed as a proof-of-concept to show how the cyber insurance model can protect blocks containing task information. Although this approach improves the time to perform each crowdsourcing task, focus is neither laid on information about contract coverage nor on interactions between customers and insurers.

Furthermore, BlockCIS [8] proposes a BC-based cyber insurance tool, which offers the insurer and the customer the possibility to reach an automated, real-time, and immutable feedback cycle for a dynamic risk assessment. For that, the system interconnects the insurer and the customer over a BC. However, BlockCIS is presented as a supporting tool and cannot be used as an individual tool to provide a cyber insurance service. For example, the paying of the premium and the payment of claims are not integrated into the system, and hence that has to be managed by external applications. However, such frameworks can well be used to assess cybersecurity correctly and, based on that, can calculate a fair premium for a cyber insurance contract.

Thus, although the demands in related work clearly indicate benefits of using BC-based approaches for cyber insurance, open issues remain, especially with regards to achieving an efficient model that considers different nuances of the market. In order to address this gap, SaCI focuses on the mapping of information and interactions, required to establish a trustworthy and automated interaction between customers and cyber insurers. Therefore, this work does contribute to the development of simplified, trustful, and efficient cyber insurance models.

3   The SaCI Approach

SaCI is proposed to handle different demands of cyber insurance in order to create a simplified, trustworthy, and automated process for cyber insurance contracts. For that, SaCI describes a JSON (JavaScript Object Notation) file structure to store relevant information about the contract and to translate it to SC code within well-defined functions allowing for interactions between customers and insurers. Therefore, the SaCI allows for the *(i)* payment of premiums and contract updates, *(ii)* request of damage coverage and dispute resolutions, and *(iii)* check of contract information and its integrity, whenever it is required (*e.g.*, in case one of the parties involved are not following the agreement defined).

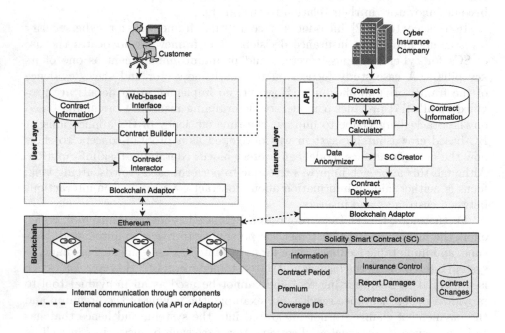

Fig. 1. SaCI architecture.

The architecture of the SaCI (*cf.* Fig. 1) determines the two different stakeholders (*i.e.*, customer and cyber insurer) at the top and enables the interaction with the system using those components running on their respective layers (*i.e.*, on their own infrastructures). The *User Layer* is composed out of a Web-based interface, with which the customer can access and add all information related to business and demands (*cf.* Table 1). This information is forwarded to the *Contract Builder* in charge of mapping these information into the JSON format. The respective JSON file is sent to the *Insurer Layer* using the SaCI 's API.

Within the *Insurer Layer* the *Contract Processor* reads information from this JSON file and stores a copy of all contract information. The *Premium Calculator* estimates the premium for this contract's coverage. While this paper does not focus on an optimal premium calculation, it provides relevant information in a standardized format, *e.g.*, as input for a base rate pricing in which modifications for the calculation can be accommodated according to insurer preferences.

Table 1. Contract information.

Category	Description	Example
Business information	Standard Information about the company, which is not relevant for the premium, but which is needed to identify the company	Company name, Company address
Contract constraints	Information about the non-technical constraints of the contract, which have to be completely defined in each contract	Duration of the contract, Payment frequency
Company conditions	Non-technical information about the company's business number, which affect the premium	Yearly revenue, Number of employees
Company security	Information about the measures of the company to increase its cyber security as well as different metrics to measure it	Risk assessment metrics, attack history, security software, security training
Company infrastructure	Information about the hardware and software used by the company	Used technologies, Critical data amount
Contract coverage	Information about what attacks and impacts are covered by the contract and by which conditions	DDoS attack: Business interruption: coverage at 50%; data breach for third-person damage: coverage: at 100%

After the premium calculation, the *Data Anonymizer* component is in charge of removing from the contract all information that can be critical to identify the company and its risks. This is essential before deploying the contract within a public BC (*e.g.*, Ethereum or Cardano). The *SC Creator* uses all other information to transform the JSON file into an SC based on previously defined one (*i.e.*, Solidity code) and fills in missing information in those fields mapped. Finally, the contract is deployed on the BC and available for interactions between all stakeholders (Actors) involved (*cf.* Table 2)

In order to define the relevant information for the creation of the cyber insurance contract, and consequently, the SC, necessary information was defined based on the related cyber insurance market. Table 1 provides an overview of these main categories considered by SaCI . Every characteristic demanded for by a customer is assigned to one of these categories. Note that this type of information has to be provided by customers, which might result in "inaccurate" information and can be impacted by companies' biases, such as metrics related to risk assessment and threats impacts.

The business information contains standard information about the company, which are most likely to be known publicly. This information is needed to identify the company, but not relevant for a premium calculation. Basic conditions (*e.g.*, contract duration) are stored in contract constraints. Company conditions comprise all non-technical characteristics and mainly include information about business numbers. The following two categories are significantly related to each other and they encompass all technical characteristics. With the information of these two categories, the probability and partially the impact of a successful attack can be estimated to better understand all risks by both actors.

Table 2. Examples of SaCI functions implemented in the SC.

Function	Actor	Parameters	Description
payPremium	Customer	–	Pays the premium converted in Ethereum's Wei, increases time of validity
reportDamage	Customer	uint date, uint amount, string type_of_attack string logfileHash, uint damage_id	Creates a damage struct on the contract
acceptDamage	Insurer	uint damage_id	Accepts damage with ID and pays out reported damage
acceptCounterOffer	Customer	uint damage_id	Accepts counter offer, which is paid out automatically
resolveDispute	Customer	uint damage_id	Resolves a dispute about a damage reported, when a solution is found off-chain
ProposeTo-UpdateContract	Both	uint new_premium, string new_file_hash	Makes a proposal to update the contract

While the company security category describes different metrics about security deployed and measures taken to improve the security, the company's infrastructure includes all information of hardware, software, and technology as well as about critical parts of those. Finally, within the contract coverage category, details about every contract's coverage are stored in an unlimited list. For every attack, the costs covered and possibly other constraints of the specific coverage (*e.g.*, maximum indemnification of insurer) are defined. The contract coverage is the most important part besides the risk assessment to calculate the premium. Listing 1.1 shows an example of a contract coverage against four different threats (*e.g.*, business interruption due to a DDoS attack and third-person damage due to a data breach) defined in the JSON file's descriptor. Finally, upon entering information of all categories, the content can be forwarded to the *Premium Calculator*, which will calculate the premium and inputs the SC generation.

At this point, the contract is deployed on the BC and can be accessed by the insurer and the customer utilizes functions available in the contract (*cf.* Table 2).

This list is not exhaustive and other functions are available in the proposed SC, too, all details are available within the implementation [11].

After the premium is paid and the contract is enacted, the actors can interact. For instance, in case an attack happened, the customer can call the *reportDamage()* function (*cf.* Listing 1.2) to ask for refunding or help. The insurer can accept or deny the coverage requested. If accepted (*i.e.*, *acceptDamage(id)*), the payment is made automatically via the SC according to what was defined previously in the contract. Note that the customer can also provide a hash of a log file as proof of the attack. This hash is also stored in the BC to further enable an integrity check. At the same time, the file itself has to be stored off-chain, especially inside the contract information datasets maintained by both actors.

```
1   "contract_coverage": [
2   { "name": "DDoS",
3     "coverage": [{
4       "name": "Business Interruption",
5       "coverage_ratio": 100,
6       "deductible": 1000,
7       "max_indemnification": 300000 }]},
8   { "name": "Data Breach",
9     "coverage": [
10    { "name": "Third-party damage",
11      "coverage_ratio": 100,
12      "deductible": 1000,
13      "max_indemnification": 300000 }]}]
```

Listing 1.1. Contract Coverage in a JSON Format.

If the parties cannot reach a conclusion, counteroffers can be made by the insurer (*i.e.*, payment for a specific loss but not for all financial losses). Figure 2 shows the state diagram of possible interactions after a *reportDamage()* is called by the customer. The report damage process has one of the following states: *New, Paid, UnderInvestigation, Dispute, Resolved*, or *Canceled*. This diagram exmplifies the different functions's use (*e.g.*, *reportDamage()*, *acceptDamage()*, and *acceptCounterOffer()*) to claim a settlement.

The *Canceled* status is an ending state, reached only if the customer cancels the request. *Paid* status defines that the insurer accepted to cover the damage, and it was automatically paid. If the contract has a lower balance than the value to pay out, the insurer has to transfer funds to the contract, when accepting the coverage. If the insurer declines the coverage payment, a reason is provided and a counteroffer is issues. If a counteroffer is not possible to be offered at that time, the status is defined as *UnderInvestigation*, which means that further manual investigations have to be placed off-chain before a counteroffer can be placed.

If the insurer provides a counteroffer (*e.g.*, a lower amount than the initially requested compensation for that incident) and the customer does not accept it, the state changes to *Dispute*. This refers to the fact that no agreement has been found yet. Either the insurer creates a better counteroffer or the two actors have to solve the dispute off-chain for which a third party may be considered. If the dispute can be solved, the final status of *Resolved* will be achieved. Using the SC function *getAllReportedDamagesWithStatus* all reported damages with a

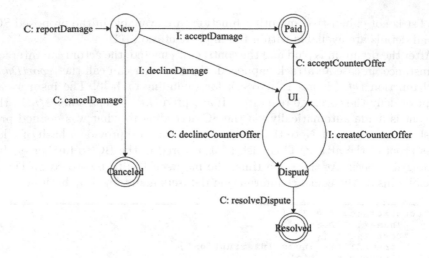

Fig. 2. Claims settlement state diagram.

specific status can be returned, which also allows verifying the history of past interactions, *e.g.*, accepted, declined, and under investigation coverage requests.

A prototype of the SaCI was implemented using Python as backend language and Solidity for the SC development. The Ethereum blockchain running on the Ganache testbed has been used for the deployment and tests of SC functionality. For SaCI 's Application Programming Interface (API) Flask was used in its latest version. Finally, for the off-chain storage, the prototype uses SQLite. The source-code and all documentation is publicly available at [11].

The code of the function to report a damage is shown, as an example, in Listing 1.2. It takes the date the damage happened, the amount of damage, the damage id, the type of attack and the logfile hash as input parameters as described in Table 2. As in the `payPremium` function first some restrictions are checked. In lines 6–9 it is verified again if the sender of the message is the customer. After that, it is checked if the contract covers the date the damage occurred. To do so, the date of the damage is compared to the contract attributes `start_date` and `valid_until` in line 11. Since damage should not be overwritten, it must be ensured that there is no damage yet, with the same damage id as the new reported damage. This check is done in lines 15–18.

When the restrictions are met, a `Reported_Damage` struct is created and mapped by the id into the contract attribute `reported_damages`. The struct is created with the values passed by the function and default values for the counter offer. The current status of the damage is set to New. The new damage id is added to the contract's list of ids in line 28, and the count of reported damages is increased by 1 in line 29.

Theoretically, it is possible to automatically pay out some damages without a check from the insurer, as shown in lines 31–33. For example, when the damage amount is quite small, and the last reported damages were all covered. This would reduce the administrative effort of the insurer and increase customers satisfaction. However, it offers an additional possibility for fraud, and the conditions when automatic payment is possible should be chosen very well. The insurer afterward also should be able to challenge paid-out damage automatically in case of fraudulent behavior. Hence, lines 31–33 are not mandatory to be included in the contract, but they offer an additional possibility to the insurer. The code of the `automaticPayOut` function that is called in line 32 is shown in Listing 1.3.

```
1    function reportDamage ( uint date_of_damage,
2                            uint amount_of_damage,
3                            uint damage_id,
4                            string memory type_of_attack,
5                            string memory logfile_hash) public{{
6        require(
7            customer_address == msg.sender,
8            "Only the registered customer can report a damage."
9        );
10       require(
11       date_of_damage > start_date && date_of_damage <= valid_until,
12            "The contract was not valid at the date of damage."
13       );
14       //check if the id is already given away
15       require(
16           reported_damages[damage_id].amount_of_damage == 0,
17           "Already exists a damage with the selected id."
18       );
19       reported_damages[damage_id]
20           = Reported_Damage( date_of_damage,
21                              amount_of_damage,
22                              StatusDamage.New,
23                              damage_id,
24                              type_of_attack,
25                              logfile_hash,
26                              "",
27                              0);
28       list_of_damage_ids[count_of_damages] = damage_id;
29       count_of_damages = count_of_damages + 1;
30       // Possibly allow an automatic payment
31       if(amount_of_damage < premium && count_of_damages < 4){
32           automaticPayOut(damage_id, false);
33       }
34   }
```

Listing 1.2. Example of the SC Function for Damage Report.

The function takes as parameter the id of the damage and a `boolean` named `is_counter_offer`. The `boolean` defines if the value of the counteroffer should be paid out or the value of the initially reported damage. As this function should not be called from outside of the contract, it is assigned to be private. The restriction in lines 3–6 checks if the damage was already paid out, canceled, or otherwise resolved to protect the insurer of unintended double payout. If the damage status is not in an ending state, the amount to pay is calculated in lines 7–12. Considering the parameter `is_counter_offer`, either the initial value of the reported damage or the value of the counteroffer is converted into Wei using the exchange rate returned from the oracle again. Afterward, it is checked if the contract currently has enough balance to pay out the damage. In the case that there is not enough balance, the insurer is notified by the error message in line 15. Otherwise, the calculated amount is transferred to the customer address stored in the contract, and the status of the damage changes to Paid.

```
1    function automaticPayOut (uint damage_id, bool is_counter_offer) private
     {
2        StatusDamage current_status = reported_damages[damage_id].status;
3        require(
4            current_status != StatusDamage.Paid && current_status !=
                 StatusDamage.Canceled && current_status != StatusDamage.
                 Resolved,
5            "This damage is already paid, deleted or resolved otherwise."
6        );
7        uint payOutInWei = 0;
8        if(is_counter_offer){
9            payOutInWei = convertEuroToWei(reported_damages[damage_id].
                 counter_offer);
10       }else{
11           payOutInWei = convertEuroToWei(reported_damages[damage_id].
                 amount_of_damage);
12       }
13       require(
14           address(this).balance >= payOutInWei,
15           "Not enough Ether available in the contract."
16       );
17       customer_address.transfer(payOutInWei);
18       reported_damages[damage_id].status = StatusDamage.Paid;
19   }
```

Listing 1.3. SC for the Automatic Payment.

4   Evaluation

While evaluations of cyber insurance models as such will cover the precision of risk models and their prediction granularity, SaCI 's evaluation here focuses on the systems' operations, which are based on a real-world case. Furthermore, cost analysis and discussion concerning its BC-based implementation are provided.

4.1   Case Study

Suppose that a customer wants to protect her business from financial loss possibly caused by Distributed Denial-of-Service (DDoS) attacks. The customer will access SaCI 's Web-based interface and fills all information related to her business and respective requirements, such as the company's conditions (*e.g.*, sector, revenue, and number of employees), security aspects (*e.g.*, attacks history, risk assessment, available protections), and coverage demands. The insurer uses this information to propose a contract offering coverage of 90% of all financial loss, if a business interruption happens due to a DDoS attack until a maximum amount of 300,000 €. For that, the deductible amount of 1,000 € is considered besides a yearly premium of 2,000 €. Figure 3 provides an overview of all interactions and actors considered for this case study.

After the customer and insurer decided about the contract off-chain, this generates a JSON file with all information and SC is created with the anonymization of private information (*cf.* Sect. 3). Finally, the contract is deployed on the BC and the hash of the JSON file with all contact information is stored together with the SC. Both actors also store a copy of the JSON file (*i.e.*, all contract information without anonymization) in private databases for further reference, while the hash stored in the BC allows for an integrity validation. The customer will finally call the function *payPremium(amount)* to initiate the coverage.

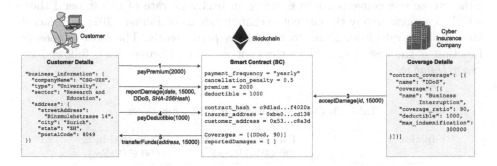

Fig. 3. Case study's information and flows.

If an attack happened at the customer's IT resulting in 15,000 € of loss, a request for coverage is placed by calling the function *reportDamage(date, amount, type_of_attack, logFile_hash)*. Based on this, the insurer automatically checks, if the request complies to the contract and calls the function *accept-Damage(amount)*, ensuring that the amount is available in the SC for the payment. The amount is automatically sent to the customer in order to pay for her losses. If the damage was not accepted, a counteroffer will be placed or further investigations are required, as discussed above. The logFile_hash allows for the verification of the attack and losses if required. Thus, the insurer can ask the customer to send log files via a secure channel, *e.g.*, containing network traces, reports, or internal analysis data explaining the incident. The hash stored in the BC provides a trustworthy record in case a dispute is required.

4.2   SC Cost Evaluation

Of key relevance for the economic efficiency of such an approach are costs related to the BC-based solution. Thus, Table 3 summarizes all costs for calling functions available in the SC, including the deployment (*i.e.*, Constructor) of the contract. These Gas costs in Ethereum were estimated using the function *estimateGas* provided by the Web3 library. Gas defines the internal pricing to run a transaction or a contract in the Ethereum BC. Gas does "measure" the computational usage in terms of monetary costs (*e.g.*, Gas per Swiss Franc or €) [3]. These functions as of today within the proof-of-concept were not yet optimized in terms of Gas costs; they can be reduced for a production deployment by *(a)* using different implementations of BC, which support SCs, and also *(b)* by optimizing the overall process, such as by increasing the time to process transactions to reduce the amount of Gas that have to be spent. Furthermore, as many BC projects (*e.g.*, Cardano and Polkadot) are promising efficient features, the can enable a cheapest and most efficient way to implement cyber insurance models that rely on SCs.

Gas costs were converted into Wei (*i.e.*, smallest denomination of Ether) using a Gas cost of 20 GWei per Gas, which is the default value of Ganache. The Ether value was converted into € using an exchange rate of 600 € per Ether, which is approximately the current exchange rate as of January 2021; in general the exchange rate from Ether to € changes permanently. The most expensive function is the one that deploys the contract (*i.e.*, Constructor), followed by *reportDamage*.

Table 3. Cost estimations of SaCI's functions.

Function	Estimation in Ether (20 GWei/Gas)	Converted in € (600 €/Ether)
Constructor	0.10893	65.36
paySecurity	0.00080	0.48
payPremium	0.00084	0.50
reportDamage	0.00435	2.61
acceptDamage	0.00109	0.65
declineDamage	0.00174	1.04
acceptCounterOffer	0.00082	0.49
proposeToUpdateContract	0.00264	1.58
agreeToUpdateContract	0.00098	0.59

Although this amount has to be paid by the actors involved, this value does not represent a high values, since it is paid only when the function is called. Therefore, 65 € are paid for the deployment of the contract and 4.5 € have to be paid, when a coverage request is done. Note that all of these values already represent the most expensive case, in which the blocks are mined as fast as possible. Taking a Gas cost of 2 GWei, which is considered a price that usually persists a transaction in a block within the next minutes in the Ethereum network [13], the final cost to deploy a contract can be divided by ten, thus, resulting in a cost of 6.5 €.

These costs can also be affected due to the choice of the BC technology to be used. For this prototype, Ethereum was used for convenience (*i.e.*, support to SC, extensive documentation, and frameworks for development). However, the approach proposed by SaCI can be implemented using any permissioned or permissionless BCs that support SCs implementation, such as Cardano, Polkadot, and Hyperledger Fabric [15]. The decision might depend upon the insurer's demands in terms of performance, privacy, and scalability.

5   Summary, Conclusions, and Future Work

This work presented SaCI , a blockchain-based approach for the creation, deployment, and life-cycle management of cyber insurance contracts. SaCI handles the translation of human-readable demands (*e.g.*, JSON file) to SC contracts executed on the BC. The approach proposed allows users' information input, provides the SC code with all functions for interactions, and deploys the contract coverage information as an SC running on the public Ethereum BC for any interactions required between customers and insurers.

Concluding, the proof-of-concept implementation of SaCI is fully operational and was developed taking into consideration real-life actors and their interactions. Moreover, the system is fully decentralized, with no intermediaries due to the usage of a BC. However, off-chain disputes are still possible to resolve open issues that require interactions, since they cannot be automated at this step (*e.g.*, analysis of log files, agreement between the premium price, and decision about the coverage payment). SaCI 's feasibility was investigated by conducting a case study and cost analysis that shows basic interactions of the approach as well as concerns regarding the costs while using public BCs. Besides the advantages introduced by this approach (*e.g.*, automation and trust), it is important to conduct further investigations to verify the role of BC in the future of cyber insurance, such as introducing trust and simplifying the process while reducing its costs.

Future work includes: *(i)* the development of a Web-based interface for the interaction with SaCI and the contract running on the BC, *(ii)* the investigation of premium calculation models that can provide a fair way to define the value of the premium and the coverage amount, and *(iii)* an analysis of different types of BCs (private and hybrid) and distributed systems (*e.g.*, Inter-Planetary File Systems) to increase the efficiency of this solution (in terms of costs, privacy, and time to process transactions), while reducing its overall complexity. Furthermore, additional studies are still required in the field of cyber insurances to map and improve all different tasks required from the creation (*e.g.*, contract underwriting and premium definition) until the termination of a contract.

Acknowledgements. This paper was supported partially by *(a)* the University of Zürich UZH, Switzerland and *(b)* the European Union's Horizon 2020 Research and Innovation Program under Grant Agreement No. 830927, the CONCORDIA Project.

References

1. Aziz, B., Suhardi, K: A systematic literature review of cyber insurance challenges. In: International Conference on Information Technology Systems and Innovation (ICITSI 2020), Padang, Indonesia, pp. 357–363 (2020)
2. Farao, A., et al.: SECONDO: a platform for cybersecurity investments and cyber insurance decisions. In: Gritzalis, S., Weippl, E.R., Kotsis, G., Tjoa, A.M., Khalil, I. (eds.) TrustBus 2020. LNCS, vol. 12395, pp. 65–74. Springer, Cham (2020). https://doi.org/10.1007/978-3-030-58986-8_5

3. Franco, M.F., Scheid, E.J., Granville, L.Z., Stiller, B.: BRAIN: blockchain-based reverse auction for infrastructure supply in virtual network functions-as-a-service. In: IFIP Networking 2019 (Networking 2019), Warsaw, Poland, pp. 1–9, May 2019

4. Gatteschi, V., Lamberti, F., Demartini, C., Pranteda, C., Santamaría, V.: Blockchain and smart contracts for insurance: is the technology mature enough? Future Internet **10**(2), 20 (2018)

5. Kenneally, E.: Ransomware: a Darwinian opportunity for cyber insurance. Conn. Ins. J. Fall Symp. Edn. **28**(1), 1–13 (2020)

6. Kshetri, N.: The economics of cyber-insurance. IT Prof. **20**(6), 9–14 (2018)

7. Kshetri, N.: The evolution of cyber-insurance industry and market: an institutional analysis. Telecommun. Policy **44**(8), 102007 (2020)

8. Lepoint, T., Ciocarlie, G., Eldefrawy, K.: Blockcis-a blockchain-based cyber insurance system. In: IEEE International Conference on Cloud Engineering (IC2E 2018), Orlando, USA, pp. 378–384 (2018)

9. Morgan, S.: Cybercrime To Cost The World $10.5 Trillion Annually By 2025, November 2020. https://cybersecurityventures.com/hackerpocalypse-cybercrime-report-2016/. Accessed June 2021

10. Nam, S.O.: How much are insurance consumers willing to pay for blockchain and smart contracts? A contingent valuation study. Sustainability **10**(4332), 1–11 (2018)

11. Noah Berni, M.F.: SaCI - Prototype and Source-Code, January 2021. https://gitlab.ifi.uzh.ch/franco/saci. Accessed June 2021

12. Pal, R., Golubchik, L., Psounis, K., Hui, P.: Will cyber-insurance improve network security? A market analysis. In: IEEE Conference on Computer Communications (INFOCOM 2014), Toronto, Canada, pp. 235–243 (2014)

13. Rajeevan, A.: Tokens, Gas and Gas limit in Ethereum, February 2019. https://arunrajeevan.medium.com/tokens-gas-and-gas-limit-in-ethereum-f07790f56d8f. Accessed June 2021

14. Rodrigues, B., Franco, M., Parangi, G., Stiller, B.: SEConomy: a framework for the economic assessment of cybersecurity. In: Djemame, K., Altmann, J., Bañares, J.Á., Agmon Ben-Yehuda, O., Naldi, M. (eds.) GECON 2019. LNCS, vol. 11819, pp. 154–166. Springer, Cham (2019). https://doi.org/10.1007/978-3-030-36027-6_13

15. Scheid, E.J., Rodrigues, B.B., Killer, C., Franco, M.F., Rafati, S., Stiller, B.: Blockchains and distributed ledgers uncovered: clarifications, achievements, and open issues. In: Goedicke, M., Neuhold, E., Rannenberg, K. (eds.) Advancing Research in Information and Communication Technology. IAICT, vol. 600, pp. 289–317. Springer, Cham (2021). https://doi.org/10.1007/978-3-030-81701-5_12 https://www.springer.com/gp/book/9783030817008

16. Wargin, J.: Insurance Company Technology Trends Transforming the Industry in 2021, January 2021. https://www.duckcreek.com/blog/insurance-technology-trends/. Accessed June 2021

17. Xu, J., Wu, Y., Luo, X., Yang, D.: Improving the efficiency of blockchain applications with smart contract based cyber-insurance. In: IEEE International Conference on Communications (ICC 2020), Dublin, Ireland, pp. 1–7 (2020)

A New Blockchain Ecosystem
for Trusted, Traceable and Transparent
Ontological Knowledge Management
Position Paper

Thanasis G. Papaioannou[1]([✉]), Vlado Stankovski[2], Petar Kochovski[2],
Anthony Simonet-Boulogne[3], Caroline Barelle[4], Alberto Ciaramella[5],
Marco Ciaramella[5], and George D. Stamoulis[1]

[1] Athens University of Economics and Business (AUEB), Athens, Greece
{pathan,gstamoul}@aueb.gr
[2] University of Ljubljana, Ljubljana, Slovenia
{Vlado.Stankovski,Petar.Kochovski}@fri.uni-lj.si
[3] iExec, Lyon, France
asb@iex.ec
[4] European Dynamics, Luxembourg City, Luxembourg
caroline.barelle@eurodyn.com
[5] IntelliSemantic, Rivoli, Italy
{alberto.ciaramella,marco.ciaramella}@intellisemantic.com

Abstract. The Internet is becoming more centralized, more asymmetric
in terms of knowledge and power distribution, more biased, less privacy-
preserving and less trustworthy. Blockchain technologies already enable
the safe and fair exchange of digital assets in a decentralized manner; however, its application to information exchange remains largely unexplored.
This article exposes our vision for a semantically-enriched blockchain software ecosystem named ONTOCHAIN, that enables the development of
trustworthy distributed applications that can empower users, guarantee
both their privacy and high quality of service, and ultimately support
pluralism and democracy. ONTOCHAIN aims primarily to attain trustworthy service exchange and trustworthy content handling by means of
advanced knowledge management mechanisms for several domains such as
health, economy, public services, energy and sustainability, news, media,
entertainment, Industry 4.0 and tourism. We present the main components of the ONTOCHAIN architecture and their functionality. Finally,
the validity of our approach is exemplified by describing how decentralized applications can be enabled by the ONTOCHAIN ecosystem.

Keywords: Trust · e-Commerce · Anonymity · Smart contract ·
Decentralized apps

This work has been funded by the European Union in the framework of the NGI
ONTOCHAIN project (H2020-957338).

K. Tserpes et al. (Eds.): GECON 2021, LNCS 13072, pp. 93–105, 2021.
https://doi.org/10.1007/978-3-030-92916-9_8

1   Introduction

The success of the Internet lies in free speech, open innovation and interoperability. However, there are growing concerns that openness, trustworthiness, privacy and security are being threatened by the seek of high performance and profit. More specifically, multiple threats have been identified when people interact with online services: centralization of power (i.e., information and knowledge being in the hands of only few actors), unknown provenance of information (e.g., fake news), anonymity in favor of criminal activity, personal privacy violations and personal data exploitation (e.g., Cambridge Analytica scandal), biases in AI algorithms (e.g., under-representation of certain social groups in training data can make AI algorithms discriminate against those social groups), no fair rewards for quality contributions (e.g., provision of credible reviews), and more threaten the fundamental rights of users.

Decentralization is a key property enabled by Distributed Ledger Technologies (DLT), such as blockchain [13]. Blockchains are "trustless", i.e., the mechanisms in place allow all parties in the system to reach a consensus on what the normative truth is without requiring any trust in any third party. Thus, the various stakeholders of the network (e.g., developers, miners, and consumers) share power and trust, instead of placing it to a single individual or entity (e.g., banks, governments, and financial institutions). However, so far, blockchain does not deal with identity management, trustworthiness assessment of data and entities, trustworthiness of data handling, smart contracts that understand data semantics, secure data exchange or secure storage. Moreover, while being run on a shared decentralized infrastructure, it suffers from the Scalability Trilemma, a term coined by Vitalik Buterin (founder of Ethereum), that refers to the tradeoffs among decentralization, security and scalability that crypto projects must make when deciding how to optimize the underlying architecture of their own blockchain.

In this paper, we describe our vision to shape a multi-layer and modular blockchain framework, to enable the implementation of a number of different next-generation real-world solutions, such as trustworthy web and social media, trustworthy crowdsensing, trustworthy service orchestration, unsupervised, decentralized online social networks, etc. and to empower practitioners to address the various challenges of the Internet (e.g., centralization of power and knowledge, unknown provenance of information, anonymous and unreliable identifiers, personal data exploitation, AI biases, data censorship, fraud, etc.) through the use of multiple ledger and semantic technologies. Our use-cases are intended to be built upon different protocols and interactions among different blockchain components. The proposed blockchain-based framework is expected to enable higher performance and scalability, through the engagement of different business logic, access methods and governance models, whereas to present scalable solutions for ensuring secure and transparent content and information exchange as well as service interoperability. Moreover, our use-cases will rely on successful Semantic Web approaches such as Linked Data, OWL Lite, OWL DL and other approaches and formats that will deliver a trustworthy, privacy-preserving, secure, transparent, democratic and traceable approach to manage access and operations over ontologies, metadata, data, knowledge and information in the ecosystem. Our technology framework will constitute a building block of the next generation Internet towards a more human-centric Internet that supports values of openness, decentralisation, inclusiveness and protection of privacy as well as giving the control back to the end-users to be able to benefit from democratic, transparent and trustworthy decision making mechanisms.

The remainder of this paper is organized as follows: In Sect. 2, we overview the background and related work. In Sect. 3, we describe our approach towards a semantically-enriched, trustworthy blockchain ecosystem. In Sect. 4, we overview the architecture of our framework under development and describe its main component. In Sect. 5, we exemplify how our technological framework enables promising use-case scenarios that tackle fundamental user needs. Finally, in 6, we conclude our work and outline future work.

2 Background and Related Work

Blockchains became popular in 2008 after Satoshi Nakamoto released the Bitcoin white paper [13], but their applications span far beyond monetary transactions; energy, mobility, logistics, supply chain, healthcare and insurance are just a few domains that drive the growth of Distributed Ledger Technologies and make it one of the most important trends in the IT industry. A blockchain is a append-only ledger of records, grouped into blocks after validation by a distributed consensus across the network's participants [9,15]. Each block typically contains a timestamp, a cryptographic hash value of the previous block and a sorted list of validated transactions. This technology builds on a combination of older technologies, e.g. peer to peer protocols, cryptographic primitives, distributed consensus algorithms and game theory. As such, the blockchain is more of a paradigm shift in the way networked applications will be built, deployed, operated, consumed and marketed than just a technology. Unlike Bitcoin which supports only simple value transfers, modern blockchains like Ethereum [19] support *smart contracts*, i.e., self-executing decentralized programs that can read and write the state of the blockchain on top of which they are deployed. Smart contracts [6] enable the specification of advanced logic and the automation of business workflows. Whereas programs used to imply trust in one or several third parties from its user, a smart contract is transparent by design: its result (i.e., the new state of the blockchain) requires a consensus of the participants, and once committed on the ledger, it cannot be forged. Depending on implementation and deployment choices, many other key properties can be insured, e.g., the resistance to censorship and tampering, pseudo-anonymity, fault-tolerance, resilience, and non-repudiation.

In this context, blockchains are foreseen as the core backbone of novel, large, inter-connected environments such as smart cities and IoT applications where security and trust in information and data processing services are paramount to adoption and to the respect of users' rights. So, the suitability of blockchain technologies has been demonstrated in numerous works [11], e.g., for the management of medical records [12], for notary [16] and public services [17], identity [20] and reputation [7] and data traceability [18]. Several initiatives are aiming to bring the benefits of DLTs to different business domains in an attempt to disrupt virtually every aspect of life. GAIA-X [2] is building a European data infrastructure for developing innovative trustworthy and sustainable data economy, by relying on standards and open-source software. The project federates services from participating providers within one user-friendly ecosystem which supports federated entities, access-control and privacy-preserving processing by design. Hyperledger Fabric [4] (HLF) is a permissioned blockchain project originally developed by IBM and distributed as free software. HLF follows a flexible modular design which allows to simply replace components (e.g. consensus, smart contract language) and adapt to various application domains. Although HLF has demonstrated fast transaction throughput, its limited scalability to a maximum of about 16 peers [8,14] and its vulnerability to compromised nodes [5] limits its applicability to small to medium enterprise consortiums. The exploitation of Hyperledger Fabric as SaaS by IBM[1] contributes to its adoption by a large variety of industries to deploy enterprise blockchain networks. EOSIO [1] offers a modular framework for creating industrial-scale permissioned or permissionless blockchains and implements a 2-layer consensus protocol which combines a Byzantine Fault Tolerant protocol and a delegated Proof-of-Stake protocol. According to its developers, EOSIO's protocol allows the chain to achieve up to 8,000 Transactions Per Second, way ahead of Hyperledger Farbic [8], although no scientific evaluation of EOSIO's performance have been conducted.

ONTOCHAIN considers several challenges to unlock the tremendous potential of blockchain technology and make it technically, economically and legally viable in business environments for ensuring trust and accountability in information sharing and data processing. The first set of challenges are technical ones; although several solutions partly address the topics of identity, privacy-preserving data processing, trustworthy information handling and data provenance, no blockchain ecosystem supports web semantics natively and enables the development of information-centric applications like ONTOCHAIN intends to. The second set of challenges is related to the development of viable business models and incentives, i.e., creating an environment of peers that all profit from fair data production and data usage and makes unfair or malicious behavior unprofitable. The last sets of challenges are of legal nature; sitting at the intersection of finance and data processing, ONTOCHAIN must incorporate the recent General Data Protection Regulation as well as upcoming and quickly changing regulations aimed at strengthening the privacy of citizens within the EU.

3   The Vision and Approach

Today, the Internet is involved in all aspects of our lives. With the number of services available constantly on the rise, we are witnesses to an ever-increasing information overload. In addition, poor content aggregation mechanisms and

---

[1] https://www.ibm.com/blockchain.

stovepipe systems are making effective collaboration and smart decision making an even bigger challenge.

Notwithstanding the ability of advanced technologies to distinguish factual from non-factual data, existing large or small WWW services are used today with the purpose of spreading misleading information that usually serve a certain purpose: to damage one's reputation, win an election, make people buy products and services. With the confluence of the WWW with the Internet of Things, the ubiquitous Artificial Intelligence, the existence of Cloud, Fog and Edge computing platforms and similar, it becomes apparent that the existing problems of misuse of information can soon achieve even more dangerous levels of potential manipulation of the people that must be prevented.

As a response to these challenges a new vision has arisen. A vision where Internet (WWW, social networks, social media and IoT, etc.) data are understood by the machines and made accessible to an array of semantic technologies, therefore allowing the machines to do more effective and value adding work when responding to service requests.

Technically, this is achieved by using ontologies, that is, "formal, explicit specification of shared conceptualizations". Ontologies make it possible to intertwine the data and information into a Web of Knowledge. Several successful companies have built on the Semantic Web ideas in the past decades and have had enormous success, with the most popular applications being in the form of knowledge graphs such as Google Knowledge Graph or IBM Socrates. However, the Semantic Web does not execute uniformly for all. In such a system actors can sometimes make completely opposed assertions, such as "that apple is red" and "that (same) apple is yellow". This concept becomes especially important in crowdsensing which allows anyone to contribute the data acquired by their own connected objects in order to build collaborative knowledge. What is currently necessary, is to be able to establish the truth from several assertions.

With the emergence of the Internet of Things (IoT), the new wave of Artificial Intelligence (AI), Orchestration and novel Cloud Continuum approaches (Edge, Fog, Data Center), we now have the potential to reach a new level of decentralization, but also of cooperation between various cyber-physical systems based on the Semantic Web principles. Blockchain technologies with their main properties of decentralisation, traceability and transparency fit perfectly to this agenda, and may contribute to achieving trusted operations of such smart applications and systems [10]. The hypothesis of this work is that with these intrinsic properties of blockchain, it is possible to establish a common, shared ledger for the management of shared ontological concepts including instances of such concepts. An important aspect of ONTOCHAIN is the ability to interlink off-chain data, information and (AI) services with on-chain information in a way that reduces the need for costly on-chain operations and provides significant new properties, such as traceability, privacy, mechanisms for democracy and other.

Membership of different entities (e.g. specific objects, persons), in specific ontological concepts can be established, for example, by means of independent evaluation of various stakeholders with the use of AI methods. These entities

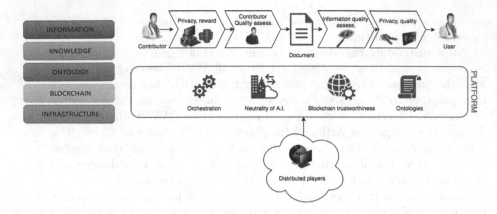

Fig. 1. Our vision and approach.

can be anonymous, but at the same time, they are able to be linked to real-word identities, when law demands it. Not only ontological concepts may be well-agreed among the participants, but also they can be directly "executable" through the employment of various semantic reasoners, operating directly on blockchain, potentially also employing trustworthy offchain real-world data (e.g., IoT) with the use of Smart Oracles and Decentralized Oracles that establish facts by using democratic, decentralised means. Overall, ONTOCHAIN's vision is depicted in Fig. 1, where trustworthy services, data and knowledge are exchanged in privacy-aware and traceable manner based on a layered approach on top of a semantically-enriched distributed ledger infrastructure.

4   The Architecture

A multi-layer approach to reach the envisioned ONTOCHAIN framework and to serve the defined use-cases and applications is followed as described in Fig. 2. This framework will enable the implementation of a number of innovative different next-generation real-world solutions, such as trustworthy web and social media, trustworthy crowdsensing, trustworthy service orchestration, unsupervised/decentralized online social networks, etc. Eventually, we predict that the diversity, the complexity and the specialization of different real-world ONTOCHAIN applications will lead practitioners to use multiple ledger technologies for implementing different solutions. This will enable higher performance and scalability, while enabling different business logic, access methods and governance models that require specific chains. ONTOCHAIN use-cases will be built upon the different protocols shown in Fig. 2. It is important to note that most of the components of the proposed architecture do not exist into any of the competitive platforms mentioned in Sect. 2. ONTOCHAIN Application and Core protocols will implement the interactions between different blockchain frameworks, while hiding them from the use-cases to support effortless inter-service

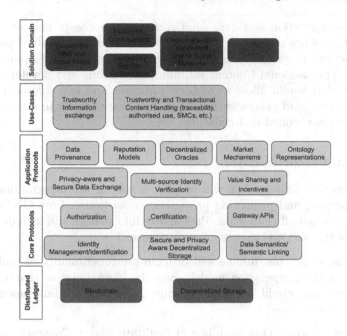

Fig. 2. The ONTOCHAIN architectural framework.

process cooperation. Moreover, data stored at different chains, may be linked together. This linkage will be stored in new ONTOCHAIN chains.

For enabling scalability, openness and high performance, we employ a modular approach. Each of the modules and functionality of each layer is built upon functionality offered by the lower layers. The functionality of the modules at each layer is described in a top-down manner below, along with the dependencies among them.

Use-Case Layer

Trustworthy Information Exchange: This use case encapsulates the tools and libraries for the secure exchange of trustworthy data among trustworthy parties. It employs and combines data provenance mechanisms, decentralized oracles and user trustworthiness to assess trustworthiness of information. Decentralized reputation models are employed to assess the trustworthiness of data sources and that of the data itself, while the secure data exchange mechanisms are employed to transfer the data securely among transacted parties through cryptographic mechanisms.

Trustworthy and Transactional Content Handling: This use case enables trustworthy data handling by means of any combination of the following: authorized access/handling of the data, data credibility assessment, implementation of copyrights, secure and privacy aware querying of the data (e.g., by means of secure multiparty computation and data sanitization approaches). This use case also deals with the secure transfer of any financial assets among involved parties in a data transaction. Regulatory alignment of data transactions, as a part of Trustworthy and Transactional Content Handling, will define and develop tools and mechanisms that would allow regulatory, judiciary and law enforcement agencies to introspect and otherwise influence data transactions in strictly defined circumstances envisioned by legislature.

Application Protocols Layer

Data Provenance: This module will provide graphical and programming interfaces for querying and presenting provenance information from ONTOCHAIN about on-chain and off-chain data. Provenance information will include the complete trail of transactions that resulted in a record.

Reputation Models: This module will provide the functionality of building different decentralized reputation models over the blockchain, so that reputation feedback is genuine, credible and anonymous. This module is built upon Identity Verification mechanisms.

Decentralized Oracles: This module will facilitate Smart Contracts to operate with off-chain data, although by design, Smart Contracts can only read and write data that is stored on their blockchain. To avoid centralization, some approaches (e.g. Substrate, ChainLink) apply multiple instances to look at a data source, and then run a consensus algorithm on-chain to validate the result. This, however, only displaces the point of centralization from the Oracle to the data source. While the idea of Decentralized Oracles is simple, its implementation is not trivial: every use-case requires different data sources, and the consensus algorithm based on multiple data types can become complex.

Market Mechanisms "as a Service": This module provides the basic support mechanisms for enabling data/service transaction, and thus enables market mechanisms. For example, this module will support trading of physical assets (e.g., tokenization) and price determination (e.g., auctions, negotiation protocols, etc.), billing, customer support, inventory management services and more. It also provides functionality for enabling the sharing economy, such as value chaining, value/cost sharing and DeFi support.

Secure Data Exchange: This module comprises the functionality of exchanging data among distributed parties, while verifying the ownership of the data and access rights, authenticity of transacted parties, the integrity of the data exchanged and the confidentiality of the data through blockchain underlying mechanisms. Most often, off-chain data will be exchanged in data transactions, while on-chain data will store public cryptographic keys and access control lists based on which elevated data access to different portions of data is authorized for specific transacted parties.

Ontology Representation: This module seeks to define new ways for implementing ontologies with the use of blockchain. Semantic agreements can be commonly agreed based blockchain-based consensus, similarly to the establishment of axiomatic statements. Moreover, new ontologies will be defined for smart contracts and decentralized services to enable service searchability and matching with service requests. This module will also include any reasoning approaches, tools and methods that can help deduce new knowledge arriving from a sensing IoT empowered environment.

Multi-source Identity Verification: This module seeks to register and verify individual digital identities of physical objects via newly designed ONTOCHAIN services. For instance, various AI methods could be introduced to operate on sensing data (IoT based, sensors, cameras and similar) to assert whether an individual belongs to a specific ontological concept.

Value Sharing and Incentives: ONTOCHAIN ecosystem is to be, by nature, a public good built upon the resources and efforts of a great number of people. Proper incentive mechanisms for rewarding the people involved, according to their contribution, should be in place. Such mechanisms could include: i) the generation of a certain number of cryptocurrencies for block mining and execution of smart contracts, ii) contribution assessment.

Core Protocols

Certification: This module refers to the confirmation of certain characteristics of an object, person, or organization. For example, a government may decide to offer certificates to cloud providers that have verified GDPR-compliant handling of private citizens' data [3]. In such case, certificates can be issued on-chain (i.e. implemented within Smart Contracts), and can be used as conditions for performing specific transactions, for example, using AI methods to analyse private data.

Secure/Privacy Aware Storage: This module encapsulates solutions already existing on blockchain. Together with decentralisation they help reduce the risk of one party having access to all private data. Moreover, various partitioning, fragmentation and redundancy methods will be used (e.g., StorJ).

Identity Management: This module deals with technologies and solutions to address parts of the digital identity puzzle. There are two conflicting requirements that drive this development: i) ability to identify oneself in specific interactions (e.g., withdrawing money in a bank), ii) preservation of one's privacy (e.g., healthcare data, online buyer's habits).

Gateways/Bridges: This module will support connections between the ONTOCHAIN blockchain and the outside world, including other blockchains in the form of Smart Contracts, as well as several higher-level wrappers for commonly used languages (e.g. JavaScript, Java and Python). Our prototype will be implemented using the Ethereum software stack, because of its important community of adopters and developers.

Data Semantics: Since ontology engineering is a complex work that usually takes many years to complete and test, this module intends to stimulate reuse of this body of generated knowledge in order to foster the use of various schemata and ontologies when describing the semantics of data. Ontologies are core building block of the Semantic Web [https://www.w3.org/]. The W3C consortium provides mechanisms for their standardisation in order to foster their use in applications world-wide, with the potential to build various artificial agents that can cross-link the information, and perform advanced queries via SPARQL. Supporting these standards in the blockchain and providing data semantic annotation, semantics extraction, linking, inference, alignment and reasoning on top of blockchains will significantly boost the business viability of future applications involving knowledge management.

Authorisation: Blockchain has stimulated the idea of self-sovereign digital identity. Various Role-Based Access Control (RBAC) systems have also existed for decades. With this module, one could easily see systems where a patient is self-identified on blockchain, while a medical doctor gains access to the medical records based on her/his role (e.g., surgeon, general practitioner).

Distributed Ledger

Blockchain Consensus Engine: Consensus making mechanisms are at the core of any blockchain. ONTOCHAIN will be designed to be scalable, open, cost and energy-efficient, and when possible even as a much improved new consensus engine. Regarding openness, ONTOCHAIN does not aim for a silo blockchain ecosystem, but for an open distributed ledger that in principle can be combined with different blockchain environments.

Decentralised Storage: Various decentralised repositories, such as Peer-to-Peer and Content Distribution Networks have existed for decades. With the emergence of blockchain, we have witnessed a new wave of participatory storage repositories that can help address the security and privacy needs, and may help store practically any kind of data (e.g., StorJ). In the near future, one could imagine new storage services, that can help store private data in encrypted and decentralised way, that can help manage data replicas for reliability and Quality of Service, while balancing the trade-offs with the storage costs.

5   Use Cases

ONTOCHAIN will enable many forthcoming applications, from B2B to C2C to G2C, in different verticals, including:

- Arts - Remunerate artistic work
- Commerce and Trading – P2P eCommerce - Proprietary data trading
- Education - Credible and authentic eScience
- Finance - Decentralized borrowing and lending

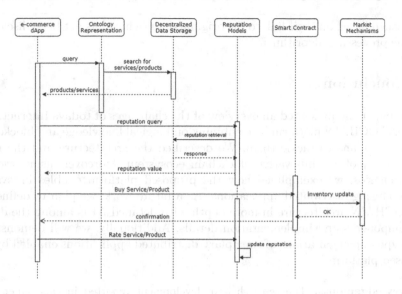

Fig. 3. P2P commerce distributed application scenario.

- Healthcare – Access to patient data – Drug control – Privacy-aware data analytics
- Industry - Privacy-aware data analytics
- Insurance - Decentralized, Transparent and Trustworthy Insurance
- Manufacturing – Supply Chain Management – Maintenance tracking
- Public Sector – Smart cities Traffic control

A use-case scenario related to P2P e-commerce is detailed as example hereafter. In this use case, users are able to search for products/services provided by business entities based on data semantics. Users receive the matching product/service from the most reputable provider. The product/service transaction is then recorded in the blockchain as well as the changes of ownership of the product or the access provision to a service. In parallel, the product/service is removed from the inventory of the seller and an invoice is automatically issued. Finally, users may submit rating data on their past transactions. Figure 3 summarizes the main interactions of this application.

Another use-case scenario concerns prorpietary-data trading. Individuals or data aggregators collect personal/proprietary data that are subject to privacy concerns and their handling is governed by GDPR. In this application, data is securely stored, uniquely identified and access to it is restricted to authorized entities for pre-specified handling. Data handling can be realized in secure enclaves through predetermined algorithms, also part of the smart contract, without any disclosure of the original data to any third party. The validity of the smart contract against GDPR is automatically validated and any processing activities to the data are recorded in the blockchain. Any data transformations that produce new data, are being treated as tradeable assets, while their provenance can be established based on their link to the original data (which has not been disclosed) and the processing algorithms.

6   Conclusion

In this paper, we presented an overview of the challenges of todays Internet, and how ONTOCHAIN platform by combining ontological knowledge and blockchain technology plans to tackle them. We described the architecture and the main functionality of our innovative blockchain ecosystem. Moreover, using two use case scenarios, we exemplified how the proposed platform enables innovative and promising distributed applications. As a future work, we plan to define the ONTOCHAIN architecture in more depth with detailed APIs among the different components and implementation details. Additionally, we will demonstrate prototype implementations of exemplary distributed applications enabled by the proposed platform.

Acknowledgements. The research and development reported in this paper have received funding from the European Union's Horizon 2020 Research and Innovation Programme under grant agreement no. 957338 (ONTOCHAIN: Trusted, traceable and transparent ontological knowledge on blockchain).

References

1. EOSIO Dawn 3.0 Now Available. https://medium.com/eosio/eosio-dawn-3-0-now-available-49a3b99242d7. Accessed 15 June 2021
2. GAIA-X: A Federated Data Infrastructure for Europe. http://www.data-infrastructure.eu/GAIAX/. Accessed 15 June 2021
3. General Data Protection Regulation. https://gdpr-info.eu/
4. Hyperledger Fabric Homepage. https://www.hyperledger.org/use/fabric. Accessed 15 June 2021
5. Bhuvana, R., Aithal, P.: Blockchain based service: a case study on IBM blockchain services and hyperledger fabric. Int. J. Case Stud. Bus. IT Educ. (IJCSBE) 4(1), 94–102 (2020)
6. Christidis, K., Devetsikiotis, M.: Blockchains and smart contracts for the Internet of Things. IEEE Access 4, 2292–2303 (2016)
7. Dennis, R., Owen, G.: Rep on the block: a next generation reputation system based on the blockchain. In: 2015 10th International Conference for Internet Technology and Secured Transactions (ICITST). IEEE (2015)
8. Dinh, T.T.A., Wang, J., Chen, G., Liu, R., Ooi, B.C., Tan, K.L.: Blockbench: a framework for analyzing private blockchains. In: Proceedings of the 2017 ACM International Conference on Management of Data (2017)
9. Hamida, E.B., Brousmiche, K.L., Levard, H., Thea, E.: Blockchain for enterprise: overview, opportunities and challenges. In: The Thirteenth International Conference on Wireless and Mobile Communications (ICWMC 2017) (2017)
10. Kochovski, P., Gec, S., Stankovski, V., Bajec, M., Drobintsev, P.D.: Trust management in a blockchain based fog computing platform with trustless smart oracles. Future Gener. Comput. Syst. 101, 747–759 (2019)

11. Maesa, D.D.F., Mori, P.: Blockchain 3.0 applications survey. J. Parallel Distrib. Comput. **138**, 99–114 (2020)
12. Mettler, M.: Blockchain technology in healthcare: the revolution starts here. In: 2016 IEEE 18th International Conference on e-Health Networking, Applications and Services (Healthcom). IEEE (2016)
13. Nakamoto, S.: Bitcoin: a peer-to-peer electronic cash system. Bitcoin White Paper (2008). https://bitcoin.org/bitcoin.pdf
14. Nasir, Q., Qasse, I.A., Abu Talib, M., Nassif, A.B.: Performance analysis of hyperledger fabric platforms. In: Security and Communication Networks, vol. 2018 (2018)
15. Singh, K., Heulot, N., Hamida, E.B.: Towards anonymous, unlinkable, and confidential transactions in blockchain. In: 2018 IEEE International Conference on Internet of Things (iThings) and IEEE Green Computing and Communications (GreenCom) and IEEE Cyber, Physical and Social Computing (CPSCom) and IEEE Smart Data (SmartData). IEEE (2018)
16. Song, G., Kim, S., Hwang, H., Lee, K.: Blockchain-based notarization for social media. In: 2019 IEEE International Conference on Consumer Electronics (ICCE), pp. 1–2. IEEE (2019)
17. Sullivan, C., Burger, E.: E-residency and blockchain. Comput. Law Secur. Rev. **33**(4), 470–481 (2017)
18. Tian, F.: An agri-food supply chain traceability system for china based on RFID and blockchain technology. In: 2016 13th International Conference on Service Systems and Service Management (ICSSSM). IEEE (2016)
19. Wood, G., et al.: Ethereum: a secure decentralised generalised transaction ledger. Ethereum Proj. Yellow Pap. **151**(2014), 1–32 (2014)
20. Yasin, A., Liu, L.: An online identity and smart contract management system. In: 2016 IEEE 40th Annual Computer Software and Applications Conference (COMPSAC), vol. 2. IEEE (2016)

Clouds, Fogs

Modelling Serverless Function Behaviours

Rafael Tolosana-Calasanz[1]([✉]), Gabriel G. Castañé[2], José Á. Bañares[1], and Omer Rana[3]

[1] Departamento de Informática e Ing. de Sistemas, Universidad de Zaragoza, Zaragoza, Spain
rafaelt@unizar.es
[2] Insight Centre for Data Analytics, University College Cork, Cork, Ireland
[3] School of Computer Science and Informatics, Cardiff University, Cardiff, UK

Abstract. The serverless computing model extends potential deployment options for cloud applications, by allowing users to focus on building and deploying their code without needing to configure or manage the underlying computational resources. Cost and latency constraints in stream processing user applications often push computations closer to the sources of data, leading to challenges for dynamically distributing stream operators across the edge/fog/cloud heterogeneous nodes and the routing of data flows. Various approaches to support operator placement across edge and cloud resources and data routing are beginning to be addressed through the serverless model. Understanding how stream processing operators can be mapped into serverless functions also offers cost incentives for users – as charging is now on a subsecond basis (rather than hourly). A dynamic Petri net model of serverless functions is proposed in this work, which takes account of the computational requirements of functions, the resources on which these functions are hosted, and key parameters that impact the behaviour of serverless functions – such as warm/cold start up times. The model can be used by developers/users of serverless functions to understand how deployment optimisation can be used to reduce application time, and to analyse various scenarios on choosing function granularity, data size and cost.

Keywords: Petri nets · Serverless economics · Dynamic models

1 Introduction and Motivation

Cloud computing has seen a transition over recent years, from virtual machines to containers to functions. This transition has mainly been driven by reducing the overhead of deploying user-based applications within a data centre. Increasing demand for short running workloads has also driven this trend towards reducing startup (referred to as *cold start time*) and deployment time. If the startup time is significantly higher than execution time of a user application, understanding how deployment optimisation can be used to reduce application execution time remains an important challenge. Variation in demand (due to dynamically

© Springer Nature Switzerland AG 2021
K. Tserpes et al. (Eds.): GECON 2021, LNCS 13072, pp. 109–122, 2021.
https://doi.org/10.1007/978-3-030-92916-9_9

changing input data streams) requires application resource scaling (up/down), forcing cloud providers to respond to this within a time-bounded manner.

Serverless computing generally refers to a cloud computing model that *hides* the concept of a server, as a serverless computing platform allows users/developers to build and deploy their code without dealing with computational resources (i.e. resource management activities). The unit of deployment is the code, which is wrapped in several functions, subsequently invoked as a composition of functions that form an application. Serverless computing provides a useful basis for reacting to dynamically changing workloads in a cost-effective manner for a user. User requests for computational resources within sub-second intervals provides a more flexible way to access cloud resources, and enables better budgeting for users. This also provides a useful business model for cloud providers to make more effective use of resources that are not used for long running workloads. Using serverless based resource allocation, cloud providers are also able to utilise their spare (under utilised) capacity in a more effective way.

Serverless computing and fog computing also benefit from increasing capability offered in user devices and sensor/actuators [5]. Cost and latency constraints prevent cloud-only processing, pushing computation closer to the sources of data, and introducing important challenges for dynamically distributing operators across heterogeneous edge/fog/cloud nodes [6], and routing of data flows to the optimum computation node [7].

Understanding how stream processing operations can be mapped into (usually short running) functions at the edge/cloud layer, and the cost incentives for users/resource providers remains a significant challenge for serverless computing. This paper proposes a dynamic Petri net model of serverless functions, which considers the computational requirements of functions, resources on which these functions are hosted, and key parameters that impact their behaviour – such as warm/cold start up times. The model can be exploited by developers/users of serverless functions to understand how deployment optimisation can be used to reduce application execution time, and to explore what-if scenarios for choosing appropriate function granularity, data size and cost.

This paper is structured as follows: Sect. 2 introduces estimated costs of using functions across different vendors. Section 3 presents the key contribution of this work – focusing on developing Petri net models of serverless functions, taking account of the costing approach adopted by various existing cloud vendors. Section 4 includes a description of how these models can be used, with evaluation in Sect. 5, followed by concluding remarks in Sect. 6.

2 Serverless Function Economics

A number of vendors offer serverless functionality – ranging from Amazon AWS, Google, Microsoft – to a number of additional vendors & open source systems such as IBM Cloud Functions, Knative based on Kubernetes deployment, Apache OpenWhisk-based function deployment, Cloudflare workers, Oracle functions, etc. A single mechanism to compare costs across different serverless offerings is very challenging, as the type of infrastructure (CPU type, execution speed), memory supported (e.g. 128 MB to 8 GB), data transfer rates supported etc., differ widely across vendors. Azure and Lambda functions are generally integrated with other services, making it challenging to do a feature to feature comparison across vendors. AWS offers the widest choice, offering serverless functions with differing resource characteristics (different RAM and underlying processor architectures). Figure 1 provides a costing undertaken on AWS Lambda using a number of different variables (e.g. user authentication, number of pages processed), and aligned with other AWS services (e.g. cloud monitoring and CDN (CloudFront)). Google function allocation is based on the size of memory and processor CPU speed, with compute time measured from the time a request is received to the time that the function is signal to be completed (successful termination, failure or a timeout). Compute time is measured in 100 ms increments, rounded up to the nearest increment (e.g. a 170 ms execution is billed as 200 ms). For Microsoft Azure functions, billing is based on a per second resource consumption basis (considering a vCPU) and number of executions carried out within a time window. Consumption plan pricing includes a monthly free grant of 1 million requests and 400,000 GBs of resource consumption per month per subscription in pay-as-you-go pricing across all function apps in that subscription.

Table 1. Serverless costs – based on [2–4].

Vendor	Billable unit (US$)	Key considerations
Amazon Lamda (128 MB)	$0.0000000021 (1 ms)	Pricing based on requests and duration
Amazon Lamda (1024 MB)	$0.0000000167 (1 ms)	
Amazon Lamda (10240 MB)	$0.0000001667 (1 ms)	
Google functions (128 MB, 200 MHz CPU)	$0.000000231 (100 ms)	Pricing based on: compute time, use of network capacity, number of invocations
Google functions (8192 MB, 4.8 GHz CPU)	$0.000006800 (100 ms)	
MS-Azure functions	$0.000016/GB-s	Number of invocations

Replacing existing container/VM-based provision with a function-based offering (e.g. AWS Lambda) can lead to significant long term savings for a typical hosting environment. For instance, consider that it takes 2 s to serve a page view based on the data from DynamoDB, we can calculate the total cost of serving 100K page requests. Even with a generous 1 GB memory allocation and relatively sluggish 2 s processing time, the total cost for AWS Lambda would be less than US$5 (calculated based on 1024 MB AWS Lamda costs from Table 1). A key challenge in function-based deployments is the *keep-alive* time of these functions between invocations. A cloud service provider may want to use synthetic data to minimise the cold start time associated with starting up a function – an important variable that influences both operational and energy costs for the provider.

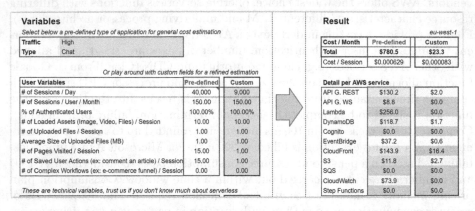

Fig. 1. Serverless costs from Amazon AWS [1].

3   Serverless Models

We develop a serverless function model that can be hosted across different types of resources – from data centre to edge nodes. The model can be used as a basis to support capacity planning for serverless functions, enabling an application designer to investigate their application requirements using the model. Petri nets are a well-established formalism and have been used extensively to model concurrent and distributed systems. Reference nets are a specific type of Petri nets that support greater levels of dynamism than ordinary Petri nets and support Java code inscriptions. In this work, we make use of Reference nets and their interpreter *Renew* to create dynamic serverless function models that can be configured over a real system's deployment. A quick introduction to the ordinary Petri net theory can be found in [12]. An example of how Reference nets can be applied to the modelling of applications and their mapping to cloud resources can be found in [13].

Figure 2 depicts Petri net (shorted to *net* in the description below) patterns to model a physical, hierarchical edge/cloud infrastructure. On the left, the net represents a node that contains computational resources to execute functions. The net in the center models data movement activity that connects two nodes, or a data source (sink) and a node. The two nets on the right represent a data source and a data sink. All these patterns can be combined to generate a model of a hierarchical (layered) physical edge infrastructure, where the lowest layer comprises IoT sensors and other user devices, and the topmost layer will represent the cloud data center. All intermediate nodes between the data sources and the cloud data center represent different fog nodes, aligning with the systems architecture proposed by the Open Fog Consortium[1].

In our model, data is always transmitted across the infrastructure along with a processing plan (or user application). The plan specifies a composition of functions in the form of a Directed Acyclic Graph (DAG) that need to be applied to its associated data. Furthermore, both the data and its plan are modelled as tokens in the physical edge model. In our model, the plan specifies the orchestration of the execution inside a node and across the nodes.

When data chunk and its associated processing plan arrive at a node, then Transition $t1$ from Fig. 2 is fired (triggering the invocation of the synchronous channel *begin* of the node). Once all function invocations in the graph are accomplished, Transition $t2$ is fired and the processing plan (Variables *app* and the data chunk d are obtained from that transition). Transitions $i11$, $i12$ and $i13$ of the node are involved in its initialization. Transition $i11$ creates an instance of the underlying serverless node components (*faasnode* net). The computational resources of the node are initialized in Transition $i12$. The model could be parameterized from a configuration file, but to enhance the readability purpose, we made the textual configuration visible within the model: We can see that 7 Raspberry Pi 2 devices with 1000 MB and 1000 MIPS are available for the node. Transition $i13$ initializes the functions that a particular user wants to place at that node. In this example, user id 1 places two functions $f1$ and $f2$ with the following parameters (from left to right): the first 4 numbers in the tuple represent the function execution time, the function warm invocation time, the function cold start time, and the time that the function will be idle in memory. The next number is the cost per millisecond of invoking the function (aligning with costs identified in Table 1), the last two numbers represent the computational requirements, expressed in MIPS and the size of memory required, respectively.

The three main internal components of a node are depicted in Fig. 3: user application (the composition of functions to be applied to a data chunk), the user functions available at the node that are managed by the function manager component (Variable fm in the model), and the machine on which the functions will be executed. As stated previously, when the pair: data chunk and its processing plan arrive at a node, Transition $t1$ of Fig. 2 is fired. During the firing, by means of the synchronous channel *begin*, Transition $t1$ of Fig. 2 synchronizes with Transition $t21$ of Fig. 3, and the token data chunk-plan is moved inside the node for processing. Once all the required functions are invoked, Transition $t22$ of Fig. 3 will be synchronized with Transition $t2$ of Fig. 2, taking the data chunk and its processing plan out of the node. The invocations of functions are accomplished by means of Transitions $t23$, which represents the start of an invocation, and $t24$ which represents the end of an invocation in Fig. 3. In these two transitions, using synchronous channels, a composition plan (*app* in the model) is paired with the function manager component (*fm* in the model). As these two transitions can be fired concurrently, a processing plan can invoke functions concurrently in the model.

---

[1] https://opcfoundation.org/about/opc-technologies/opc-ua/.

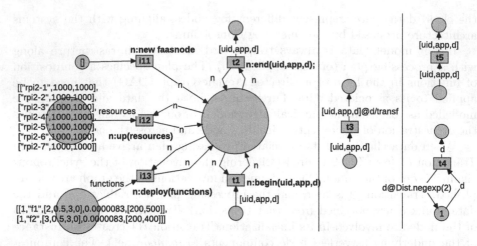

Fig. 2. Node infrastructure net patterns: (left) FaaS-based edge/cloud node, (center) data transfer representation, and (right) data source modelling.

A function needs to meet some conditions to be invoked: (i) it needs to find a computational resource with enough memory and CPU capacity, (ii) the function needs to be loaded in memory. Transition $t26$ binds a computational resource to a function, a computational resource that matches the function memory and CPU requirements. It should be noticed that these constrains are enforced by the inscription: $guardmips >= mipsrq \& mem >= memrq$. This inscription will only enable Transition $t26$ when there is a machine whose MIPS and memory are enough to host the function. Transition $t27$ frees the computational resources, it means that the function was removed from memory and placed back on disk.

From Fig. 3, transition $t27$ enables users to deploy functions, transitions $t28$ and $t29$ enable allocation and deallocation of computational resources respectively. Computational resources are represented by a tuple comprising: (i) resource identifier, (ii) resource CPU performance (in MIPS) and (iii) the memory size.

The dynamic behaviour is achieved through the function manager component, which is inside the node (Fig. 3). While multiple data chunks and their processing plans can exist simultaneously inside the node model in Fig. 3, there is only one instance of the function manager component. This component controls the life cycle of functions and manages their invocations. It consists of two concurrent processes, the function as a service life cycle process (specified in Fig. 4) and the function invocation process (in Fig. 5). A function is deployed in the model at Transition $t41$ in Fig. 4. This transition synchronizes with Transition $t25$ in Fig. 3 and with Transition $i13$ in Fig. 2 simultaneously, by chaining different synchronous channels that enable the functions to arrive from the model in Fig. 2 to Fig. 4. The deployed functions will eventually arrive at the place "Compiled & Idle in Disk" in Fig. 4, waiting for an invocation. Once an invocation occurs, a function instance is loaded in memory (Transition $t43$ fires), this is

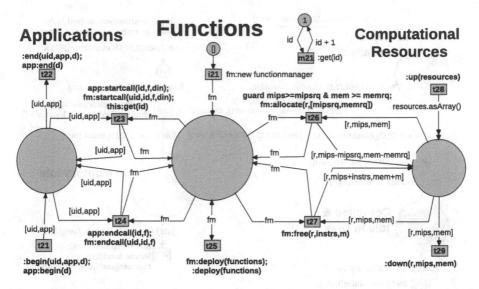

Fig. 3. Node modelling: a node consists of applications, functions and computational resources.

called a cold start invocation. At that point, a function in memory is ready to be called, the actual invocation happens when Transition $t45$ is fired, and the invocation finishes when Transition $t46$ is fired. In the model, after the call, the function remains in memory idle for some period of time (function parameter $t3$), ready to be invoked again. In such a case, the invocation is called warm function invocation, and it involves firing Transition $t44$. If the period of time elapses without an invocation Transition $t47$ will be fired.

Cold and warm function invocations can have significant impact on function performance, and cold invocations typically have a higher time than warm invocations. This is reflected in the model by the time inscriptions on the arcs – the output arc of Transition $t43$ (cold invocation) has the time inscription $[uid, f, [tex, t1, t2, t3], ecost, hwrq]@t2$, while the output arc of Transition $t44$ (warm invocation) has $[uid, f, [tex, t1, t2, t3], ecost, hwrq]@t1$. In both cases, a token will be available after $t2$ and $t1$ units of time after the firing. The model allows cold and warm times for each function to be parameterized. Similarly, the actual function execution is modelled by the output arc of Transition $t45$, $[uid, f, [tex, t1, t2, t3], ecost, hwrq]@tex$, which indicates that after the invocation, the token will be available after tex units of time. While all these time inscriptions are on output arcs, the model also uses time inscriptions at input arcs. Once a function is idle in memory, it will remain for a period of $t3$ units of time. If no invocation occurs, the function will be removed from memory and the computational resources freed. This is modelled by the input arc of Transition $t47$: $[uid, f, [tex, t1, t2, t3], ecost, hwrq]@t3$. The effect of the time inscription at the input arc is that once a function instance is idle in memory, Transition $t47$ will be only enabled after $t3$ units of time.

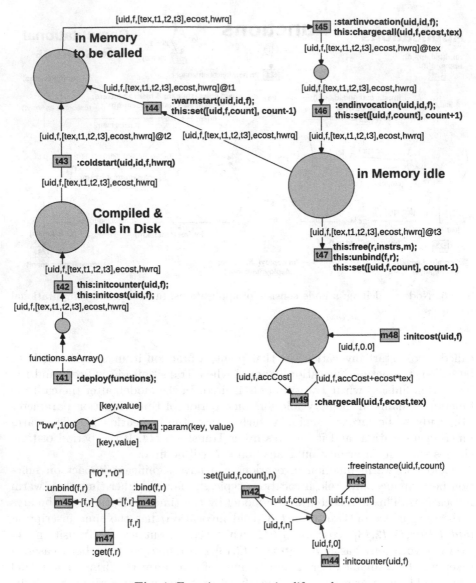

Fig. 4. Function as a service life cycle.

Another important aspect of the model in Fig. 4 is the consideration of the economic cost. Serverless infrastructures typically charge users on a per millisecond basis. This is reflected in the model in Transition $t45$ that, once fired, invokes Synchronous Channel $this: chargecall(uid, f, ecost, tex)$. The callee channel is in Transition $m49$, which retrieves the accumulated cost for function f of user uid ($[uid, f, accCost]$) and adds the incurred cost for the actual invocation $[uid, f, accCost + ecost * tex]$, where $ecost$ is the cost associated with function

f, and it is a parameter of the function in the model. This pricing model is based on computing time on per millisecond basis, which one of the models described on Sect. 2. Other models can be implemented by updating that cost formula.

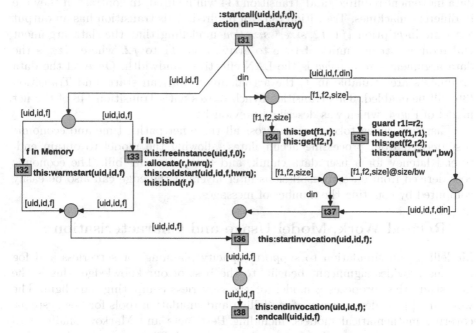

Fig. 5. Function invocation and data movement.

When a function invocation occurs in the model of Fig. 3, Transition $t23$ is fired. It involves invoking the synchronous channel *startcall* of the function composition, and the synchronous channel "startcall" of the function manager component. In Fig. 5, it corresponds to Transition $t31$, where the invocation process starts. At this point, the model considers two *concurrent* activities: the function invocation, and the transmission of the arguments of the function through the local area network links of the node. It is important to highlight that the time elapsed in both activities will overlap.

The function invocation involves Transitions $t32$ and $t33$. Transition $t32$ will only be enabled if there is any function instance f idle in memory in the net of Fig. 4 (warm invocation). Otherwise, Transition $t33$ will be enabled (cold invocation). In case of a cold invocation, computational resources need to be allocated. Transition $t33$ will allocate the required computational resources by means of synchronous channel: $allocate(r, hwrq)$. It will synchronize with Transition $t26$ of Fig. 3, which was described previously.

The data movement activity may only have an impact on the function performance time if the transmission time is significant, considering the argument size and the LAN bandwidth. There is no need to move data if the functions are hosted in the same machine. From the user function composition, the model obtains the data dependencies for function f. All these dependencies are placed at the input place of Transitions $t34/t35$. If the origin function $(f1)$ and the destination function $(f2)$ are hosted on the same machine (r), then there is no data movement required, and Transition $t34$ will be fired. In contrast, if they are in different machines, Transition $t35$ will be fired. This transition has an output arc time inscription $[f1, f2, size]@size/bw$ modelling that the data argument will require $size/bw$ units of time to arrive from $f1$ to $f2$, where $size$ is the data argument size and bw is the LAN effective bandwidth. Once all the data arguments are available in f, the actual invocation can start, and Transition $t38$ will be enabled. This transition synchronizes with Transition $t48$ of the net model of Fig. 4, which was described previously.

Therefore, when tokens move across all these net paths, time and economic cost derived from processing accumulates, allowing the model to obtain end-to-end latency for a user data chunk, and the processing bill. The economic cost derived from data transmissions inter layers of the edge can also be easily computed by counting the number of messages.

4   Related Work, Model Usage and Characterisation

Modelling and simulation to support capacity planning for serverless and fog systems provides significant benefit, to the best of our knowledge, this is the first study that proposes a model for the serverless computing paradigm. The work in [8] provides a survey of modelling and simulation tools for Fog systems, covering mathematical models, including Petri nets and Markov Chains, and various cost parameters that need to be considered. The survey concludes that only a few simulation tools take account of cost metrics, and that this aspect is still in its infancy.

Performance and cost modeling of cloud computing has been extensively covered, but only recently the modelling of Serverless Function has received attention. In [9], limited user control over resources on FaaS platforms on the cloud is emphasised, and a formal model of serverless workflows to estimate performance and cost is proposed. However, Fog computing nodes have limited resources, which can introduce an added complexity in the modelling of serverless function behaviors that now must consider the heterogeneity of cloud and edge/fog nodes – with varying resource capacity. The need to represent the dependency of serverless applications on data storage and other resources on the cloud is identified in [10]. In this paper, authors present a dependency graph for serverless applications that helps to optimize an existing system by identifying hot spots, supports the generation of test cases and can be used to monitor an existing system. The problem of scheduling operators between the Cloud and the Fog is also the focus of several research efforts – these consider both computational and network resource usage costs [6,11], and propose analytical models and operator placement strategies to reduce end-to-end latency, data transfer times and messaging costs between edge and cloud systems.

The Reference/Petri net models presented in Sect. 3 enables us to support capacity and cost planning for deployment of serverless functions. By varying costs and times associated with execution of functions, and the types of resources on which these functions are hosted, it is possible for a user to plan their application design and deployment. The models we propose go beyond existing cost calculators provided by cloud providers, as we are able to derive a finer grained analysis taking account of actual deployment and use – achieved by combining the modelling and simulation capability made possible by the use of a Petri net model.

5   Evaluation

In addition to the formal semantics provided by Petri nets, another advantage of using Reference nets is that they can be interpreted by the Renew tool[2]. In order to show how the model can be exploited, we provide an example of usage here in this section. From two synthetic applications, we conducted different simulations to analyse the impact of cold and warm function invocations on its performance and the amount of computational resources required. We made use of simple Reference nets, and the time inscriptions where simulated with action delays[3]. For the physical infrastructure, we modeled two nodes: an edge node with up to 5 Raspberry Pi 2 devices, connected to a Cloud data center, with multiple Intel Xeon servers. The edge node is connected to two data sources that generate data continuously at constant rates (every 5 s to 6.75 s), having each data chunk a size of 1 MB and remaining constant through the simulation.

We designed two synthetic streaming applications: f and g. Application f is a sequential composition of 5 functions (f_1 to f_3, at the edge and f_4 to f_5 at the cloud) and it consumes data generated from a data source. The other source of data is processed by application g, which consists of 3 functions (g_1, g_2 at the edge and g_3 at the cloud). Table 3 summarizes the characterization and requirements of the functions: the average execution time, the average memory size requirements and the average amount of instructions that require its execution. We simulated 4 different scenarios with different combinations of warm/cold function invocation times, and keep alive periods, as well as the number of computational resources allocated to each application, as specified in Table 2.

Figure 6 depicts a graphical representation of the main idea of our simulations, a chronograph corresponding to the edge of two possible scenarios of applications f ($f_1 \rightarrow f_2 \rightarrow f_3$) and g ($g_1 \rightarrow g_2$): (a) on top, without keep alive periods of time for functions, whenever a function finishes, the involved computational resources are released. Therefore, as the two applications are sequential compositions, each application only requires one computational resource at a time. In contrast, the case (b) reflects that when introducing keep alive periods of functions, as functions are kept in memory, the number of computational resources required increases significantly (five at this early stage of execution of

---

[2] http://renew.de/.

[3] The models in Reference nets and the simulation environment are made available through a Docker container with the aim of enhancing the reproducibility of experiments: https://github.com/rtolosana/fog-modelling.

applications f and g). Choosing between one or another option, or intermediate alternatives will depend on the actual cold/warm function invocation times, on the QoS to be enforced and on the computational capacity available, which might be scarce at the edge.

Table 2. Simulation parameters (in secs)

Case	Warm invocation	Cold invocation	Keep alive
1	0.01	10	10
2	0.01	0.05	10
3	0.01	10	0
4	0.01	0.05	0

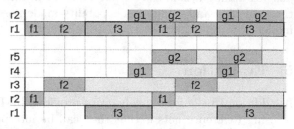

Fig. 6. Chronograph: (a) without keep-alive (top) (b) with keep alive (down)

The results of the simulations can be seen in Fig. 7. Although the simulations involve the execution of compositions f and g, for clarity purposes and space, Fig. 7 only depicts the performance of composition f. On the x-axis, the timeline, and on the y-axis, the end-to-end latency both in seconds. The end-to-end latency includes processing times, waiting times, overheads, and data transmissions. When the cold function invocation time is higher than the execution time (cases 1 and 3), it has a significant impact on performance time, unless the function is kept alive in memory (case 3). Therefore, in case 3, the impact of high cold invocations on performance only appears the first time the functions are invoked. However, this is at the expense of consuming more computational resources. As our models do not consider invocation overheads for the economic cost, and they only include the actual invocation time, the 4 scenarios show the same cost. For composition f for all the simulation time, the economic cost is 0.24 USD, as each function pricing tariff costs 0.0000083 USD per msec.

Table 3. Function characterization

F	Tex (secs)	Mem (MB)	MIPS
f1	0.2	600	600
f2	0.4	600	700
f3	0.6	600	800
f4	0.04	600	600
f5	0.04	600	600
g1	0.2	200	700
g2	0.4	300	500
g3	0.05	600	600

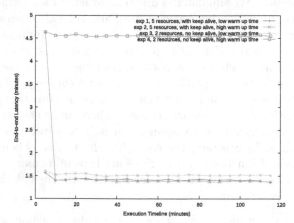

Fig. 7. End-to-end latency for f over time.

6 Conclusions

We develop a dynamic Petri net model of a serverless function, demonstrating how a combination of these functions can be hosted across edge and cloud data centre-based resources. With the significant flexibility that a serverless model offers to users, in both costs of use and deployment, many see a transition to serverless as a natural progression from VM and container based invocations. The model proposed in this work includes a number of parameters that can be characterised from a practical deployment, and can be used for designing an application across different types of resources. Our proposed approach can be used to undertake a number of *what-if* scenarios to explore various configuration options available to a developer, ranging from: computational complexity of hosting nodes (characterised as MIPS and memory), cold and warm start times associated with initiating a function, data size associated function execution, time to move function executable to/from disk and computational requirements (also modelled as MIPS and memory) of the function itself. This approach can also be used to undertake comparison of executing the same function across different cloud vendors – who may offer different pricing/power tradeoffs for function developers.

References

1. Lefevre, X.: Is serverless cheaper for your use case? Find out with this calculator. https://medium.com/serverless-transformation/is-serverless-cheaper-for-your-use-case-find-out-with-this-calculator-2f8a52fc6a68. Accessed June 2021
2. Microsoft: Azure Function Pricing. https://azure.microsoft.com/en-gb/pricing/details/functions/. Accessed June 2021
3. Amazon: AWS Lambda Pricing. https://aws.amazon.com/lambda/pricing/. Accessed June 2021
4. Google: Google Function Pricing. https://cloud.google.com/functions/pricing. Accessed June 2021
5. González, L.M.V., Rodero-Merino, L.: Finding your way in the fog: towards a comprehensive definition of fog computing. Comput. Commun. Rev. **44**(5), 27–32 (2014)
6. Renart, E.G., Da Silva Veith, A., Balouek-Thomert, D., De Assuncao, M.D., Lefevre, L., Parashar, M.: Distributed operator placement for IoT data analytics across edge and cloud resources. In: 2019 19th IEEE/ACM International Symposium on Cluster, Cloud and Grid Computing (CCGRID), pp. 459–468 (2019)
7. Peña, M.A.L., Fernández, I.M.: SAT-IoT: an architectural model for a high-performance fog/edge/cloud IoT platform. In: 5th IEEE World Forum on Internet of Things, WF-IoT 2019, Limerick, Ireland, 15–18 April 2019, pp. 633–638. IEEE (2019)
8. Margariti, S.V., Dimakopoulos, V.V., Tsoumanis, G.: Modeling and simulation tools for fog computing a comprehensive survey from a cost perspective. Future Internet **12**(5), 89 (2020)
9. Lin, C., Khazaei, H.: Modeling and optimization of performance and cost of serverless applications. IEEE Trans. Parallel Distrib. Syst. **32**(3), 615–632 (2021)

10. Winzinger, S., Wirtz, G.: Model-based analysis of serverless applications. In: 2019 IEEE/ACM 11th International Workshop on Modelling in Software Engineering (MiSE), pp. 82–88 (2019)
11. Ntumba, P., Georgantas, N., Christophides, V.: Scheduling continuous operators for IoT edge analytics. In: Proceedings of the 4th International Workshop on Edge Systems, Analytics and Networking, pp. 55–60. Association for Computing Machinery (2021)
12. Murata, T.: Petri nets: properties, analysis and applications. Proc. IEEE **77**(4), 541–580 (1989)
13. Tolosana-Calasanz, R., Bañares, J.Á., Pham, C., Rana, O.F.: Enforcing QoS in scientific workflow systems enacted over cloud infrastructures. J. Comput. Syst. Sci. **78**(3), 1300–1315 (2012)

Knowledge Management Framework for Cloud Federation

Wahiba Mellaoui[(✉)], Richard Posso, Yodit Gebrealif, Erik Bock, Jörn Altmann[(✉)], and Hyenyoung Yoon

Technology Management, Economics and Policy Program, College of Engineering, Seoul National University, Seoul, South Korea
jorn.altmann@acm.org, hyyoon00@snu.ac.kr

Abstract. A cloud federation (CF) is an alliance of cloud service providers (CSPs) working together to overcome scalability and portability barriers. However, there are some business challenges (e.g., lack of trust, lack of schemes for revenue sharing, and lack of schemes for resource sharing) and technological challenges (e.g., missing schemes for resource provisioning, lack of coordinated resource management, and little load balancing), causing instability in CFs. As CF alliances pursue strategic goals, they require intensive knowledge sharing. In fact, practitioners have confirmed a positive impact of knowledge management on stability and success of strategic alliances (SA). According to the literature, SAs may also face learning issues such as non–controlled information revelation or unbalanced dissemination of core competencies. These findings pose challenges about the nature of the knowledge and how to share it within a CF. Nonetheless, there is only scarce literature on KM in CF. Thus, the purpose of the paper is to propose a KM framework for CFs with the aim of strengthening stability and potential CF commercialization.

Keywords: Cloud federation · Knowledge management · Strategic alliance

1 Introduction

In cloud federations (CFs), various cloud service providers (CSPs) are collaborating, when it comes to delivering services. However, there are issues and challenges that hamper the commercialization of CFs; lack of trust between CSPs is considered one of the reasons hindering CFs [1]. Although trust among CSPs is the basic element for commercializing CFs, trust-building technologies have not been seen in market yet [2]. Trust between CSPs could be created in several ways. One solution is providing an accountable and measurable platform, in order to share CSPs information and knowledge among the CSPs in a CF [3].

Scholars have not explored the relation between knowledge management (KM) and CF sufficiently. Only few articles discussed about KM relation with CF such as [4, 5]. This led to the exploration of the relation between KM and SA instead of KM and CF. From the research on this relation, evidence was gained of a strong relation between KM

© The Author(s) 2021
K. Tserpes et al. (Eds.): GECON 2021, LNCS 13072, pp. 123–132, 2021.
https://doi.org/10.1007/978-3-030-92916-9_10

and stability of a SA [6–8]. Based on this newly discovered information, a search was started for a model that explains the relation between KM and SA stability with trust as the main enabler of knowledge sharing. The search resulted in the adoption of the model of inter-organizational system collaboration [9]. Furthermore, it was enhanced by detailing the KM components.

The goal of this paper is to provide insight into how KM helps CFs come closer to being commercialized [14]. Thus, the following research questions were elaborated:

- What are the requirements of applying KM to CF?
- How should a framework on KM for CF be defined?
- What is the impact of KM on the stability of CF as a SA?

To answer the research questions, a literature review was conducted with the goal to understand what is behind CFs' challenges and the motivations to become part of a CF. The results showed that a lack of trust is one of the main reasons why CFs are not commercialized, whereas the motivation could be explained with the resource dependent theory and the resource-based view. Besides, we consider that KM could influence CFs according to the knowledge-based theory. The contribution of this paper is a proposal for a KM Framework for CFs, in order to strengthen stability of the underlying SA by improving trust among the CSPs. Section 2 gives the background on CFs and its challenges that prevent it from being commercialized. Section 3 explains how a CF can be viewed as a SA, and how this can explain instability of CFs. Based on this, the requirements for applying the concept of KM to CF as a SA are defined. Section 4 contains the proposed framework for KM in CFs. In Sect. 5, the article is wrapped up with a discussion and ideas on how to evaluate the model in the future. Lastly, Sect. 6 presents the conclusion.

2 Background

CF is a group of CSPs working together to overcome scalability problems, which are of concern in the cloud computing area [10]. Basically, CSPs collaborate to form a single large CF without merging or changing the individual CSPs functionalities and strategies. The difference is that, whereas a standalone CSP might have trouble meeting users' needs, a CSP in a CF can use available resources of its partners, to meet its customers' demands [11]. Another benefit from CFs is that it allows for smaller CSPs to compete with larger ones [12]. CSPs such as Amazon and Microsoft already control over 50% of the cloud computing market [13]. Nevertheless, despite the benefits CF brings, it has been difficult to commercialize CFs [14], particularly because of the following issues and challenges. Resource Provisioning: A CF requires to integrate various CSPs with heterogeneous infrastructures. Dynamic service delivery also raises an issue on the efficient resource provisioning techniques for a CF [15]. Resource Management: Reliable and flexible management of SLA in CF is needed, to deliver efficient and flexible services [11]. Security: There is a need for solid user identity management [16], security protocols, authentication, and authorization [16]. Data Management: CFs have to provide data transfer protocols between CSPs and must guarantee long-term storing and interoperable sharing among CSPs [17]. Trust and Confidence: boosting trust and confidence between CSPs are important towards the implementation [1, 17] and commercialization of CF [10].

3 Requirements for Knowledge Management in Cloud Federations

This section describes three requirements for applying the proposed KM framework to CFs: (1) identifying and defining common strategic objectives among CSPs, (2) identifying the nature of knowledge to be shared, and (3) protecting the knowledge to be shared.

3.1 Cloud Federation as a Strategic Alliance

Prior research supports the idea of representing a CF as a SA [18]. A CF is a projection of SA, specifically, a joint venture between CSPs. The latter is similar to CF establishments, because both embed signed agreements to join and work in alliance.

Table 1. Mapping motives for CF creation and alliance formation (based on [19]).

Underlying theory	Specific motive	Seminal authors
Resource Dependency Theory	Lack of Self-sufficiency Leads to Dependence, Vertical Links	Pfeffer and Salancik (1978), Pfeffer and Novak (1976), Glaister and Buckley (1996)
Resource Based View (RBV)	Resource Exchange-Access to Complementary/Supplementary Resources	Dan and Teng (2000a), Tsang (1998)
Knowledge-Based Theory	Inter-organizational Learning	Larsson et al. (1998), Hamed (1991), Gils and Zwart (2004)

Moreover, SAs are motivated by some theories such as: comprising resource dependence theory [20], transaction cost economics [21], resource-based view [22], institutional theory [23], and network theory [24]. The motivation to establish a CF can be projected on those cited theories. However, according to the basic definition of CF, it is first linked to the resource dependence theory, followed by the resource-based view (Table 1). It is also proposed to extend existing motivations for a CF creation by utilizing knowledge-based theory.

3.2 Strategic Alliance Instability in the Context of Cloud Federations

Despite the growing trend of SA formations, the rate of failure is high [22]. Resource dependence theory [20] explains one of the motivations for SA formations. Ultimately, the target of this kind of alliance is to control the resource dependence as well as the risk. After firms satisfy their needs, and succeed in acquiring the requested resources, the alliance motivation dies, and the inter-firm relationship may end [22]. In the case of CFs, the residual mutual resource needs of CSPs may play in favor of the stability of the CF and create a certain immunity against such turbulences.

Soft facts, such as trust, could be crucial to the stability of the SA. Moreover, hard facts, such as strategic compatibility and appropriate governance mechanisms, may strengthen the SA and could have a tangible positive influence on alliance stability [25]. Thus, the lack of trust and the lack strategic compatibility may lead to instability of the SA. In addition to that, at the SA level, Bhattacharya et al. [26] defined four trust-inducing ways: (1) alignment of interests and strategic goals, (2) value alteration, (3) selectivity in transactions, and (4) research and knowledge revelation. Furthermore, theory often emphasizes the importance of sharing knowledge, when it comes to building trust [27]. These findings drive the focus on the relation between knowledge sharing among CSPs and the identification of the common strategic objectives, which are considered the first requirement for constructing our KM framework, aiming at raising the stability of CFs.

3.3 Strategic Alliances and Knowledge Management in the Context of Cloud Federations

Previous literature has also examined the impact of KM on stability and success of SAs [6–8]. Moreover, as CF leverages SAs [5], the relationship between KM, SA, and CFs can be depicted as shown in Fig. 1. In addition to this, both academics and practitioners work on understanding how to develop alliance capabilities, in order to raise the rate of alliance success [6]. In particular, the manner, in which the inter-organizational learning process is managed, has an important role into determining success or failure of the SAs [7].

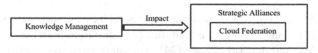

Fig. 1. Impact of knowledge management on the success of CFs as a SAs.

A project named Basmati was designed to strengthen the support of applications and services that run in a CF environment. It improves the service quality perceived by end users [5, 28]. Within this project, knowledge sharing between components has been considered but is limited to resource information. If there were more diversified knowledge sharing between CSPs than only sharing resource information's, the CF may gain further stability and trust among CSPs.

The knowledge theory [27–29] is considered one of the most important theories that motivates the formation of SAs [19]. In addition, many empirical studies gave evidence that KM (i.e., codifying, sharing, articulating, and internalizing) has a positive relation with the overall stability and success of SAs [6]. SAs face some learning issues, such as non–controlled information revelation, or unbalanced dissemination of core competences between the SA actors [29, 30]. These issues push to think about the nature of the knowledge to be shared within the CF. Buckley et al. (2009) argued that combining specific knowledge benefits firms when implementing common goals, which cannot be implemented individually [31]. Figure 2 describes this process in a CF environment, in which CSPs identify a common goal C, identify the knowledge to share while keeping individual goals A and B separate. Developing the capability of knowing the nature of the knowledge to be shared within the CF represents the **second requirement** to build the KM framework for CFs.

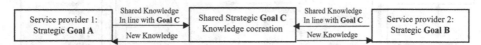

Fig. 2. Relation between the nature of the shared knowledge and the strategic objectives within CFs (adapted from [31]).

3.4 Strategic Alliances and Knowledge Protection in the Context of Cloud Federations

Most studies claim to share and protect knowledge, yet, at the same time, reveal certain incompatibilities of knowledge sharing and protecting [32]. However, few studies argue that sharing and protecting knowledge is crucial to the overall success of SAs [33]. Guo et al. [34] demonstrate the existence of a complementarity between applying knowledge sharing and knowledge protection simultaneously, in addition to the positive effect of this ambidexterity on SAs [34]. Therefore, the protection of knowledge to be shared among CSPs has a positive impact on the stability of CFs. Based on this finding, the third requirement is the protection of the knowledge to be shared.

4 Knowledge Management Framework

Based on the requirements and the literature review aforementioned, various KM frameworks were examined. Among them, the Inter-Organizational System (IOS) addresses trust and KM relationships, as well as their impact on stability of alliances [9]. Thus, the proposed KM model for CFs is an extension of the IOS collaboration model, with respect to following requirements: (1) identifying the common strategic objectives among CSPs, (2) identifying the nature of the knowledge to be shared, in line with the defined common strategic objectives, and (3) selecting the methods of knowledge protection based on its nature and existing commitment between a CF and the participating CSPs.

The proposed framework aims to raise trust and commitment among the participants, and it also encourages knowledge sharing among CSPs to strengthen the SA [9, 34, 35]. The adopted and extended model (Fig. 3) presents the relation between KM, trust, and commitment within an IT and communication infrastructure. This choice helps building on existing software modules used by CFs, dedicated exclusively to managing the information related to resource management (prediction, planning, and allocation). As argued by [9], the relation between KM and trust-commitment is bidirectional. Therefore, it can be stated that the more CSPs trust each other, the more they share knowledge and cooperate, and that the more CSPs share knowledge, the more they create added value and trust each other.

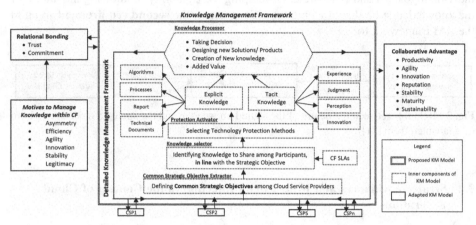

Fig. 3. Knowledge management framework for CF (adapted from [9] [31]).

In the proposed framework (Fig. 3), the starting point is to identify CSPs common strategic objectives, through the **"Common Strategic Objectives Extractor"**. It also represents the foundation of a relation built on trust, transparency, and guarantees that all the members pursue the same goals. Some common objectives may change by the dynamic environment, or by individual CSPs' goals. Then, the **"Knowledge Selector"** component enables CSPs to identify the nature of the knowledge to be shared, in line with common strategic goals and service level agreements between federation members. In the next stage, the **"Protection Activator"** enables CSPs to select an appropriate protection mechanism depending on the nature of the knowledge. This knowledge could be tacit (i.e., knowledge based on experience, perception, judgement) or explicit (i.e., knowledge based on data, algorithms, technical documents). Once the knowledge to be shared is identified, and its protection method has been defined, the knowledge is shared, and directed to the fourth component, **"Knowledge Processor"**. Within this component, new knowledge is created, and new solutions or products are designed. The output induces to several collaborative advantages, namely agility, productivity, reputation, and, most importantly, the stability of the CF. The final knowledge output goes back to the CSPs and CF, while also raising commitment and trust among the CSPs.

5   Discussion and Future Work

The paper proposes a KM framework for CFs to increase stability and potential CF commercialization. For the methodology, a literature review was conducted to understand CFs' challenges and motivations. The results showed that a lack of trust is one of the main reasons why CFs are not commercialized whereas the motivations were the resource dependent theory and the resource-based view. Besides, it is argued that KM influences CFs based on the knowledge-based theory.

To clarify the whole process of KM framework, consider a couple of CSPs collaborating in a CF. Although every CSP faces a myriad of cyber-attacks, the security mechanism of each CSP varies from each other due to the difference in their security infrastructure [36, 37]. This kind information, like security mechanism or attack patterns, is too sensitive to share with any third party [38]. However, within a CF, there is trust, which makes the sharing of such information possible. By using the proposed KM framework, each CSP shares their cyber threat information with each other, allowing them to develop a strong security method. This can be granted as a common strategic objective. By sharing their explicit knowledge (e.g., necessary cyber threat information and protection technology) and tacit knowledge (e.g., expertise and skill) a new stronger security technique can emerge and be used by all CF members.

The framework limitation is the evaluation stage. Thus, it opens a window to research about evaluation and test methods. The empirical evidence through tests can be split in two categories: 1) Analysis of existing case studies of KM in SAs and comparing the KM dynamics with the present proposal. Similarities and differences with respect to success or failure of the selected SA will bring further insight towards the validity of the proposed framework; 2) Perform surveys or interviews with experts in the CF field.

6   Conclusion

This article addressed the trust between cloud service providers (CSPs) in cloud federations (CFs), for its importance in keeping CSPs in CFs. It also analyzed the impact of knowledge management (KM) on CF stability from a strategic alliance (SA) perspective. Based on an extensive SA literature review, a KM framework was proposed and discussed.

Acknowledgment. This research was supported by the BK21 FOUR (Fostering Outstanding Universities for Research) funded by the Ministry of Education (MOE, Korea) and National Research Foundation of Korea (NRF). This work was also supported by the National Research Foundation of Korea (NRF) grant (No. NRF-2019R1F1A1058487) funded by the Ministry of Science and ICT (MSIT) of Korea.

References

1. Kanwal, A., Masood, R., Shibli, M.A.: Evaluation and establishment of trust in cloud federation (2014). https://doi.org/10.1145/2557977.2558023
2. Jones, S., Irani, Z., Sivarajah, U., Love, P.E.D.: Risks and rewards of cloud computing in the UK public sector: a reflection on three organisational case studies. Inf. Syst. Front. **21**(2), 359–382 (2017). https://doi.org/10.1007/s10796-017-9756-0
3. Romero Coronado, J.P., Altmann, J.: Model for incentivizing cloud service federation. In: Pham, C., Altmann, J., Bañares, J.Á. (eds.) GECON 2017. LNCS, vol. 10537, pp. 233–246. Springer, Cham (2017). https://doi.org/10.1007/978-3-319-68066-8_18
4. Nguyen, P.D., Thoai, N.: DrbCF: a differentiated ratio-based approach to job scheduling in cloud federation. In: Proceedings - 2016 10th International Conference Complex, Intelligent, Software Intensive Syststem. CISIS 2016, pp. 31–37 (2016). https://doi.org/10.1109/CISIS.2016.93
5. Altmann, J., et al.: BASMATI: an architecture for managing cloud and edge resources for mobile users. In: Pham, C., Altmann, J., Bañares, J.Á. (eds.) GECON 2017. LNCS, vol. 10537, pp. 56–66. Springer, Cham (2017). https://doi.org/10.1007/978-3-319-68066-8_5
6. Kale, P., Singh, H.: Building firm capabilities through learning: the role of the alliance learning process in alliance capability and firm-level alliance success. Strateg. Manag. J. **28**(10), 981–1000 (2007). https://doi.org/10.1002/smj.616
7. Larsson, R., Bengtsson, L., Henriksson, K., Sparks, J.: The interorganizational learning dilemma: collective knowledge development in strategic alliances. Organ. Sci. **9**(3), 285–305 (1998). https://doi.org/10.1287/orsc.9.3.285
8. Meier, M.: Knowledge management in strategic alliances: a review of empirical evidence. Int. J. Manag. Rev. **13**(1), 1–23 (2011). https://doi.org/10.1111/j.1468-2370.2010.00287.x
9. Chi, L., Holsapple, C.W.: Understanding computer-mediated interorganizational collaboration: a model and framework. J. Knowl. Manag. **9**(1), 53–75 (2005). https://doi.org/10.1108/13673270510582965
10. Aryal, R.G., Altmann, J.: Dynamic application deployment in federations of clouds and edge resources using a multiobjective optimization AI algorithm. In: 2018 3rd International Configuration Fog Mobile Edge Computing. FMEC 2018, pp. 147–154 (2018). https://doi.org/10.1109/FMEC.2018.8364057
11. Aryal, R.G., Altmann, J.: Fairness in revenue sharing for stable cloud federations. In: Pham, C., Altmann, J., Bañares, J.Á. (eds.) GECON 2017. LNCS, vol. 10537, pp. 219–232. Springer, Cham (2017). https://doi.org/10.1007/978-3-319-68066-8_17
12. Aryal, R.G., Marshall, J., Altmann, J.: Architecture and business logic specification for dynamic cloud federations. In: Djemame, K., Altmann, J., Bañares, J.Á., Agmon Ben-Yehuda, O., Naldi, M. (eds.) GECON 2019. LNCS, vol. 11819, pp. 83–96. Springer, Cham (2019). https://doi.org/10.1007/978-3-030-36027-6_8
13. Stalcup, K.: AWS vs Azure vs Google Cloud Market Share 2021: What the Latest Data Shows – ParkMyCloud. ParkMyCloud (2021). https://www.parkmycloud.com/blog/aws-vs-azure-vs-google-cloud-market-share/. Accessed 19 June 2021
14. L. Code: Economic Models for Incentivizing the Federations of IaaS Cloud Providers (2021)
15. Rajarajeswari, C.S.: Challenges in Federated Cloud, vol. 4, pp. 2394–2697 (2017)
16. Villari, M., Brandic, I., Tusa, F.: Achieving federated and self-manageable cloud infrastructures: Theory and practice. IGI Global (2012)
17. Ahmed, U., Raza, I., Hussain, S.A.: Trust evaluation in cross-cloud federation: survey and requirement analysis. ACM Comput. Surv. **52**(1), 1–37 (2019). https://doi.org/10.1145/3292499

18. Haile, N., Korea, S.: College of Engineering Technology Management , Economics , and Policy Discussion Paper Series Risk-Benefit-Mediated Impact of Determinants on the Adoption of Cloud Federation, January 2015

19. Dhaundiyal, M., Coughlan, J.: Understanding strategic alliance life cycle: a 30 year literature review of leading management journals. Bus. Theory Pract. **21**(2), 519–530 (2020). https://doi.org/10.3846/btp.2020.11530

20. Reitz, H.J., Pfeffer, J., Salancik, G.R.: The external control of organizations: a resource dependence perspective (New York: Harper & Row, 1978). Acad. Manag. Rev. **4**(2), 309–310 (1979)

21. Kogut, B.: Joint ventures: theoretical and empirical perspectives. Strateg. Manag. J. **9**(4), 319–332 (1988). https://doi.org/10.1002/smj.4250090403

22. Das, T.K., Teng, B.S.: Instabilities of strategic alliances: an internal tensions perspective. Organ. Sci. **11**(1), 77–101 (2000). https://doi.org/10.1287/orsc.11.1.77.12570

23. Tina Dacin, M., Oliver, C., Roy, J.P.: The legitimacy of strategic alliances: an institutional perspective. Strateg. Manag. J. **28**(2), 169–187 (2007). https://doi.org/10.1002/smj.577

24. Gulati, R.: Alliances and networks. Strateg. Manag. J. **19**(4), 293–317 (1998). https://doi.org/10.1002/(SICI)1097-0266(199804)19:4%3c293::AID-SMJ982%3e3.0.CO;2-M

25. Hoffmann, W.H., Schlosser, R.: Success factors of strategic alliances in small and medium -sized enterprises - An empirical survey. Long Range Plan. **34**(3), 357–381 (2001). https://doi.org/10.1016/S0024-6301(01)00041-3

26. Bhattacharya, R., Devinney, T.M., Pillutla, M.M.: A formal model of trust based on outcomes. Acad. Manag. Rev. **23**(3), 459 (1998). https://doi.org/10.2307/259289

27. Das, T.K., Teng, B.S.: Trust, control, and risk in strategic alliances: an integrated framework. Organ. Stud. **22**(2), 251–283 (2001). https://doi.org/10.1177/0170840601222004

28. Kim, S.: HORIZON2020 FRAMEWORK PROGRAMME TOPIC EUK-03-2016 Federated Cloud resource brokerage for mobile cloud services (2016)

29. Hamel, G.: Competition for competence and inter- partner learning within international. Strateg. Manag. J. **12**, 83–103 (1991)

30. Bresser, R.K.F.: Matching collective and competitive strategies. Strateg. Manag. J. **9**(4), 375–385 (1988). https://doi.org/10.1002/smj.4250090407

31. Buckley, P.J., Glaister, K.W., Klijn, E., Tan, H.: Knowledge accession and knowledge acquisition in strategic alliances: the impact of supplementary and complementary dimensions. Br. J. Manag. **20**(4), 598–609 (2009). https://doi.org/10.1111/j.1467-8551.2008.00607.x

32. Yang, S.M., Fang, S.C., Fang, S.R., Chou, C.H.: Knowledge exchange and knowledge protection in interorganizational learning: the ambidexterity perspective. Ind. Mark. Manag. **43**(2), 346–358 (2014). https://doi.org/10.1016/j.indmarman.2013.11.007

33. Wu, F., Sinkovics, R.R., Cavusgil, S.T., Roath, A.S.: Overcoming export manufacturers' dilemma in international expansion. J. Int. Bus. Stud. **38**(2), 283–302 (2007). https://doi.org/10.1057/palgrave.jibs.8400263

34. Guo, W., Yang, J., Li, D., Lyu, C.: Knowledge sharing and knowledge protection in strategic alliances: the effects of trust and formal contracts. Technol. Anal. Strateg. Manag. **32**(11), 1366–1378 (2020). https://doi.org/10.1080/09537325.2020.1769840

35. Castelfranchi, C.: Trust mediation in knowledge management and sharing. In: Jensen, C., Poslad, S., Dimitrakos, T. (eds.) iTrust 2004. LNCS, vol. 2995, pp. 304–318. Springer, Heidelberg (2004). https://doi.org/10.1007/978-3-540-24747-0_23

36. Rashid, Z., Noor, U., Altmann, J.: Economic model for evaluating the value creation through information sharing within the cybersecurity information sharing ecosystem. Futur. Gener. Comput. Syst. **124**, 436–466 (2021). https://doi.org/10.1016/J.FUTURE.2021.05.033

37. Rashid, Z., Noor, U., Altmann, J.: Network externalities in cybersecurity information sharing ecosystems. In: Coppola, M., Carlini, E., D'Agostino, D., Altmann, J., Bañares, J.Á. (eds.) GECON 2018. LNCS, vol. 11113, pp. 116–125. Springer, Cham (2019). https://doi.org/10.1007/978-3-030-13342-9_10

38. Noor, U., Anwar, Z., Altmann, J., Rashid, Z.: Customer-oriented ranking of cyber threat intelligence service providers. Electron. Commer. Res. Appl. **41**, 100976 (2020). https://doi.org/10.1016/j.elerap.2020.100976

Self-organizing Energy-Minimization Placement of QoE-Constrained Services at the Edge

Matteo Mordacchini[2]($\boxtimes$) [ID], Luca Ferrucci[1] [ID], Emanuele Carlini[1] [ID], Hanna Kavalionak[1] [ID], Massimo Coppola[1] [ID], and Patrizio Dazzi[1] [ID]

[1] ISTI-CNR, Pisa, Italy
{luca.ferrucci,emanuele.carlini,hanna.kavalionak,massimo.coppola,
patrizio.dazzi}@isti.cnr.it
[2] IIT-CNR, Pisa, Italy
matteo.mordacchini@iit.cnr.it

Abstract. The wide availability of heterogeneous resources at the Edge of the network is gaining a central role in defining and developing new computing paradigms for both the infrastructures and the applications. However, it becomes challenging to optimize the system's behaviour, due to the Edge's highly distributed and dynamic nature. Recent solutions propose new decentralized, self-adaptive approaches to face the needs of this scenario. One of the most challenging aspect is related to the optimization of the system's energy consumption. In this paper, we propose a fully decentralized solution that limits the energy consumed by the system, without failing to match the users expectations, defined as the services' Quality of Experience (QoE). Specifically, we propose a scheme where the autonomous coordination of entities at Edge is able to reduce the energy consumption by reducing the number of instances of the applications executed in system. This result is achieve without violating the services' QoE, expressed in terms of latency. Experimental evaluations through simulation conducted with PureEdgeSim demonstrate the effectiveness of the approach.

Keywords: Edge computing · Self-organizing

1 Introduction

Traditional Cloud solutions are facing increasing difficulties in coping with novel sets of applications, like latency-sensitive ones. The Edge/Cloud continuum paradigm allows to overcome these limits by seamlessly integrating one (or more) Cloud(s) and wide numbers of Edge resources, geographically distributed.

This work has been partially supported by the European Union's Horizon 2020 Research and Innovation program, under the project ACCORDION (Grant agreement ID: 871793).

However, several challenges are emerging for the management, coordination and optimization of these large sets of heterogeneous and dispersed resources [25]. Among those challenges, a sensitive problem concerns the reduction of the overall energy consumption of the system. One way to achieve this results is to optimize the placement of the instances of the applications requested by the users. This is a non-trivial task, since it has to take into account the functional needs of the applications, the computational limits of Edge resources and the non-functional requirements associated with the users' Quality of Experience (QoE).

Distributed [1], self-organizing [10,14,20] and adaptive [3,5] solutions have been advanced for facing these kind of challenges at the Edge. In this paper, we propose a decentralized, self-organizing and QoE-aware scheme for the optimization of the energy consumed by the system. Specifically, Edge entities interact among themselves and exchange information in order to determine whether the users of each application can be served using a lower number of instances. This behaviour allows to reduce the number of instances executed in the system, thus reducing the overall energy consumed. When taking the decision to shut down a potential redundant instance, the entities exploit the data they have exchanged to evaluate whether this decision is in accordance with the services' QoE and the computational limits of Edge resources. Experimental results through simulation show that the proposed solution is able to reduce the energy required by the system up to nearly 40%.

The rest of this paper is organized as follows. Section 2 contextualizes this work in the related scientific literature. Section 3 presents our the definition of the problem and the approach we propose. Section 4 describes the experimental evaluation of the proposed solution. Finally, Sect. 5 draws concluding remarks and highlights future work directions.

2   Related Work

Edge-based systems are the object of many investigations that try to optimize their performance by limiting the communications to/from centralized Clouds [23,24]. In fact, these communications could introduce significant overhead and could potentially degrade the performance of many Edge-based applications, like locality and context-based services. A common way to overcome this problem is to use decentralized and/or self-organizing solutions [11,16,18]. These solutions achieve their goal by moving the applications [9,15,21] and/or data closer to users. When the data is moved in the system, the aim is to make it easy for the users to access it [6,8,19,22]. In this case, the general strategy is to shorten the distance between the data storage devices or the data producers and their respective consumers [2,13]. To achieve an optimization of the energy consumption levels of the entities at the Edge, we use a method which does not move data and/or applications closer to each other and/or closer to their users.

The optimization of the usage of Edge resources is proposed by Kavalionak et al. [12]. In this proposal, the devices fulfill their tasks by sharing and balancing the required computational costs. Beraldi et al. propose CooLoad [4], a scheme

Table 1. Table of symbols.

Symbol	Meaning
EMC	Edge Mini-cloud
$E = \{EMC_1, \ldots, EMC_m\}$	Set of all the EMCs in the system
$A = \{A_1, \ldots, A_n\}$	Set of all the applications in the system
u_{ij}	Number of users of a_{ij}
U_i	Total number of users of A_i
l_{ij}	Maximum latency experienced by the users of a_{ij}
L_i	Maximum latency admitted by A_i's QoE
$\mathcal{L}(j,k)$	Maximum latency between EMC_j and EMC_k
w_{ij}	Weight (resource occupancy) of a_{ij}
e_{ij}	Energy consumed by a_{ij}
W_j	Max weight that can be sustained by EMC_j
W_j^t	Resource occupancy of EMC_j at time t
$c(a_{ij})$	Function that returns $True$ if a_{ij} is QoE-compliant
$\mathcal{E}_i$	Set of EMCs that can host (w.r.t. QoE) an instance of A_i
$\mathcal{A}_j$	Set of apps that can hosted (w.r.t. QoE) by EMC_j

where Edge datacenters re-direct their requests to other adjacent data centers whenever they become congested. Carlini et al. [7] propose a decentralized system, where autonomous entities in a Cloud Federation communicate to exchange computational services, trying to maximize the profit of the whole Federation. Differently from the previous solutions, in this paper, the efficient exploitation of the resources at the Edge is obtained by optimizing the energy consumption of the system as a whole. As we explain in depth in the rest of the paper, this result is achieved through point-to-point interactions between Edge entities, known as Edge Miniclouds (EMCs). These entities use their communications to detect potential redundant instances of the applications requested by the users. As a result, the users are directed to use only a limited set of instances, thus allowing to shut down the others. However, an user request could be served by a different instance running on another EMC only if the associated QoE constraints remain satisfied. The outcome of the collective behaviour of the entities at the Edge is a notable reduction of the energy needed by the system performing the computational tasks requested by its users.

3 Problem Definition and Proposed Solution

In this paper, we face the problem of how to optimize the execution of applications at the Edge, in order to minimize the energy consumption level of the system as a whole, while respecting the applications' QoE constraints. For the rest of this paper, we will make use of the symbols reported in Table 1.

Specifically, consistently with the definitions of the EU ACCORDION project (https://www.accordion-project.eu/), we consider that the system at the Edge is a federation of so-called *Edge mini-clouds* (EMCs). Each EMC is an entity that supervises a set of other devices with limited resources, like IoT devices, sensors, etc. Applications are sent to an EMC, which is in charge to orchestrate their execution among the devices it controls.

We consider that $E = \{EMC_1, \ldots, EMC_m\}$ is the set of all the EMCs in the system, with $|E| = M$. The set $A = \{A_1, \ldots, A_n\}$ is the set of all the types of applications that can be executed in the system, with $N = |A|$. Each $A_i \in A$ represents a distinct type of service, with specific requirements in term of resources. In order to meet the requests of the users, several instances of an application A_i can be deployed among the various EMCs. The symbol a_{ij} denotes the instance of the application A_i executed by EMC_j. Running a_{ij} has a weight (in terms of resource occupancy) w_{ij}. This weight is composed of a base weight w_i^{fix} and a variable component w_{ij}^{var}, where the variable component depends on the number of users served by a_{ij}. Therefore, if we denote with u_{ij} the number of users of a_{ij}, we have that $w_{ij}^{var} = u_{ij} w_i^u$, where w_i^u is the weight-per-user of A_i. Thus, $w_{ij} = w_i^{fix} + u_{ij} w_i^u$. The overall number of users served by all the instances of A_i is U_i, while W_j is the maximum weight that can be supported by EMC_j for running all the instances that are assigned to it. In addition to the functional requirements, in order to meet the required QoE, each application has also additional non-functional requirements. These requirements limit the EMCs where an instance can be deployed. We assume that the QoE is expressed in terms of latency, where any service A_i constraints it to be lower than a value L_i. In fact, latency is one of the main factors that influence a user's perception of the quality of a service. Based on this assumption, we also assume that each time a user requests a service, an instance of it is activated on the user's closest EMC (in terms of latency). In this way, the latency is initially minimized. As a consequence, this allocation scheme can also generate a set of redundant instances of the same service. In fact, sets of users initially assigned to different EMCs can be served by just one, properly selected instance, without violating the service's QoE. This allows to shut down the other instances and reduce the amount of energy consumed for serving the same users. Always relaying on the direct intervention of a distant Cloud orchestrator to reach this result could be a source of delay and degradation of the QoE. To overcome this limit, we propose an adaptive self-optimization scheme, based on the autonomous actions of the EMCs. The global goal of the actions of the EMCs' orchestrators is to identify and stop redundant instances of the running applications, thus reducing the system overall energy consumption. The result is achieved by allowing pairs of neighboring EMCs, that share instances of the same application, to evaluate whether they can direct their users to exploit just one of the instances, thus allowing to turn off the other one. In the next, following the pseudocode given in Algorithm 1, we describe the steps executed by a generic EMC_j. We consider that EMC_j has a set $\mathcal{N}$ of neighboring EMCs (EMCs within the communication range of EMC_j). The latency between EMC_j and any of its neighbors $EMC_k \in \mathcal{N}$ is $\mathcal{L}(j,k)$. I_j^t is the set of application types running on the instances on EMC_j at time t. Each application $A_i \in I_j^t$ has a maximum agreed latency L_i, and a set

---

Algorithm 1. Actions performed by a generic EMC_j at each time step t

---

Input: $\mathcal{N}$ = set of neighbors of EMC_j

Randomly choose $EMC_k \in \mathcal{N}$
Request I_k^t, W_k, W_k^t to EMC_k
Compute $I_{jk} = \{A_i | A_i \in I_j^t \cap I_k^t\}$
if $I_{jk} \neq \emptyset$ **then**
    if $W_j^t \geq W_k^t$ **then**
        $\mathcal{A}_{jk} = \{A_i \in I_{jk} | \tilde{c}(a_{ik}) = True\}$
        Order $\mathcal{A}_{jk}$ in ascending order using w_{ij}
        Let m be the index of the first application $A_m \in \mathcal{A}_{jk}$ s.t. $W_k^t + w_m^u u_{mj} \leq W_k$
        Direct the users of a_{mj} to use a_{mk}
        Turn off a_{mj}
    else
        $\mathcal{A}_{jk} = \{A_i \in I_{jk} | \tilde{c}(a_{ij}) = True\}$
        Order $\mathcal{A}_{jk}$ in ascending order using w_{ik}
        Let m be the index of the first application $A_m \in \mathcal{A}_{jk}$ s.t. $W_j^t + w_m^u u_{mk} \leq W_j$
        Direct the users of a_{mk} to use a_{mj}
        Tell EMC_k to turn off a_{mk}
    end if
end if

---

of users u_{ij}, which experiences a maximum latency l_{ij}. At regular time intervals, EMC_j randomly chooses one neighbor $EMC_k \in \mathcal{N}$, using a uniform probability distribution. This distribution is a good baseline for an initial evaluation of the approach, while other choices are left for future works. It then asks EMC_k for the list of its running applications I_k^t with their number of users, its maximum capacity W_k and its actual resource occupancy W_k^t. The solution tries to gather the users of both the instances on the EMC with the lowest actual occupancy.

$I_{jk} = \{A_i | A_i \in I_j^t \cap I_k^t\}$ is the set of shared applications. If $I_{jk} \neq \emptyset$, s is the *source* EMC (the one from which the users will be moved), with d the EMC receiving that users. Thus, $W_s^t \geq W_d^t$. EMC_j builds a set $\mathcal{A}_{sd} = \{A_i \in I_{sd} | l_{is} + \mathcal{L}(s, d) \leq L_i\}$ containing the instances whose users can be moved without violating the QoE. EMC_j traverses $\mathcal{A}_{sd}$ in descending order (on the basis of the instances weights in EMC_s), choosing for the exchange the first application whose users can be transferred without exceeding W_d. In the special case where both the EMCs select each other for an exchange, having equal loads and selecting the same service, the EMC with the lowest ID rejects to receive the exchange, asking for another application. Once the users are directed to another instance, the instance on EMC_s is turned off. This action allows both to save energy and to free space for other potential exchanges or new instances.

4   Experimental Evaluation

In this section, we present a validation of the proposed solution. The results are obtained through a simulation of a target scenario. We use PureEdgeSim [17],

Table 2. w^{fix} and w^u for each application type

Type	VCPU	Ram	BW	VCPU (user)	Ram (user)	BW (user)
Balanced	1	200	20	1 each 10 users	20	2
Comp bound	2	200	20	1 each 5 users	20	2
Mem bound	1	400	20	1 each 10 users	40	2
I/O bound	1	200	40	1 each 10 users	20	4

a discrete-event simulator for Edge environments, that well matches the EMC-based structure of our scenario, allowing also to easily measure energy consumptions. While each EMC is composed of a set of heterogeneous Edge devices, it is viewed as a single entity, resulting from the aggregation of the resources of the devices it manages. At the beginning of the simulation, each user requests a single application to its closest EMC. In case an instance of the requested application type already exists on that EMC, the user is simply added to the instance's local set of users.

In the next, we present results coming from different experiments. In each experiment the number of users varies in the set $\{60, 120, 180\}$. Each user device is placed randomly in a bi-dimensional area of 200×200 m. In all the experiments the number of EMCs is fixed to 4. They are placed at predefined locations inside the simulation space. We assume that any EMC can host any type of application. Moreover, each EMC is able to communicate with the others. There are three types of resources available in the system (at the EMCs): the number of VCPU; the amount of Ram; the amount of network bandwidth (BW).

In the simulations, we use four different types of applications. Application types differ on the resources they request and, as a consequence, the energy footprint they produce when their instances are executed. The application types are divided as *Computational Bound* (i.e., computational intensive), *Memory Bound* (memory intensive) and *I/O Bound* (networking intensive) applications, where "intensive" means having double the requirements of the basic *Balanced* application type. The load of an EMC is calculated as the mean of the percentage of availability of the three resources. The fixed weight w_i^{fix} and the weights per user w^u associated with the different application types is shown in Table 2. Ram and BW are in Mbytes and Mbit/s, respectively. In addition to these parameters, we also use three different values for the maximum application latency L_i: 0.2, 0.3, 0.5 s. Therefore, we have 12 possible combinations of parameters for the applications: 4 types of applications times 3 different latency constraints. All the results presented in the next are the average of 10 independent runs.

The first and main result of our evaluation is presented in Fig. 1a. This figure presents the evolution over time of the energy required by all the EMCs in the system, including the energy needed for inter-EMCs communications. The results are presented as the ratio between the energy needed at a time $t > 0$ and the energy consumed by the system at the beginning of the simulation. It is possible to observe that the level that is required to serve the very same number of users drops by a minimum of 20% (with 180 users) up to nearly 40% (with 60 users); this drastic reduction in the energy footprint of the system demonstrates the high level of efficiency of the proposed approach.

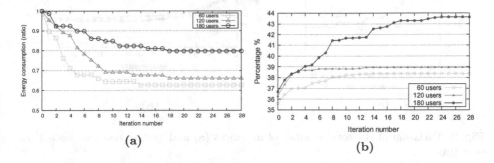

Fig. 1. Temporal evolution of the levels of energy (a) and average latency (b)

In Fig. 1b we investigate how the configurations adopted by the system are able to remain compliant with the applications' QoE. A simulated latency function is calculated for each user's device, which is the composition of a fixed part, which is dependent from the communication channel type, and a linear part, proportional to the Euclidean distance between the EMC hosting the instance of the serving application and the user's device. The average latency is measured as the percentage of the maximum average latency, as constrained by the applications' limits. It is possible to note that there is only a limited increase on the average latency. Therefore, the proposed solution shows its ability to remarkably reduce the energy needed to run the instances that serve a given population of users, while remaining well below the limits of the required QoE.

In order to better understand how these results are achieved, the next set of figures analyses how the system collectively adapts its behaviour and how it changes the exploitation of the available resources. Specifically, Fig. 2a presents the variation over time of the number of running instances in the system. Clearly, these entities are the source of energy consumption. The ability of the system to detect and eliminate redundant instances is the basis for the energy minimization scheme. It is possible to observe a clear and sharp decrease of this quantity. The final number is nearly the half of the original number of instances. Figure 2b presents the global level of exploitation of the resources. The y axis presents the percentage of all the resources that are required to run the application instances. As in the previous case, we can observe a clear reduction. The amount of this reduction is lower than that of the number of instances, since users are moved from a redundant instance to an active one. As we highlighted in Sect. 3, each user bring an additional cost in terms of resources. Despite this fact, the overall level of occupied resources is decremented, since the fixed costs needed for running redundant instances are saved.

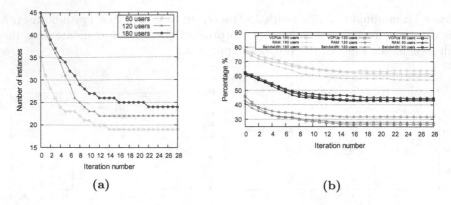

Fig. 2. Variation of the total number of instances (a) and system resource loads (b), over time

5   Conclusions

This paper presents a solution for application placement performing edge-to-edge exchanges to reduce the resource usage, while guaranteeing the QoE of applications by keeping the communication latency below given thresholds. The paper provides a definition of the problem and the pseudo code of the proposed approach. An experimental evaluation via simulation shows the validity of our solution. While the solution is quite a promising one, there is space to improve the results in the near future. It is worth e.g. considering alternative local search criteria and heuristics for the selection criteria of the EMC and application for the swap proposal. This may improve the asymptotic cost savings and is likely to improve the achieved savings as well as the convergence speed of our algorithm.

References

1. Anastasi, G.F., Carlini, E., Dazzi, P.: Smart cloud federation simulations with CloudSim. In: Proceedings of the first ACM Workshop on Optimization Techniques for Resources Management in Clouds, pp. 9–16 (2013)
2. Aral, A., Ovatman, T.: A decentralized replica placement algorithm for edge computing. IEEE Trans. Netw. Serv. Manage. **15**(2), 516–529 (2018)
3. Baraglia, R., Dazzi, P., Guidi, B., Ricci, L.: GoDel: Delaunay overlays in P2P networks via gossip. In: IEEE 12th International Conference on Peer-to-Peer Computing (P2P), pp. 1–12. IEEE (2012)
4. Beraldi, R., Mtibaa, A., Alnuweiri, H.: Cooperative load balancing scheme for edge computing resources. In: 2017 Second International Conference on Fog and Mobile Edge Computing (FMEC), pp. 94–100. IEEE (2017)
5. Bruno, R., Conti, M., Mordacchini, M., Passarella, A.: An analytical model for content dissemination in opportunistic networks using cognitive heuristics. In: Proceedings of the 15th ACM International Conference on Modeling, Analysis and Simulation of Wireless and Mobile Systems (2012)

6. Carlini, E., Coppola, M., Dazzi, P., Laforenza, D., Martinelli, S., Ricci, L.: Service and resource discovery supports over P2P overlays. In: 2009 International Conference on Ultra Modern Telecommunications & Workshops, pp. 1–8. IEEE (2009)
7. Carlini, E., Coppola, M., Dazzi, P., Mordacchini, M., Passarella, A.: Self-optimising decentralised service placement in heterogeneous cloud federation. In: 2016 IEEE 10th International Conference on Self-adaptive and Self-organizing Systems (SASO), pp. 110–119 (2016)
8. Carlini, E., Ricci, L., Coppola, M.: Integrating centralized and peer-to-peer architectures to support interest management in massively multiplayer on-line games. Concurr. Comput. **27**(13), 3362–3382 (2015)
9. Dazzi, P., Mordacchini, M.: Scalable decentralized indexing and querying of multi-streams in the fog. J. Grid Comput. **18**(3), 395–418 (2020)
10. Ferrucci, L., Ricci, L., Albano, M., Baraglia, R., Mordacchini, M.: Multidimensional range queries on hierarchical Voronoi overlays. J. Comput. Syst. Sci. **82**, 1161–1179 (2016)
11. Gennaro, C., Mordacchini, M., Orlando, S., Rabitti, F.: MRoute: a peer-to-peer routing index for similarity search in metric spaces. In: 5th VLDB International Workshop on Databases, Information Systems and Peer-to-Peer Computing (DBISP2P 2007) (2007)
12. Kavalionak, H., et al.: Distributed video surveillance using smart cameras. J. Grid Comput. **17**(1), 59–77 (2019)
13. Li, C., Wang, Y., Tang, H., Zhang, Y., Xin, Y., Luo, Y.: Flexible replica placement for enhancing the availability in edge computing environment. Comput. Commun. **146**, 1–14 (2019)
14. Lulli, A., Carlini, E., Dazzi, P., Lucchese, C., Ricci, L.: Fast connected components computation in large graphs by vertex pruning. IEEE Trans. Parallel Distrib. Syst. **28**(3), 760–773 (2016)
15. Maia, A.M., Ghamri-Doudane, Y., Vieira, D., de Castro, M.F.: Optimized placement of scalable IoT services in edge computing. In: 2019 IFIP/IEEE Symposium on Integrated Network and Service Management (IM), pp. 189–197 (2019)
16. Marzolla, M., Mordacchini, M., Orlando, S.: A P2P resource discovery system based on a forest of trees. In: 17th International Workshop on Database and Expert Systems Applications (DEXA 2006), pp. 261–265. IEEE (2006)
17. Mechalikh, C., Takta, H., Moussa, F.: PureEdgeSim: a simulation toolkit for performance evaluation of cloud, fog, and pure edge computing environments. In: 2019 International Conference on High Performance Computing & Simulation (HPCS), pp. 700–707 (2019)
18. Mordacchini, M., Conti, M., Passarella, A., Bruno, R.: Human-centric data dissemination in the IoP: large-scale modeling and evaluation. ACM Trans. Auton. Adapt. Syst. **14**(3), 1–25 (2020)
19. Mordacchini, M., Dazzi, P., Tolomei, G., Baraglia, R., Silvestri, F., Orlando, S.: Challenges in designing an interest-based distributed aggregation of users in P2P systems. In: 2009 IEEE ICUMT, pp. 1–8. IEEE (2009)
20. Mordacchini, M., et al.: Crowdsourcing through cognitive opportunistic networks. ACM Trans. Auton. Adapt. Syst. **10**(2), 1–29 (2015)
21. Ning, Z., et al.: Distributed and dynamic service placement in pervasive edge computing networks. IEEE Trans. Parallel Distrib. Syst. **32**, 1277–1292 (2020)
22. Ricci, L., Genovali, L., Carlini, E., Coppola, M.: AOI-cast in distributed virtual environments: an approach based on delay tolerant reverse compass routing. Concurr. Comput. Pract. Exp. **27**(9), 2329–2350 (2015)

23. Salaht, F., Desprez, F., Lebre, A.: An overview of service placement problem in fog and edge computing. ACM Comput. Surv. **53**(3), 1–35 (2020)
24. Santoso, G.Z., et al.: Dynamic resource selection in cloud service broker. In: 2017 International Conference on High Performance Computing & Simulation (HPCS), pp. 233–235. IEEE (2017)
25. Taleb, T., Samdanis, K., Mada, B., Flinck, H., Dutta, S., Sabella, D.: On multi-access edge computing: a survey of the emerging 5g network edge cloud architecture and orchestration. IEEE Commun. Surv. Tutor. **19**(3), 1657–1681 (2017)

RapidSwap: a Hierarchical Far Memory

Hyunik Kim ID, Changyeon Jo ID, Jörn Altmann ID, and Bernhard Egger(✉) ID

Seoul National University, Seoul, Korea
{hyunik,changyeon,bernhard}@csap.snu.ac.kr, jorn.altman@acm.org

Abstract. As more and more memory-intensive applications are moved into the cloud, data center operators face the challenge of providing sufficient main memory resources while achieving high resource utilization. Solutions to overcome the unsatisfying performance degradation of traditional on-demand paging include memory disaggregation that allows applications to access remote memory or compressing memory pages in local DRAM; however, the former's extended failure domain and the latter's low efficacy limit their broad applicability. This paper presents RapidSwap, a hierarchical far memory manager that exploits the wide availability of phase-change memory (Intel Optane memory) in data centers to achieve quasi-DRAM performance at a significantly lower total cost of ownership (TCO). RapidSwap migrates infrequently accessed data to slower and cheaper devices in a hierarchy of storage devices by tracking applications' memory accesses. Evaluated with several real-world cloud benchmarks, RapidSwap achieves a reduction of 20% in operating cost at minimal performance degradation and is 30% more cost-effective than pure DRAM solutions. The results demonstrate that proper management of new memory technologies can yield significant TCO savings in cloud data centers.

Keywords: Memory hierarchy · Far memory · Cloud data center

1 Introduction

Over the past two decades, big data and artificial intelligence techniques have been adopted by numerous application domains such as data analysis, drug discovery, video processing, and autonomous driving [7,18,21]. A common characteristic of such workloads is their need for large amounts of main memory to process the big data sets [23]. As these workloads are moved into the cloud, cloud service providers have started to offer virtual machine (VM) instances optimized for such memory-intensive workloads. Amazon, Google Cloud, and Microsoft Azure, for example, support VM instances with up to 24 terabytes of main memory [5,6,19]. Ideally, data center operators would equip their machines with sufficient DRAM to store all data; however, this approach negatively impacts the TCO of a warehouse.

ⓒ Springer Nature Switzerland AG 2021
K. Tserpes et al. (Eds.): GECON 2021, LNCS 13072, pp. 143–151, 2021.
https://doi.org/10.1007/978-3-030-92916-9_12

One way to lower memory pressure is to impose a price penalty on using DRAM and induce the use of cheaper low-tier storage devices. According to the pricing policy of different Amazon EC2 instances as of June 2021 [4], DRAM storage is 45 times more expensive than solid state drive (SSD) storage at the same capacity. A better approach than offloading the burden of using less DRAM to the customer is to provide the required performance through an optimized storage hierarchy that can offer the same service (performance) at a lower price. Common techniques involve demand paging to local storage [15] and memory disaggregation. Based on the principle of locality [2], both techniques keep frequently accessed pages (also called *hot pages*) in the fast and expensive DRAM and relegate infrequently accessed parts (the *cold pages*) to slower and cheaper storage tiers. Both techniques suffer from a significant performance slowdown the more memory is paged out. This is caused by (1) the large access latency of far storage tiers and (2) inflexible and slow system software that fails to exploit new and fast storage technologies such as phase change memory (PCM) [14].

In this paper, we present RapidSwap, a framework built for modern storage hierarchies to achieve a lower TCO at near-DRAM performance. RapidSwap classifies pages into different temperatures based on their access history. Hot pages are kept in DRAM and gradually downgraded to slower devices as they cool down. RapidSwap's awareness of the storage hierarchy and its optimized software stack minimize the page reclaim overhead and achieve a significantly lower TCO and cost effectiveness than existing solutions.

2   Background and Motivation

2.1   Tiered Storage and Novel Storage Devices

Tiered storage, also known as hierarchical storage, is a widely adopted technique in computing devices [8]. Faster and more expensive devices are placed at the upper side of the storage hierarchy, while slower and cheaper media are located below. Placing the data of all workloads in high-performance devices yields the best performance at the expense of larger operating costs. One possibility to decrease the cost while maintaining performance is to monitor and classify memory pages by their access frequency into different temperatures from *hot* to *cold*. The principle of locality dictates that, in general, the colder a page gets, the less likely it is to be accessed and can thus be migrated to slower storage devices without causing a large performance drop.

Recently, new storage technologies with dramatically improved performance characteristics have entered the market. Non-volatile memory (NVM) devices such as phase change memory (PCM) used in Intel's Optane product line have a read/write theoretical latency of 10 μs [11]; three orders of magnitude below that of conventional Hard Disk Drives (HDD). The NVDIMM interface allows direct load/store accesses by the CPU and is thus able to benefit from caches.

Table 1. Comparison of existing techniques and RapidSwap.

Type	Granularity	Failure domain	Overhead
Software-defined far memory [16]	Page	Local	CPU
Hydra [17]	Page	Remote	CPU & Network
RackMem [14]	Page	Remote	Network
RapidSwap	Page	Local	Minimal CPU
Optane PMEM Memory Mode [9]	Cache-line	Local	No SW overhead

2.2   Techniques Proposed to Lower Memory Pressure

Transparent Memory Compression. compresses cold pages *in memory* with a lightweight algorithm [3]. Support in the Linux kernel is provided by *zswap* [24]. Pages that do not benefit from compression are sent to local storage devices. *Zswap* is expected to work well if the read latency from DRAM plus the decompression time is significantly shorter than the read latency of the backing store, however, its efficiency depends on the compressibility of the data in memory. A practical implementation of zswap is provided by Google's Far Memory [16]. Applied in their data centers, Google Far Memory classifies around 20% of all pages as cold, and among those, about 70% achieve 3x compression and are kept in DRAM. The remaining 30% are stored on traditional storage devices. Google reports a 4–5% reduction of their TCO.

Memory Disaggregation. pools memory resources from different physical nodes over a low latency and high throughput network to overcome the limitations of the node-centric computation model. A significant disadvantage of memory disaggregation is the extension of the failure domain from a single local to multiple remote machines. Replication, erasure coding [17], or hybrid approaches [22] are used to achieve fault tolerance, however, these approaches requires additional storage or computational resources.

2.3   Tiered Storage as a Promising Alternative

Current approaches such as Linux demand paging, transparent memory compression, and memory disaggregation all have shortcomings. On the other hand, RapidSwap eliminates the deficiencies of existing approaches and implements a high-performance demand paging system to a local storage hierarchy consisting of various types of devices with different characteristics. Data is stored in one of the local storage tiers according to RapidSwap's page classification. Pages are assigned a temperature ranging from hot to cold, representing how recently the page has been accessed. Pages are migrated between the different storage tiers depending on their temperature to store each page in the most beneficial device. Table 1 summarizes state-of-the-art techniques and RapidSwap.

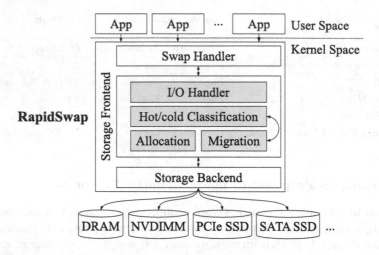

Fig. 1. Overall architecture of RapidSwap.

3 RapidSwap

This section discusses the design and implementation of RapidSwap. RapidSwap is composed of three main components: an optimized *swap handler*, a *storage frontend*, and a *storage backend*. Figure 1 shows the overall architecture.

3.1 Swap Handler

Linux's virtual memory management has been demonstrated to be too slow for modern storage devices [13,14]. RapidSwap's optimized swap handler follows the design of RackMem [14] and manages pages with two quasi-ordered lists: the *active* and the *inactive* page list. To quickly react to page allocation requests, the inactive list is kept populated by pro-actively paging data out. If the *inactive* list becomes empty under high load, victim pages are taken from the head of the *active* page list.

3.2 Storage Frontend

RapidSwap's *storage frontend* manages the different tiered storage devices and exposes a uniform paging device to the *swap handler*. Consecutive pages are grouped into *slabs* to minimize metadata and I/O overhead. The storage frontend swaps in/out slabs from/to different storage devices and maintains a mapping of virtual pages to their locations in the storage hierarchy.

Slabs are classified into *hot*, *warm*, or *cold*. A newly allocated slab is considered hot, then transitions over warm to cold if it is not accessed for a certain period of time. Cold slabs are periodically migrated to the next lower level in the storage hierarchy. A page fault causes the associated slab to be immediately migrated up to the fastest storage below DRAM.

Table 2. Yahoo! Cloud Serving Benchmark (YCSB) workloads [1].

Workload type	Distribution	Details
A: Update heavy	Zipfian	50% Reads, 50% Writes
B: Read mostly	Zipfian	95% Reads, 5% Writes
C: Read only	Zipfian	100% Reads
D: Read latest	Latest	Read from the fresh data
E: Short ranges	Zipfian/Uniform	95% Scans, 5% Writes
F: Read-modify-write	Zipfian	50% Reads, 50% Read-modify-writes

3.3 Storage Backend

The *storage backend* provides a uniform abstraction for physical storage devices. When the *storage backend* registers a device, RapidSwap's *storage frontend* gathers information about the storage device including its capacity and the latency of allocation, deallocation, and 4 KiB read/write operations. RapidSwap uses this information to establish a hierarchy among the attached storage devices.

4 Results

4.1 Experimental Setup

RapidSwap is evaluated on a data center server node equipped with an Intel Xeon Silver 4215R processor with 8 cores (16 threads) and 64 GiB of DRAM. The node contains a two-tiered storage hierarchy consisting of a 960 GB Intel 905P Optane NVMe PCIe (SSD) and an 128 GB Intel Optane Persistent Memory 200 Series (PMEM). The base operating system is Ubuntu Server 20.04. The slab size is set to 1 MB (256 pages per slab). Slabs are demoted to the next colder level after a threshold of 5 s.

We use six different workloads from the Yahoo! Cloud Serving Benchmark (YCSB) suite [1] to measure the performance of RapidSwap. Benchmarks A, B, C, D, and F follow a *Zipfian* access pattern where 80% of the total accesses go to 20% of the data. Workload D predominantly reads from just inserted data that is not physically contiguous. Workload E selects the key with a Zipfian distribution, then scans a uniformly distributed number of records.

The performance of RapidSwap is evaluated by measuring the query response latency as reported by YCSB. Memory scarcity is simulated by artificially limiting the available DRAM to a certain percentage of the benchmark's overall maximum memory requirements (resident set size, RSS). RapidSwap is compared against a Linux baseline with PMEM and SSD paging devices where the former is prioritized, i.e., the SSD is only used when the PMEM paging device is completely full. The size of the available PMEM device is identical to that in RapidSwap. We also compare RapidSwap against compressed DRAM.

Table 3. Maximum number of PMEM slabs allocated by local memory size.

Workload type	Local: 50%	Local: 60%	Local: 70%	Local: 80%
A	2388	1403	330	222
B	2374	1438	402	215
C	2345	1433	273	225
D	1459	795	405	292
E	2549	2184	396	332
F	2340	1456	366	309

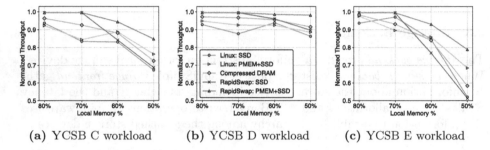

(a) YCSB C workload   (b) YCSB D workload   (c) YCSB E workload

Fig. 2. Normalized throughput over DRAM of RapidSwap and prior work.

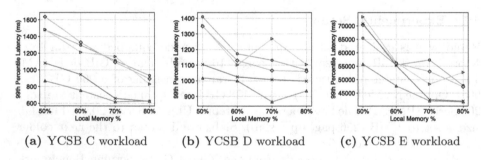

(a) YCSB C workload   (b) YCSB D workload   (c) YCSB E workload

Fig. 3. 99th percentile latency of RapidSwap and prior work.

4.2   RapidSwap Performance

Degradation Over DRAM. Figure 2 plots the normalized throughput of the different implementations and with local memory limits set to 80, 70, 60, and 50 As the amount of DRAM is reduced, all implementations experience a performance degradation. Workloads exhibit three different patterns with minor (workloads A, B, C, and F; C is shown as a representative), average (workload D), and high sensitivity (workload E) to the available local memory. Table 3 shows the maximal number of allocated slabs in PMEM for the different benchmarks. RapidSwap outperforms the other approaches in all configurations.

CPU Overhead and I/O Latency. The CPU overhead is gathered by calculating the average system level utilization throughout the workload execution. The system CPU overhead caused by all three methods is less than 1% compared to the ideal case with 100% local memory. The average 99th percentile latency reported by RapidSwap is presented in Fig. 3. Compared to the Linux baseline and compressed DRAM, RapidSwap exhibits significantly lower latencies thanks to its optimized page fault handler and pro-active page reclamation.

4.3 Cost of Storage Tier

To analyze the benefits of RapidSwap on the cost of the entire storage tier, we surveyed the current market prices of the different storage backends [10,12,20]. The cost is obtained by multiplying the peak utilization in all storage tiers by the cost of the respective device. The total cost is obtained by adding the cost of the allocated DRAM. We consider only the fractional cost of a storage device (as opposed to the cost of the entire device) to reflect the pricing models of cloud data centers. RapidSwap achieves cost savings for all workloads and all configurations. At 70%, a 18–20% cost reduction in the storage hierarchy is achieved. As the amount of local memory is reduced, more data gets paged out to secondary storage which, in turn, leads to a higher cost in the storage hierarchy.

4.4 Cost Effectiveness

The total cost of the storage tier does not consider the cost incurred by performance degradation. A more sensible metric is the *cost effectiveness*, i.e., performance per cost. We compared the cost effectiveness of compressed DRAM and RapidSwap relative to a DRAM-only solution. Our first observation is that RapidSwap achieves a significantly better cost effectiveness than other solutions for all workloads and all configurations. Compared to DRAM, RapidSwap achieves an up to 40% higher cost effectiveness with 70% of the data kept in DRAM and 30% paged out. As the amount of DRAM is reduced, workloads experience a higher performance degradation and require larger amounts of storage.

5 Conclusion and Future Work

Motivated by the broad availability of novel storage technologies and the shortcomings of existing approaches to resource overcommitment, we have presented RapidSwap, a hierarchical far memory implementation that is built for diverse storage tiers composed of faster and slower devices. Paging only to local devices, RapidSwap does not extend the failure domain, and its awareness of the storage hierarchy allows it to significantly outperform other techniques that swap out data locally. The results demonstrate that proper management of new memory technologies can yield significant cost savings in data centers.

One direction of future work is application-specific resource management. As shown in previous work [16], RapidSwap can also benefit from a machine learning based approach to adjust the amount of local memory and the policies to degrade slabs to colder storage. Also, we have not yet compared RapidSwap against the memory mode configuration of PMEM, which offers similar functionality as RapidSwap, implemented in hardware at cache-line granularity.

Acknowledgments. We thank our shepherd Carl Waldspurger and the anonymous reviewers for their helpful feedback and guidance. This work was supported by the Korean government (MSIT) through the National Research Foundation by grants 0536-20210093 and 21A20151113068 (BK21 Plus for Pioneers in Innovative Computing - Dept. of Computer Science and Engineering, SNU). ICT at Seoul National University provided research facilities for this study.

References

1. Cooper, B.F., Silberstein, A., Tam, E., Ramakrishnan, R., Sears, R.: Benchmarking cloud serving systems with YCSB. In: Proceedings of the 1st ACM Symposium on Cloud Computing, SoCC 2010, pp. 143–154. Association for Computing Machinery, New York (2010). https://doi.org/10.1145/1807128.1807152
2. Denning, P.J.: Thrashing: its causes and prevention. In: Proceedings of the December 9–11, 1968, Fall Joint Computer Conference, Part I, AFIPS 1968 (Fall, part I), pp. 915–922. Association for Computing Machinery, New York (1968). https://doi.org/10.1145/1476589.1476705
3. Douglis, F.: The compression cache: using on-line compression to extend physical memory. In: USENIX Winter 1993 Conference (USENIX Winter 1993 Conference). USENIX Association, San Diego, January 1993. https://www.usenix.org/conference/usenix-winter-1993-conference/compression-cache-using-line-compression-extend-physical
4. EC2 On-Demand Instance Pricing - Amazon Web Services. https://aws.amazon.com/ko/ec2/pricing/on-demand/
5. Amazon EC2 high memory instance types. https://aws.amazon.com/ec2/instance-types/
6. SAP HANA Planning Guide | Google Cloud. https://cloud.google.com/solutions/sap/docs/sap-hana-planning-guide
7. Harel, S., Radinsky, K.: Accelerating prototype-based drug discovery using conditional diversity networks. In: Proceedings of the 24th ACM SIGKDD International Conference on Knowledge Discovery & Data Mining, KDD 2018, pp. 331–339. Association for Computing Machinery, New York (2018). https://doi.org/10.1145/3219819.3219882
8. Herodotou, H., Kakoulli, E.: Automating distributed tiered storage management in cluster computing. Proc. VLDB Endow. **13**(1), 43–56 (2019). https://doi.org/10.14778/3357377.3357381
9. Why is the Intel Optane persistent memory in memory mode. https://www.intel.com/content/www/us/en/support/articles/000055895/memory-and-storage/intel-optane-persistent-memory.html
10. Intel NMB1XXD128GPSU4 Intel Optane 200 128GB DDR-T Persistent Memory Module. https://www.itosolutions.net/Intel-Optane-200-128GB-DDR-T-Persistent-Memory-p/nmb1xxd128gpsu4.htm

11. Intel Optane SSD 905P Series. https://www.intel.com/content/www/us/en/products/memory-storage/solid-state-drives/consumer-ssds/optane-ssd-9-series/optane-ssd-905p-series.html
12. Intel Optane 905P 1.50 Tb Solid State Drive. https://www.newegg.com/intel-optane-ssd-905p-series-1-5tb/p/0D9-002V-003X1
13. Jo, C., Kim, H., Egger, B.: Instant virtual machine live migration. In: Economics of Grids, Clouds, Systems, and Services, GECON 2020, Springer, Cham (2020). https://doi.org/10.1007/978-3-030-63058-4_14
14. Jo, C., Kim, H., Geng, H., Egger, B.: RackMem: a tailored caching layer for rack scale computing. In: Proceedings of the ACM International Conference on Parallel Architectures and Compilation Techniques, PACT 2020, pp. 467–480. Association for Computing Machinery, New York (2020). https://doi.org/10.1145/3410463.3414643
15. Kilburn, T., Edwards, D.B.G., Lanigan, M.J., Sumner, F.H.: One-level storage system. IRE Trans. Electr. Comput. EC-**11**(2), 223–235 (1962). https://doi.org/10.1109/TEC.1962.5219356
16. Lagar-Cavilla, A., et al.: Software-defined far memory in warehouse-scale computers. In: Proceedings of the Twenty-Fourth International Conference on Architectural Support for Programming Languages and Operating Systems, ASPLOS 2019, pp. 317–330. Association for Computing Machinery, New York (2019). https://doi.org/10.1145/3297858.3304053
17. Lee, Y., Maruf, H.A., Chowdhury, M., Shin, K.G.: Mitigating the performance-efficiency tradeoff in resilient memory disaggregation. CoRR abs/1910.09727 (2019), http://arxiv.org/abs/1910.09727
18. Lin, S.C., et al.: The architectural implications of autonomous driving: constraints and acceleration. In: Proceedings of the Twenty-Third International Conference on Architectural Support for Programming Languages and Operating Systems, ASPLOS 2018, pp. 751–766. Association for Computing Machinery, New York (2018). https://doi.org/10.1145/3173162.3173191
19. Linux Virtual Machines | Microsoft Azure. https://azure.microsoft.com/en-us/pricing/details/virtual-machines/linux/
20. Samsung M386A8K40BM1-CPB 64GB DDR4-2133 4Rx4 LP ECC LRDIMM Server Memory. https://www.amazon.com/Samsung-M386A8K40BM1-CPB-DDR4-2133-LRDIMM-Server/dp/B017A8FJEG
21. Shi, W., et al.: Real-time single image and video super-resolution using an efficient sub-pixel convolutional neural network. In: CVPR, pp. 1874–1883 (2016). https://doi.org/10.1109/CVPR.2016.207
22. Wang, Z., et al.: Craft: an erasure-coding-supported version of raft for reducing storage cost and network cost. In: 18th USENIX Conference on File and Storage Technologies (FAST 2020), pp. 297–308. USENIX Association, Santa Clara, February 2020. https://www.usenix.org/conference/fast20/presentation/wang-zizhong
23. Zaharia, M., Xin, R.S., Wendell, P., Das, T., Armbrust, M., Dave, A., Meng, X., Rosen, J., Venkataraman, S., Franklin, M.J., Ghodsi, A., Gonzalez, J., Shenker, S., Stoica, I.: Apache spark: a unified engine for big data processing. Commun. ACM **59**(11), 56–65 (2016). https://doi.org/10.1145/2934664
24. zswap - The Linux Kernel documentation. https://www.kernel.org/doc/html/latest/vm/zswap.html

Regulation, Compliance

Analyzing the Wehe Network Neutrality Monitoring Tool

Ximun Castoreo[1], Patrick Maillé[2], and Bruno Tuffin[1]

[1] Inria, Univ Rennes, CNRS, IRISA, Rennes, France
ximuncastoreo@disroot.org, bruno.tuffin@inria.fr
[2] IMT Atlantique, IRISA, UMR CNRS 6074, 35700 Rennes, France
patrick.maille@imt.fr

Abstract. Network Neutrality is protected by law in many countries over the world, but monitoring has to be performed to ensure operators conform to the rules. The Wehe application, jointly developed by Northeastern University and the French regulator ARCEP, allows users to take measurements and analyze them to detect possible traffic differentiation.

In this paper, we investigate the playroom left for ISPs to still differentiate traffic, when tested with the Wehe detection tool. Our contributions include the design of a test bed to evaluate the detection capacities of Wehe, and its use to provide some elements of response: By computing the detection probabilities and estimating the potential benefit of a revenue-interested operator, we fine-tune and compare the main differentiation types (throughput, packet loss and delay) that an operator could implement.

Keywords: Network Neutrality · Monitoring tool · Detection evasion

1 Introduction

1.1 Network Neutrality

The Internet is used by a vast and heterogeneous group of users (individuals, companies, governments, associations, etc.) who communicate with each other through inter-connected networks owned by Internet Service Providers (ISPs). These providers own the network architecture and control the way they convey traffic.

The Network Neutrality [17] principle aims to ensure a fair network experience for every user. The pieces of legislation protecting Network Neutrality over the world mostly agree on the following interpretation of that principle: no traffic differentiation based on traffic origin, destination, protocol or service is accepted [6, 10, 14].

The first benefit of Network Neutrality is a wide and complete access to the different public resources of the network, regardless of the user's specifics (geographical and cultural origin, working situation, political beliefs, etc.).

K. Tserpes et al. (Eds.): GECON 2021, LNCS 13072, pp. 155–167, 2021.
https://doi.org/10.1007/978-3-030-92916-9_13

At the same time, innovation can thrive on the network without monopoly or unfair competition, as all online services are equally accessible. Network Neutrality also helps innovation in the networking domain, because it prevents putting forward certain protocols or applications. New protocols can be freely tested and adopted without compatibility issues.

Network Neutrality is seen by its opponents as a pure ISP limitation. Being unable to manage the traffics flowing through their network, ISPs cannot propose *differentiated* offers, apply revenue management for a better return on investment, or make deals with companies for preferential treatment. Moreover, they cannot ensure Quality of Service requirements from demanding types of traffic. Network Neutrality is also limited if protection laws apply in some countries while traffic may transit through other places applying differentiation, hence barring end-to-end equality of treatment [13].

1.2   Measurement Tools

Even if Network Neutrality is enforced by law, ISPs do not always comply with it. Pointed violations [1,5,8] have shown that operators tend to differentiate traffic for commercial reasons. At the other extreme, blocking is sometimes asked by governments for security or political reasons [3,18], or for legal reasons such as for example with peer-to-peer being accused of infringing copyright rules.

Hence there is a need for *tools* to monitor ISPs behavior: such tools are required for regulators, guarantors of the law, to ensure ISPs conform to the enacted rules, but also for end users to evaluate ISPs and possibly switch operator if the current one appears to violate Network Neutrality.

The research community and user associations have created various tools to check Network Neutrality (see [2,9] for a full list). The existing tools differ in various ways: the checked violation, the measured metrics, the interaction they have with the network infrastructure, the measure type, the tool architecture, etc. For example, the POPI tool [12] makes passive measurements, and aggregates measures from different nodes into an inference analysis model to detect packet forwarding prioritisation. This highly differs from Switzerland [4], that uses active measures to check packet integrity between a client and a server.

But as mentioned in [2], the available tools are limited in number and in scope, and are rarely maintained. One standing out is Wehe [15,16], stemming from a joint development between Northeastern University and the French regulator ARCEP. That tool has been highly advertised because of the participation of a regulatory body, and is maintained. We therefore choose to focus on it in this paper.

1.3   Paper Focus: What Room for Differentiation Under Wehe Monitoring?

The main result provided by Wehe is binary, indicating whether differentiation has been detected or not. In this paper, we aim at investigating the sensitivity of that detector, to analyze how reliable its results are, and whether it could still be beneficial for an operator to perform some carefully-designed differentiation, if that differentiation can be monetized. For those reasons, a key step is to determine, through a test bed, how much differentiation can be introduced before being detected by Wehe, for different types of differentiation: throughput limitation, packet loss and packet delay. We are then able to present which differentiation means is the most beneficial for an ISP and if a significant gain can be derived from it.

The remainder of the paper is organized as follows. Section 2 briefly presents the Wehe tool and its main characteristics; Sect. 3 introduces the testing platform we have developed; the experimental results are given and analyzed in Sect. 4; and finally Sect. 5 concludes and suggests directions for future work.

2   Wehe: A Differentiation Detection Tool

Wehe is a Network Neutrality monitoring tool aiming at studying differences in terms of throughput for some traffic sent both "as is" and in a way that the operator cannot identify the flow (the tool assumes non-differentiation in that latter case). It has been presented in 2015 [15] as a joint venture between Northeastern University and the French communication regulator ARCEP. The application targets mobile devices because of known mobile network issues (wide group of users, resource scarcity, network opacity). The interest of Wehe resides in its genericity: it theoretically allows the user to test any traffic (classic traffic, user-customised traffic, encrypted traffic...) even if specific traffic types are targeted in the application to ease usage.

2.1   Wehe Functioning Principles

Wehe is based on active measures between a client and a Wehe server, and works as follows: the tool replays twice a prerecorded traffic between the client (an app installed by the user on their device) and the server (a specific server running the Wehe service). The first replay is identical to the original traffic while the second traffic's payload is modified (by randomizing or encrypting it). In both cases, the replayed traffic has the same shape as the original one: same packet sizes with same IP and TCP/UDP protocol headers (minus the IP addresses) and same inter-packet timings (see replay similarity in [15]), but with an unidentifiable payload in the latter case (through encryption, or just by replacing the application data with random bits).

Therefore, the modified replay traffic cannot be identified by the means of Deep Packet Inspection (DPI), and cannot be differentiated afterwards when assuming that an ISP does DPI-based differentiation (e.g., targeting a specific application like YouTube that is very bandwidth-consuming): only the unmodified replay would suffer differentiation. During replays, the client and the server measure the throughput of each traffic. Then, the throughput distributions are compared using a statistical test inspired by the Kolmogorov-Smirnov test [15]. If the test does not reject the assumption of throughput samples being from the same distribution, Wehe does not raise any warning about a potential non-neutral behavior. Otherwise, Wehe considers that a differentiation occurred on the original traffic and signals it to the user.

More details on how those replays are built and performed are given below.

2.2 Wehe Replay

Wehe records an original traffic that has been conveyed through the network. It is separated in two traces: the client trace and the server trace. These two represent the packets each side has to send to simulate the original traffic. To keep the simulation accurate, the Wehe designers have added two constrains to packet transmission: a packet cannot be sent before the prior one was received (happen-before dependency), and it also waits the duration given in the original transmission (time dependency). This way, a replay's shape is identical to the original's shape.

The actual replays are initiated by the client application: it connects to the server, specifies the traffic it is going to replay and waits the server to be ready. Then they start transmitting their trace for each replay (original and randomized), respecting the dependencies. Wehe measures the throughput of the two replayed traffics. Each side of the replay periodically measures the sent and received data amount. When the replays finish, the client asks the server for analysis.

2.3 A Detection "Grey Zone"

Wehe is conservative: after a few iterations of such indecisive analysis, Wehe declares that no differentiation was found. This reduces false positive results which might result in legal complaints from ISPs, an important component from regulators point of view. But it also increases the possibilities for an operator to fool the tool, highlighting the relevance of the present work.

3 Building a Test Bed to Evaluate Wehe

To analyze the performance of the Wehe tool, we designed a simple test bed, with a controlled environment, to perform different kinds of ISP traffic differentiation and investigate whether Wehe detects them.

3.1 Test Bed Setup

The test bed's simple topology is composed of three parts: the client side, the server side and the core network part. The client and server sides are two devices where Wehe applications are installed. We use the proof-of-concept code available from https://github.com/NEU-SNS/wehe-server.

The core network part, meaning the existing ISP networks between a client and a Wehe server, is emulated by a single device running a Linux Traffic Control utility with a netem queueing discipline [7] for classifying and differentiating traffic. We call this device the test bed middlebox. Modeling the whole network between source and destination with a unique device is common practice and sufficient since the Wehe tool only makes end-point measurements. With this setting, the network is represented by a single node, as often done in many models in the literature. While it is a simplified network emulation, we believe that it helps to capture the main differentiation features that can be implemented in a network, and to point out that there is a notable variability in service limitation thresholds before detection depending the differentiation type.

The tc-netem queueing discipline allows to control the throughput, the packet loss rate and the delay applied to classified packets. This way, we are able to choose between general but precise traffic deterioration (with throughput) or more random performance loss (using a packet loss rate, losses being then decided independently for each packet).

Figure 1 summarizes the test bed and the important parts of a Wehe test. The packet classifier is started on the middlebox. Then the two replays are run through the test bed. When the classifier identifies the unmodified replay (because its data correspond to the original traffic's data), it applies the differentiation. At the end of the Wehe run, the values of throughput calculated during the transmissions are sent back to the server for analysis.

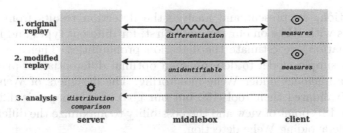

Fig. 1. The three parts of the Test bed *(horizontally)* and the steps of a Wehe run *(vertically)*. What is "replayed" are packet exchanges recorded beforehand.

To differentiate a traffic, it must be identified beforehand. To do so, we use a keyword present in the targeted traffic. When the keyword is found by the middlebox, the differentiation is triggered for every packet of the corresponding flow (a flow is defined by the IP addresses and port numbers).

3.2 Traffic and Differentiation in the Experiments

Our experiments are carried out for the traffic corresponding to a **file transfer**, a basic but essential traffic type that for example corresponds to a web page request, and represents a significant part of the Internet traffic. That traffic is captured and saved beforehand, to be replayed during the tests. The file transfer is a simple web page retrieval of a random 1 GB file (here, an HTTP GET request).

We implemented several types and levels of differentiation (described below). Repeated independent experiments allowed us to plot the detection probability in terms of the differentiation parameter value, together with a confidence interval. The differentiation can take three different forms, whether it affects the transmission throughput, the packet loss rate, or the packet delay. Those three types of differentiation are supported by tc-netem:

i) **Throughput limitation** (called traffic shaping) delays packets when the measured throughput of the transmission exceeds a certain value. If too many packets are delayed and the waiting queue fills up, the following packets are dropped.

ii) **Packet loss rate** differentiation applies an independent drop probability to each transmitted packet. Random packet losses can happen in a physical network, but we here simulate a deliberate loss applied by the network operator.

iii) **Packet delay** retains all the transmitted packets for a predefined amount of time. Delay can be observed when congestion hits the network, but in the same way as for packet losses, we emulate an intentional behavior that affects all the classified packets.

4   Experimental Results and Analysis

In this section, we present and analyze the detection results from extensive experiments with Wehe on our test bed. First, for different types and intensities of differentiation, we estimate the detection probabilities. Then we use those results in a simple model to determine an optimal differentiation plan that an ISP could implement under Wehe monitoring. The designers of Wehe already tested and validated their tool [15], but our goal in this paper is different: we focus on the ISP point of view and the possibility to maximize the differentiation impact while avoiding Wehe detection.

4.1   Raw Results: Wehe Detection Probabilities

The detection accuracy is the key to further investigate how an ISP could still differentiate under Wehe monitoring. As the Wehe statistic decision model is based on the client-side calculated throughput that can be slightly different on each test, we run numerous tests for each setting and estimate the detection probability of the tool. These probabilities will then be used later to build a ISP differentiation benefit model.

To detect the parameter ranges where (non-)detection is not systematic, we first ran tests for a broad range of differentiation parameter values, and then we focused on shorter differentiation value intervals experiencing more variability in terms of detection. We present here the results on these shorter intervals for the three differentiation types. In each case, the results given are for a sample of size 150, a number large enough to get a reasonable estimation of the probability detection (with, in the worst cases, a precision of 0.1 at confidence level 99%).

The graphs in Fig. 2 respectively display the Wehe differentiation detection probabilities versus the traffic throughput reduction, packet loss rate, and delay, for a file transfer traffic. We also run our experiment for another traffic type, namely video streaming, for which results are given in Fig. 3.

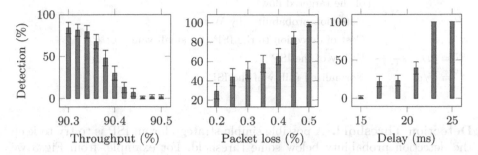

Fig. 2. Wehe detection probability estimations in the case of file transfer for three types of differentiation, with 95% confidence intervals.

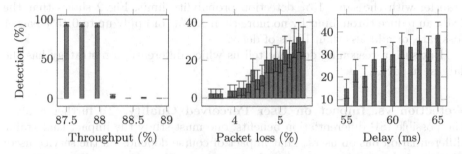

Fig. 3. Wehe detection probability estimations in the case of video streaming for three types of differentiation, with 95% confidence intervals.

The figures illustrate the expected tendency that as more differentiation is applied, the detection probability increases.

4.2 Differentiating While Monitored by Wehe: An Economic Model

Given the detection probability measurements obtained in the previous subsection, we now focus on whether traffic differentiation can significantly impact traffic and therefore users, while being only rarely detected. Taking the ISP point of view, that would indicate what level(s) of differentiation can be implemented, and how valuable it would be. That value might originate from freeing network resources, or from slowing down traffic for commercial purposes.

To that end, we propose a simple model to built a reasonable objective function for the ISP, encompassing both the detection probability and the gains from differentiating traffic. The variables we will use in that model are summarized in Table 1.

Table 1. Notations used in the economic model.

Notation	Interpretation
D	Quality degradation due to differentiation
g	Marginal gain from quality degradation (e.g., from competitors of the targeted flow)
P_d	Detection probability (by Wehe)
s	Cost of detection to the ISP (for small values of P_d)
$U = gD - s\frac{P_d}{1-P_d}$	Utility of the ISP
$\tilde{U} = U/g$	Normalized utility of the ISP

Detection Threshold. A possible simple strategy for an ISP is to try to keep the detection probability below some threshold. For example, from Fig. 3 we deduce that to deteriorate video streaming traffic with a detection probability no larger than 15%, the ISP can reduce throughput by no more than 12%, or apply up to 4.6% packet loss rate, or add less than 55 ms of delay. For file transfer with the same 15% detection probability limit, Fig. 2 shows that the ISP can reduce throughput by no more than 8.58%, or apply up to 0.15% packet loss rate, or add less than 16 ms of delay.

But such a reasoning does not tell us which differentiation strategy has the largest impact.

Detection vs. Impact on User Perceived Quality. To further analyze the possible ISP differentiation benefits, one must study the impact that traffic differentiation has on users. That impact of course depends on the service used: file transfer and video streaming, for example, will not be equally sensitive to differentiation from a user point of view.

In the rest of this section, we focus on file transfers, for which an appropriate and simple quality metric can be provided: the total transfer time. More specifically, we will consider as the degradation metric the **relative transfer time increase**, which we will denote by D, when differentiating traffic: if differentiation leads to a total expected transfer time T_d instead of T_n, then our degradation metric D is

$$D := \frac{T_d - T_n}{T_n}. \tag{1}$$

In our experiments, that degradation is estimated for the transfer of a 1 GB file. Figure 4 shows the impact of the three types of differentiation on the transfer time ratio, in the parameter intervals that were previously identified as "interesting" (with low but non-zero detection probabilities).

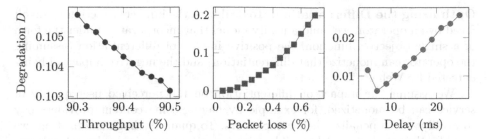

Fig. 4. Impact of the three types of differentiation on the degradation level D (relative increase of transfer time of a 1 GB file).

Since the trade-off faced by an ISP willing to monetize differentiation would be between the degradation and the detection probability, we display those two values on a common graph for all types of differentiation, combining the results from Figs. 2 and 4, in Fig. 5.

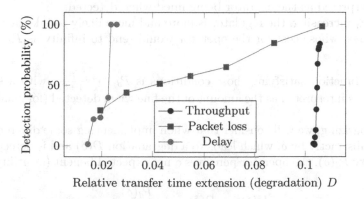

Fig. 5. Detection probability as a function of differentiation impact (relative transfer time extension) for each type of differentiation, varying its intensity.

The figure highlights the differences between the three types of differentiation: directly degrading the throughput allows an ISP to extend the transfer time by nearly 10% without being detected by Wehe, while by affecting packet losses or delay, the detection probability is significant before reaching such an impact on the transfer time. Among the three types, playing on delay appears to be the least effective, as the detection probability increases very fast with the degradation: with only about 2% degradation the differentiation is detected. Playing with packet losses leads to a smoother curve, but again, with only 2% degradation the detection probability already exceeds 25%.

Optimizing the Differentiation. To deal with the impact-detection trade-off faced by an operator, we build a utility model that incorporates, under the form of a single objective function, the positive impact of differentiation (assuming the operator can monetize that differentiation) and the negative impact of being detected by Wehe.

We assume the impact of differentiation on the perceived user quality of service can be monetized, for example by having some content providers pay to avoid it or to penalize their competitors. To quantify that monetization, we consider the simplest model possible, with a constant marginal value g for degradation, i.e., the differentiation can yield the operator some gain gD, with D the degradation level (given in (1) for the case of file transfer).

On the other hand, being detected is bad for the operator, at this may come with a fine to pay, a loss of reputation, or even possibly an interdiction to further operate. To represent this variety of interpretations, we consider a cost function that will depend on the probability to be detected, which we will denote by P_d, and such that:

- for low values of P_d, the cost is (approximately) proportional to P_d, and can be interpreted as the operator being fined when detected;
- with P_d increasing, the regulator is more and more likely to take more severe measures, whose cost for the operator would tend to infinity as P_d tends to one.

A simple function satisfying those conditions is $P_d \mapsto s\frac{P_d}{1-P_d}$, with a sanction parameter s interpreted as the amount of the fine when detected (for small values of P_d).

Summarizing, we will consider that when implementing some differentiation, denoted abstractly by δ, which leads to a degradation $D(\delta)$ and is detected with probability $P_d(\delta)$, the operator perceives a net expected benefit (or utility) $U(\delta)$, equal to

$$U(\delta) = gD(\delta) - s\frac{P_d(\delta)}{1 - P_d(\delta)}. \tag{2}$$

Note that finding a utility-maximizing differentiation δ to implement depends only on the ratio s/g, so we will focus on the quantity

$$\tilde{U}(\delta) = D(\delta) - \frac{s}{g}\frac{P_d(\delta)}{1 - P_d(\delta)}. \tag{3}$$

Using our detection and degradation measures in the case of file transfers, we plot in Fig. 6 the values of $\tilde{U}$ for each type and intensity of differentiation, with different values of the ratio $\frac{s}{g}$.

This illustrates how a utility-maximizing ISP may reason to manage the differentiation/detection trade-off, once the ratio s/g is known:

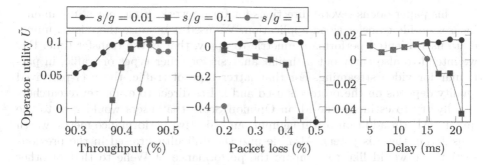

Fig. 6. ISP utility function $\tilde{U}$ when differentiating for file transfers.

- First, for a given differentiation type, the formulation (3) can be used to find the optimal differentiation level. For example, if $s/g = 0.01$, then
  - when playing on throughput the optimal reduction is around 90.45%;
  - if differentiation is through packet losses, the optimal loss rate to introduce is 0.4%
  - if instead differentiation means delaying packets, the optimal delay to add is 19 ms.
- Second, once each differentiation type is optimized, the analysis helps to compare them decide which one maximizes the overall utility $\tilde{U}$ in (3). Here, again for $s/g = 0.01$, playing on throughput can yield a value of $\tilde{U}$ above 0.1, while with packet losses or delay $\tilde{U}$ remains below 0.06 and 0.017, respectively. Hence for the specific case of file transfers, it seems that affecting the throughput is the most effective.

5   Conclusions

In this paper, we have analyzed the traffic differentiation detection tool Wehe, that is recommended by some regulators to detect net neutrality violations. To do so, we have designed a test bed that allows us to run Wehe in a controlled environment, where three types of differentiation are implemented (transmission throughput, packet loss rate and packet delay). For each differentiation type, we have carried out intensive simulations of the detection tool, to estimate the Wehe detection probabilities and indicate thresholds over which differentiation is significantly pointed out.

For the case of file transfers, we have quantified the impact that the differentiation types have on the total transfer time, a natural metric users are sensitive to. This has enabled us to build a model, assuming operators can monetize that differentiation, where an operator weighs that possible gain with the risk associated to detection. A utility function taking into account those two aspects can be used to manage the trade-off, determining the optimal type and level of differentiation to implement. Such a reasoning can for example help regulators set the sensitivity of their monitoring tools.

This paper opens several directions for future work. First, our study mainly focuses on file transfer as an application. We used it because there is an immediate user-oriented performance metric to apply, that is the transfer time. But we intend to also carry out a similar analysis for other types of traffic, in particular for video streaming. For that latter type of traffic, the user-perceived quality depends on the protocols used and is less direct to evaluate: researchers usually try to estimate the Mean Opinion Score that users would give to the quality [11] (in addition to throughput, an objective performance metric worth considering there is jitter). Also, despite the difficulties raised in the previous section, we would like to compare the performance of Wehe to that of other differentiation-detecting tools.

Finally, we are aware that our use of a network emulator in a single machine (the middlebox) constitutes a simplification with respect to the complex topologies (and types of other traffic using the same links) that can be found on the Internet. This is likely to impact what differentiation can look like (e.g., the distribution of the losses) and thus the detection probability, probably leaving ISPs more space to play with before being detected. As a consequence, our work here could be seen as upper-bounding the detection probability, and re-creating more specific topologies could help refine our estimations.

References

1. AirFrance: AirFrance Connect WiFi on Board. https://www.airfrance.fr/FR/en/common/transverse/footer/wifi-a-bord.htm. Accessed 23 Oct 2020
2. Castoreo, X., Maillé, P., Tuffin, B.: Weaknesses and challenges of network neutrality measurement tools. In: Proceedings of the 16th IEEE International Conference on Network and Service Management (CNSM). Virtual Conference, April 2020. https://hal.inria.fr/hal-02542689
3. Clayton, R., Murdoch, S.J., Watson, R.N.M.: Ignoring the great firewall of China. In: Danezis, G., Golle, P. (eds.) PET 2006. LNCS, vol. 4258, pp. 20–35. Springer, Heidelberg (2006). https://doi.org/10.1007/11957454_2
4. Eckersley, P.: Switzerland Design, May 2008. https://www.eff.org/files/2018/06/21/design.pdf. Accessed 23 Oct 2020
5. Electronic Frontier Foundation: Packet Forgery by ISPs: A Report on the Comcast Affair. https://www.eff.org/wp/packet-forgery-isps-report-comcast-affair. Accessed 23 Oct 2020
6. European Parliament & Council: Regulation (EU) 2015/2120 of the European Parliament and of the Council, November 2015. https://eur-lex.europa.eu/legal-content/EN/TXT/?uri=CELEX%3A32015R2120. Accessed 23 Oct 2020
7. The Linux Foundation: netem. https://wiki.linuxfoundation.org/networking/netem. Accessed 23 Oct 2020
8. Gannes, L.: AT&T Changes TOS to Limit Mobile Video. https://gigaom.com/2009/04/02/att-changes-tos-to-limit-mobile-video/. Accessed 23 Oct 2020
9. Garrett, T., Setenareski, L.E., Peres, L.M., Bona, L.C.E., Duarte, E.P.: Monitoring network neutrality: a survey on traffic differentiation detection. IEEE Commun. Surv. Tutor. **20**(3), 2486–2517 (2018). https://doi.org/10.1109/COMST.2018.2812641

10. Indian Department of Telecommunications: National Digital Communications (2018). https://dot.gov.in/sites/default/files/Final%20NDCP-20180.pdf. Accessed 23 Oct 2020

11. Khokhar, M., Ehlinger, T., Barakat, C.: From network traffic measurements to QoE for internet video. In: Proceedings of IFIP Networking, Warsaw, Poland (2019)

12. Lu, G., Chen, Y., Birrer, S., Bustamante, F.E., Li, X.: POPI: a user-level tool for inferring router packet forwarding priority. IEEE/ACM Trans. Netw. **18**(1), 1–14 (2010)

13. Maillé, P., Tuffin, B.: Neutral and non-neutral countries in a global internet: what does it imply? In: Djemame, K., Altmann, J., Bañares, J.Á., Agmon Ben-Yehuda, O., Naldi, M. (eds.) GECON 2019. LNCS, vol. 11819, pp. 111–123. Springer, Cham (2019). https://doi.org/10.1007/978-3-030-36027-6_10

14. Ministerio de Transportes y Telecomunicaciones de Chile: Subsecretara de Telecomunicaciones: Ley 20.453: consagra el principio de neutralidad en la red para los consumidores y usuarios de Internet, August 2010. https://www.leychile.cl/Navegar?idNorma=1016570. Accessed 23 Oct 2020

15. Molavi Kakhki, A., et al.: Identifying traffic differentiation in mobile networks. In: Proceedings of the 2015 Internet Measurement Conference, IMC 2015, pp. 239–251. Association for Computing Machinery, New York (2015). https://doi.org/10.1145/2815675.2815691

16. Northeastern University: wehe-server. https://github.com/NEU-SNS/wehe-server. Accessed 23 Oct 2020

17. Wu, T.: Network Neutrality FAQ. http://www.timwu.org/network_neutrality.html. Accessed 23 Oct 2020

18. Xynou, M., Filastò, A.: Togo: Instant messaging apps blocked amid 2020 presidential election. https://ooni.org/post/2020-togo-blocks-instant-messaging-apps/. Accessed 23 Oct 2020

Towards Software Compliance Specification and Enforcement Using TOSCA

Mohammed Mubarkoot$^{(\boxtimes)}$ (iD) and Jörn Altmann$^{(\boxtimes)}$ (iD)

Seoul National University, 1, Gwanak-ro, Gwanak-gu, Seoul 08826, Korea
mubarkoot@snu.ac.kr, jorn.altmann@acm.org

Abstract. According to the laws of software evolution, the size and complexity of software systems continue to increase over time and, simultaneously, if not maintained rigorously, the quality decreases. Quality degradation typically happens due to changes in policies, regulations, and industry requirements, which, in turn, complicates compliance management over time. Among the key challenges in managing the evolution of software are the modelling and the enforcement of compliance rules. Moreover, the gap between compliance experts and software engineers has worsened the problem. The topology and orchestration specifications for cloud applications (TOSCA), which is an OASIS standard, has the potential to offer a relief by enabling different levels of abstractions for modeling and enforcing compliance policies. This work aims at investigating the potential of using TOSCA service templates for modelling and enforcing non-functional requirements and policies. Then, it proposes an approach that maximizes involvement of stakeholders in modeling and auditing such requirements and policies. Findings can help enterprises and policy makers achieve better governance and compliance on software services.

Keywords: Software compliance · Non-functional requirements · Software evolution · Stakeholders' involvement · TOSCA blueprint

1 Introduction

Compliance management is one of the critical challenges in all stages of the software development life cycle (SDLC). In particular, the E-type software evolves over time as a response to real world changes. This continuous change increases the complexity and, as a result, leads to a degradation in quality if not maintained well [1]. In addition to that, the continuous changes of policies and industry-specific requirements further complicates governance and compliance management of a software. Lehman's laws of software evolution, namely continuing change and growth, increasing complexity, declining quality and feedback system, still apply and cannot be ignored [1]. Therefore, such continuous changes make it difficult to track whether the overall changes made in the software adhere to corporate policies and compliance requirements; and more importantly, getting insights on the status of policy modeling and enforcement at different levels of abstraction for different stakeholders.

© The Author(s) 2021
K. Tserpes et al. (Eds.): GECON 2021, LNCS 13072, pp. 168–177, 2021.
https://doi.org/10.1007/978-3-030-92916-9_14

The recent decades experienced a huge change in the software industry in areas of distributing development, crowdsourcing, service-oriented approaches, and microservice practices [23]. This change is also powered by a big shift to cloud computing, which leads to more standardized software services [2]. The laws that govern software evolution do not seem to have adapted to the new paradigm shifts [1].

In this regard, many cloud modeling languages were introduced to address issues related to modeling and specification of cloud applications. Bergmayr et al. [1] conducted a systematic review on existing cloud modeling languages. They found that the majority of the existing modeling languages focus primarily on design-time aspects and very few consider the provisioning and runtime aspects. The topology and orchestration specifications for cloud applications (TOSCA) can contribute to the convergence of different cloud modeling languages, besides its abilities to describe processes for creating, terminating cloud services and for managing them throughout their whole lifetime [3]. According to the Organization for the Advancement of Structured Information Standards (OASIS) [3], TOSCA provides strong typing for artifacts in addition to the ability to extend to new types without extending the language definition [4]. Compared to other modeling languages, TOSCA supports the decomposition of software and definition of policies and non-functional behavior of a system [4]. It also implements management plans using existing workflow languages, namely the business process model and notation (BPMN) and the business process execution language (BPEL) [5]. This makes it promising for modeling non-functional requirements and enhancing evolution management of a software.

The aim of this paper is to explore how TOSCA enhances evolution management of software as well as address compliance modeling of non-functional requirements. The paper proposes an approach that maximizes involvement of stakeholders in setting up and monitoring TOSCA-based blueprints. A key contribution of the paper is that it brings the focus of a new application of TOSCA in compliance modeling, and how to utilize that within the entire ecosystem of software development and provisioning.

The subsequent sections are structured as follows: Sect. 2 presents a background on non-functional requirements and TOSCA as well as related work. Section 3 introduces the proposed approach and explains with an example on how TOSCA handles modeling of non-functional requirements, and how it fits into our approach. Finally, Sect. 4 summarizes and explains validation of the proposed approach.

2 Background and Related Work

2.1 Non-functional Requirements

E-Type software, which automates human or societal activities and involves real world problem solving [6], must change and continuously adapt to real world requirements [1]. While this evolution is regulated by a feedback system, it typically results in an increase in complexity and decline in quality driven by the need to maintain familiarity [7]. The challenge comes with the objective of controlling the continuous evolution in a systematic way. One solution is to adopt model-driven engineering (MDE), since it allows abstraction of unnecessary details, and to focus on more important aspects (e.g., domain-specific needs) [8]. Another way is to use modeling languages to standardize software design and improve the management of software evolution [4]. In all this, it is critical to differentiate between functional and non-functional requirements, as they require different tools and skills for modeling let alone the resources needed.

While there is no formal definition or a complete list of non-functional requirements [9], Glinz [9] surveyed existing literature on the definition, classification and representation of non-functional requirements. Their study presents a taxonomy to define non-functional requirements of three categories: performance requirements, specific quality requirements, and constraints. Performance requirements include timing, speed, volume and throughput. Specific quality requirements include reliability, usability, security, availability, portability, and maintainability. Constraints include physical, legal, cultural, environmental, design, implementation, and interface. The international organization for standardization (ISO) [10] however categorizes software quality requirements into eight categories. It does not classify them into functional and non-functional due to overlaps in some requirements. These requirements are functional suitability, reliability, performance efficiency, usability, security, compatibility, maintainability, and portability. ISO also defined sub-characteristics for each of these requirements. As we focus mainly on non-functional requirements, functional suitability and usability, which are more related to functional requirements of a system are excluded from our discussion.

Among non-functional aspects, which can be modeled using TOSCA, are: (i) enhancement of reliability through scalability thresholds that ensure availability and allow re-instantiating failed components [10, 11]; (ii) improvement of performance and resource utilization [11]; (iii) support of security-by-design (e.g., enforcement of certain encryption mechanisms and access policies) [12]; (iv) increase of compatibility and standardized blueprints [13]; (v) enhancement of maintainability through modularity, reusability, and analyzability of an application [2, 14]; and (vi) ensuring portability and provider-agnostic deployment [12, 15].

2.2 Related Work on Modeling Non-functional Requirements with TOSCA

Many studies in the literature discuss applications of TOSCA in modeling of policies and non-functional requirements. Waizenegger et al. [16] introduced two approaches to model and enforce policies, and provide different levels of abstraction depending on the level of details needed. Built on TOSCA policies and management plans, these approaches focus on providing global knowledge of services as well as enforcement at a component level. They also highlight the importance of reusability of artifacts to minimize the efforts of modeling and provide a wider range of options to customers.

Koetter et al. [17] introduced a Generic Compliance Descriptor, to address the gap between IT and law, linking IT and law to implementation rules that facilitate responses to changes. To do so, they used different technologies at different application life cycles. For example, they collect compliance rules during the design time and link them to the compliance requirements for enforcement during run-time. They used the TOSCA Policy template for modeling security aspects, to ensure that their database and its underlying system is located within the same country. Similarly, and in the context of third-party deployment models, Zimmermann et al. [18] proposed an approach that uses TOSCA, to enforce third-party deployment models to be executed within a company's network. As enforcement of this kind of security policy is critical, third-party applications have to be enforced to be executed within a company's network, ensuring that vital information does not leave the company [18]. In a slightly wider perspective, Krieger et al. [19] use TOSCA, to automate compliance checking of deployment models with the aim of addressing the issues of changing rules and regulations at the corporate level. Their approach allows separating modeling of compliance rules from modelling of deployment models, so that modelers do not need to know all constraints and requirements to specify compliant deployment models.

Motivated by the growing trend of home-based healthcare, which poses challenges in data collection, transferring, and sharing due to geographical distance between the patients and their care providers, Li et al. [20] apply TOSCA for heterogeneous home-edge-core clouds. They intend to bridge the gap between the availability of software defined infrastructure and meeting regulatory compliance. In the same context, Carrasco et al. [21] introduced a provider-agnostic TOSCA-based model, to allow specification of characteristics and requirements of any system for deployment in the cloud. Besides facilitating the reusability of cloud services, such standardized description of applications, cloud resources, and service APIs can significantly reduce the issues of portability, interoperability, and vendor lock-in.

Despite these works on modeling non-functional aspects of software, exploitation of TOSCA is still under-represented [4]. In addition to that, the extent to which TOSCA can enhance the evolution management of software, is not fully explored.

3 Proposed Approach

3.1 Background on the Workings of TOSCA

While the main purpose of TOSCA is to enhance automation of deployment and management of cloud applications, its functionality can be extended to include modeling and specification of policies, architectural specification of a software service, topology design, service template design, and other non-functional requirements [14]. A TOSCA topology template defines the structure of an application and the orchestration artifacts. While the structure defines application components and the relationships between them, the orchestration artifacts define the deployment and management plans of the application components [16]. Figure 1 shows a topology template for a web application based on OpenTOSCA[1]. The topology describes the components of the application and relationships between them. DjWebApp connects to the DjDB database and depends on Python APIs. The template states that DjWebApp should be hosted on a NGINX server running in a Docker container. DjDB is of type MySQL 5.5 and should be hosted on a separate container. All containers run on a Docker engine hosted on a Linux server of type Ubuntu 18.04. The numbers on each node specify a minimum and maximum number of instances to be created. For example, the AppContainer node can scale up to 10 instances, when the load on the application reaches its peak, and can scale down to 1 instance, if resources are no longer needed. While this description of the topology is at a high level and abstract, detailed specifications of each node and relationship are further elaborated and modeled at a lower level.

[1] https://www.opentosca.org.

A detailed specification of each node and relationship is elaborated using a TOSCA document definition. Such specifications include policies and constraints to be enforced at node and relationship levels. While the TOSCA definition document contains type definitions of Node Types, Relationship Types, Artifact Types, and Policy Types, a TOSCA topology template contains instances of these definitions with assigned values, ready for execution by a TOSCA-compliant orchestrator.

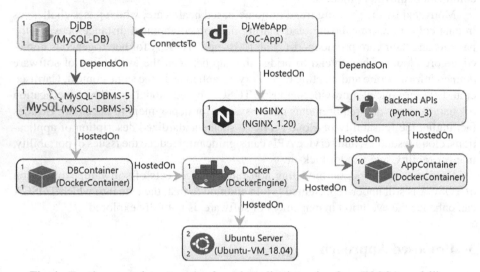

Fig. 1. Topology template example of a web application using OpenTOSCA modelling.

According to OASIS [3], TOSCA can be extended to new types, relationships, policies, and management plans. This allows extensibility of orchestrators' functionality to process these new definitions. The snippet in Fig. 2 shows the syntax of nodes and policy templates in a YAML format. Policy templates define policies and actions to trigger in case of any violation, which in turn enhances the overall reliability and performance. In general, the TOSCA template can serve as a reference architecture with different levels of abstraction. In addition to that, the decomposition of an application into small units along with clear relationships allows for an enhanced evolution management of a software.

3.2 Proposed Architecture for Handling Non-functional Requirements

Software related policies and constraints are mostly the concern of more than one stakeholder [22], who are in charge of different aspects of compliance. The different levels of abstraction that TOSCA provides [14] makes it possible to engage stakeholders of different levels of expertise in the design of software blueprints. The level of abstractions depends on stakeholders' roles and expertise. Preparing a TOSCA blueprint involves stakeholders like IT managers, compliance experts, and software architects. The approach that is presented in Fig. 3 aims at enhancing the evolution management of a software, while controlling compliance to the agreed upon blueprint. The first step is the

```
my_company.my_types.DjWebApp:
    derived_from: tosca.nodes.SoftwareComponent
    properties:
      my_app_password:
        type: string
        constraints:
          - min_length: 6
          - max_length: 10
    attributes:
      web_app_port:
        type: integer
        default: 80, 443
    requirements:
      - Database:
        capability: EndPoint.Database
        node: DjDB
        relationship: ConnectsTo
```

```
my_company_placement_policy:
    type: tosca.policies.Placement.Geolocation
    description: geographic placement of nodes
    properties:
      region: region_endpoint

my_company_scaling_policy:
    type: tosca.policies.scaling
    description: node autoscaling policy
    properties:
      min_instances: 1
      max_instances: 10
      default_instances: 2
    targets: DjWebApp
```

Fig. 2. Example of TOSCA custom definitions of non-functional requirement on the right; and policy definition on the left, based on [3].

development of a TOSCA-based blueprint. This step requires the concerned stakeholders to specify the new policies to model or revise an existing one. The deliverable of this step is a new TOSCA-based blueprint or an updated version. In the second step, the blueprint is stored into the Blueprint Repository, making it available for the development and operations (DevOps) teams to proceed based on that. The DevOps teams are granted only read access on the blueprint so that any fundamental changes at the topology and policy levels have to be reviewed by all stakeholders before deploying them onto production. The third step is to match the active blueprint with the one running in the provisioning. This involves enforcing and auditing the blueprint, and reporting to stakeholders whenever they inquire. Such a task can be performed by extending the functionality of TOSCA-compatible orchestrators (e.g., Kubernetes, which is one of the promising technologies for automating deployment, scaling, and management of applications).

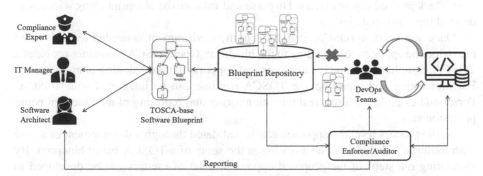

Fig. 3. Proposed architecture for handling compliance of non-functional requirements.

The Blueprint Repository and the Compliance Enforcer/Auditor (Fig. 3) are key components in the proposed approach. The Blueprint Repository stores and keeps track of changes of software blueprints over time through versioning the releases. This enhances reusability of blueprints and simplifies management of the growing complexity of a software. The Compliance Enforcer/Auditor validates and enforces the assigned blueprint during provisioning. It matches components deployed against the predefined blueprint. If any mismatches are found, the orchestrator stops application provisioning and reports the mismatch right away. As a result, the low-level teams cannot modify the architectural level of the software during the development and provisioning. Changes that require modification on the blueprint topology cannot take place unless a consensus is made among stakeholders on updating the blueprint and, then, pushing it into the repository to be available for enforcement at the production. To keep stakeholders informed, reporting is triggered on the following scenarios: (i) once a new release of the software is made available for production; (ii) upon stakeholders' inquiry on status of the deployed services and how well they align to the blueprint; or (iii) on a regular basis for the purpose of auditing and monitoring depending on corporate policy.

Practically, to keep up with the ever-growing business requirements, the continuing changes and the complexity of an E-type software poses a need for a new way of controlling the evolution and non-functional requirements. While most existing modeling languages focus mainly on functional aspects and the behavior of a software, the proposed approach helps address the non-functional aspects, giving a better visibility of the architectural topology of a software to stakeholders with different levels of abstraction. Distributed software development is a potential application of the proposed approach.

4 Conclusion and Future Work

4.1 Future Validation of the Proposed Approach

The approach proposed needs to be evaluated at technical and process levels. At the technical level, Eclipse Winery[2] or any other TOSCA modeling tool can be used to design a TOSCA-based blueprint and model the non-functional requirements.

Once the blueprint is ready, it has to be validated. TOSCA-Parser[3], which is an OpenStack project, can be extended to parse and validate the blueprint along with newly defined types and policies.

Once validated, a TOSCA-conform runtime environment is needed to deploy and provision the application according to the blueprint. OpenTOSCA Container provides a TOSCA-compliant runtime environment and supports the provisioning of applications. For monitoring and reporting, the TOSCA runtime can be integrated with TOSCA-Parser and extended to allow real time monitoring and reporting of the blueprint being provisioned.

At the process level the approach can be validated through a development of a case with multiple stakeholders collaborating in the setup of a TOSCA-based blueprint. By simulating the steps of the proposed approach, a set of metrics can be developed to evaluate its effectiveness and identify possible improvements.

---

[2] https://winery.readthedocs.io/en/latest.
[3] https://wiki.openstack.org/wiki/TOSCA-Parser.

4.2 Summary

In this paper, we explored the potential of using the TOSCA standard for modeling non-functional requirements. In particular, we described its potential for compliance specification and enforcement. We also proposed an approach that maximizes involvement of stakeholders in setting up compliance specifications of non-functional requirements in the form of a TOSCA-based blueprint. This blueprint can then be used by DevOps teams as a base and a reference architecture through all stages of the software development life cycle (SDLC). It can also serve as a compliance checking and reporting while provisioning. Moreover, keeping track of changes in topologies over time is expected to give more control over the evolution process of the software. The approach can be useful for managing software projects, which change and grow at a high rate. Examples are cloud native applications, whether on-premise cloud or on clouds.

Besides validating the proposed framework at technical and process levels, as described above, it is planned to extend the application of TOSCA to modeling and specification of other requirements including regulations and industry-specific ones.

Acknowledgements. This research was supported by the BK21 FOUR (Fostering Outstanding Universities for Research) funded by the Ministry of Education (MOE, Korea). This work was also supported by the National Research Foundation of Korea (NRF) grant (No. NRF-2019R1F1A1058487) funded by the Ministry of Science and ICT (MSIT) of Korea.

References

1. Herraiz, I., Rodriguez, D., Robles, G., Gonzalez-Barahona, J.M.: The evolution of the laws of software evolution: a discussion based on a systematic literature review. ACM Comput. Surv. **46**(2), 28:1–28:28 (2013). https://doi.org/10.1145/2543581.2543595
2. Nieuwenhuis, L.J.M., Ehrenhard, M.L., Prause, L.: The shift to Cloud Computing: the impact of disruptive technology on the enterprise software business ecosystem. Technol. Forecast. Soc. Chang. **129**, 308–313 (2018). https://doi.org/10.1016/j.techfore.2017.09.037
3. "TOSCA Version 2.0." OASIS (2020). https://docs.oasis-open.org/tosca/TOSCA/v2.0/TOSCA-v2.0.pdf. Accessed 07 May 2021
4. Bergmayr, A., et al.: A systematic review of cloud modeling languages. ACM Comput. Surv. **51**(1), 22:1–22:38 (2018). https://doi.org/10.1145/3150227
5. Bellendorf, J., Mann, Z.Á.: Specification of cloud topologies and orchestration using TOSCA: a survey. Computing **102**(8), 1793–1815 (2019). https://doi.org/10.1007/s00607-019-00750-3
6. Lehman, M.M.: Programs, life cycles, and laws of software evolution. Proc. IEEE **68**(9), 1060–1076 (1980)
7. Lehman, M.M., Ramil, J.F.: Software evolution and software evolution processes. Ann. Softw. Eng. **14**(1), 275–309 (2002). https://doi.org/10.1023/A:1020557525901
8. Liebel, G., Marko, N., Tichy, M., Leitner, A., Hansson, J.: Model-based engineering in the embedded systems domain: an industrial survey on the state-of-practice. Softw. Syst. Model. **17**(1), 91–113 (2016). https://doi.org/10.1007/s10270-016-0523-3
9. Glinz, M.: On non-functional requirements. In: 15th IEEE International Requirements Engineering Conference (RE 2007), pp. 21–26, October 2007. https://doi.org/10.1109/RE.2007.45

10. ISO/IEC 25010:2011(en): Systems and software engineering — Systems and software Quality Requirements and Evaluation (SQuaRE) — System and software quality models. https://www.iso.org/obp/ui/#iso:std:iso-iec:25010:ed-1:v1:en. Accessed 11 June 2021

11. Kim, D., Muhammad, H., Kim, E., Helal, S., Lee, C.: TOSCA-based and federation-aware cloud orchestration for Kubernetes container platform. Appl. Sci **9**(1), Art. no. 1 (2019). https://doi.org/10.3390/app9010191

12. Antonacci, M., et al.: Digital repository as a service: automatic deployment of an Invenio-based repository using TOSCA orchestration and Apache Mesos. EPJ Web Conf. **214**, 07023 (2019). https://doi.org/10.1051/epjconf/201921407023

13. Cankar, M., Luzar, A., Tamburri, D.A.: Auto-scaling using TOSCA infrastructure as code. In: Muccini, H., et al. (eds.) ECSA 2020. CCIS, vol. 1269, pp. 260–268. Springer, Cham (2020). https://doi.org/10.1007/978-3-030-59155-7_20

14. Brogi, A., Soldani, J., Wang, P.: TOSCA in a nutshell: promises and perspectives. In: Villari, M., Zimmermann, W., Lau, K.-K. (eds.) ESOCC 2014. LNCS, vol. 8745, pp. 171–186. Springer, Heidelberg (2014). https://doi.org/10.1007/978-3-662-44879-3_13

15. Binz, T., Breiter, G., Leyman, F., Spatzier, T.: Portable cloud services using TOSCA. IEEE Internet Comput. **16**(3), 80–85 (2012)

16. Waizenegger, T., et al.: Policy4TOSCA: a policy-aware cloud service provisioning approach to enable secure cloud computing. In: Meersman, R., et al. (eds.) OTM 2013. LNCS, vol. 8185, pp. 360–376. Springer, Heidelberg (2013). https://doi.org/10.1007/978-3-642-41030-7_26

17. Koetter, F., Kochanowski, M., Weisbecker, A., Fehling, C., Leymann, F.: Integrating compliance requirements across business and IT. In: 2014 IEEE 18th International Enterprise Distributed Object Computing Conference, pp. 218–225, September 2014. https://doi.org/10.1109/EDOC.2014.37

18. Zimmermann, M., Breitenbucher, U., Krieger, C., Leymann, F.: Deployment enforcement rules for TOSCA-based applications. In: Proceedings of The Twelfth International Conference on Emerging Security Information, Systems and Technologies (SECURWARE 2018), pp. 114–121 (2018)

19. Krieger, C., Breitenbücher, U., Képes, K., Leymann, F.: An approach to automatically check the compliance of declarative deployment models. In: IBM Research Division, pp. 76–89 (2018)

20. Li, P., Xu, C., Luo, Y., Cao, Y., Mathew, J., Ma, Y.: CareNet: building a secure software-defined infrastructure for home-based healthcare. In: Proceedings of the ACM International Workshop on Security in Software Defined Networks & Network Function Virtualization, New York, NY, USA, pp. 69–72, March 2017. https://doi.org/10.1145/3040992.3041007

21. Carrasco, J., Cubo, J., Durán, F., Pimentel, E.: Bidimensional cross-cloud management with TOSCA and Brooklyn. In: 2016 IEEE 9th International Conference on Cloud Computing (CLOUD), pp. 951–955, June 2016

22. Rashid, Z., Noor, U., Altmann, J.: Economic model for evaluating the value creation through information sharing within the cybersecurity information sharing ecosystem. Future Gener. Comput. Syst. **124**, 436–466 (2021). https://doi.org/10.1016/j.future.2021.05.033

23. Mohammed, M., Altmann, J.: Software compliance in different industries: a systematic literature review. In: CIISR 2021, International Workshop on Current Compliance Issues in Information Systems Research, March 2021

New Idea Papers

Energy Efficiency in Edge Environments: a Serverless Computing Approach

Karim Djemame$^{(\boxtimes)}$ 🆔

School of Computing, University of Leeds, Leeds, UK
K.Djemame@leeds.ac.uk
https://eps.leeds.ac.uk/computing/staff/187/professor-karim-djemame

Abstract. The paper revisits the Internet Architecture by leveraging Software Defined Networks (SDN) with Network Function Virtualisation (NFV) technologies to allow efficient and on-demand placement of Virtual Network Functions (VNF) on a serverless platform for energy-aware function provisioning in edge environments. Edge computing is seen as critical for supporting the next generation of services and applications that demand high speeds and low-latencies though energy consumption is a matter of concern. Serverless computing as a paradigm in virtualisation is considered as a low-latency and a rapidly deployable alternative to traditional virtualisation approaches. Event-triggered serverless functions incentivise energy efficient resource usage and provide granular reporting on a function level. The research will develop a new building block that satisfies the services performance while reducing the energy consumption in edge environments.

Keywords: Serverless computing · Energy efficiency · Software Defined Networks · Network Function Virtualisation

1 Context

There is proliferation of applications benefiting from edge computing solutions: scalability, reliability, cost-effectiveness, which are being adopted in various domains such as autonomous vehicles, traffic management, edge video orchestration, industrial Internet of Things (IIoT) to name a few. Edge computing pushes the intelligence, processing power and communication capabilities of an edge gateway or appliance directly into edge devices, ensuring it is closer to where the data originates from, e.g. sensors.

Virtualisation servers running containers (or unikernels) are usually deployed at multiple locations at the edge of the network. This virtualisation infrastructure hosts not only mobile application services to execute on edge and cloud nodes, but also other related services, namely Network Function Virtualization (NFV) and Software Defined Networking (SDN) to reserve and set up a portion of the underlying networking infrastructure appropriately for guaranteeing the desired runtime behaviours for each application operating on the edge. Such deployment

© Springer Nature Switzerland AG 2021
K. Tserpes et al. (Eds.): GECON 2021, LNCS 13072, pp. 181–184, 2021.
https://doi.org/10.1007/978-3-030-92916-9_15

would reduce the deployment costs, and provide a common management and orchestration infrastructure for all virtualised services.

SDNs facilitate the containerised applications and network traffic consolidation to optimise performance and energy consumption. Leveraging SDN together with NFV technologies allows for efficient and on-demand placement and chaining of VNFs, making orchestration and consolidation of services easy and dynamic deployment of network services possible. Moreover, the consideration of Virtualized Network Functions (VNFs) is key to enable 5G application use-cases with specific processing and networking capability requirements. Moreover, a serverless computing system [4] is an ideal solution to build and optimise any IoT operation with zero infrastructure and maintenance costs and little-to-no operating expense [3] as it allows IoT businesses to offload all of a server's typical operational backend responsibilities.

Energy consumption in the Internet architecture is one of the highest operating costs. Energy is becoming even more important due to climate change and sustainability considerations. The advent of 5G mobile-network technology is bringing a significant increase in data traffic and the infrastructure to support it, which consequently will consume more energy. However, applications' performance lies with not only efficient node-level execution but energy consumption as well as these applications may operate in a low energy computing environment. The energy increase coming from applications and infrastructure calls for action. Network load optimisation and efficient resource management are essential to ensure a reduction in total energy consumption.

2   Ambition

This research aims to reduce energy consumption of applications deployment and operation in edge computing by addressing the challenges in resource management to support disruptive applications through large scale connected devices operating in low energy environments. The proposed Internet architecture renovation will be able to automate the deployment, monitoring, scaling of containers running serverless functions ensuring interoperability in an energy-aware edge environment. To do so, it considers the SDN architecture, leveraged with NFV to enable the network to be intelligently and centrally controlled using software applications. Therefore, it addresses the control layer to configure the infrastructure and the application layers to support autonomous energy efficiency in edge computing. The serverless platforms does not take into account energy savings in resource management decisions, and to the best of our knowledge, there is currently no work that addresses performance concerns combined with availability and energy efficiency concerns in serverless computing.

The innovation lies in the incorporation of serverless architectures with 1) SDN controllers which are highly event-driven, modular, and concurrent (with minimal sharing of state between the modules) 2) NFV for orchestrating VNF as well as applications that require running short, on-demand tasks operating on data collected from the data plane. VNFs launched and orchestrated in a serverless manner incentivises efficient resource usage and provides granular reporting on a function level: functions take up the most execution time can be identified, which equals *cost*. This is essentially a *proxy* for energy usage as a unit of (serverless) compute, making VNFs instantiation and orchestration significantly energy and resource efficient.

The SDN controllers are a great fit for the serverless computing paradigm as they are highly event-driven, modular and parallel [1]. Moreover, Serverless computing provides a resource-efficient, low overhead alternative to Virtual Machines (VMs) and containers, and can effectively support the NFV architecture.

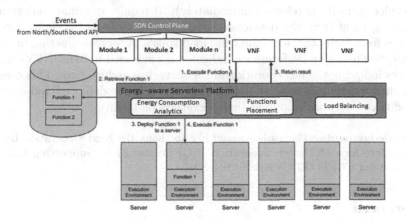

Fig. 1. Proposed solution.

3   Solution: Technical Approach

Architecture. The execution of SDN modules are triggered by events coming from the southbound API, e.g. OpenFlow as well as events received via the northbound API, which interfaces with network applications running on top of the controller, e.g. security services, applications orchestration across edge resources. The SDN controller modules in the SDN architecture are implemented as separate, stand-alone serverless functions (Fig. 1), including the flow management on network switches, exercising direct control over the state in the switches via OpenFlow APIs. Serverless functions are used to orchestrate multiple VNFs for short-lived sessions. The open-source serverless platform (e.g. Apache Openwhisk) [2] will be extended to support resource mapping and load balancing to increase resource utilisation by distributing the function executions to available resources with the aim to minimise power consumption. A load balancing strategy considers functions interactions by assigning the function executions belonging to the same session to the same server. Latency sensitive communication services require careful placement of VNFs by allowing locality requirements for grouping functions as a single application. Containers image sizes are reduced to speed up the start of a function execution thus avoiding cold start.

Expected Results. The research new building block is made of 1) a methodology combining SDN, NFV and serverless architectures; 2) placement algorithms for serverless functions to minimise energy consumption; 3) the underlying software implementation. SDN and NFV make communication networks adaptive and scalable. Their combination with the serverless platform provides the required agility, robustness, and scalability for the services executed and will 1) match the demand of a service by scaling up fast to provision additional compute resources for the service (even if that traffic is increasing rapidly); 2) make efficient use of the available resources (services are never over-provisioned and idle service capacity is released immediately); 3) require minimal configuration and management from the developers; 4) isolate services and their provisioned resources from each other e.g. faults and load spikes. A target reduction in energy consumption as a Key Performance Indicator is envisaged in SDN/NFV-enabled networks following the incorporation of the serverless architecture. This comparison is drawn against a use case application as a baseline deployed and operated on traditional network resources (non-serverless platform).

Acknowledgements. The author would like to thank the Next Generation Internet Program for Open INTErnet Renovation (NGI-Pointer 2) for supporting this work under contract 871528 (EDGENESS Project).

References

1. Aditya, P., et al.: Will serverless computing revolutionize NFV? Proc. IEEE **107**(4), 667–678 (2019)
2. Djemame, K., Parker, M., Datsev, D.: Open-source Serverless architectures: an evaluation of Apache OpenWhisk. In: 2020 IEEE/ACM 13th International Conference on Utility and Cloud Computing (UCC), pp. 329–335 (2020)
3. Großmann, M., Ioannidis, C., Le, D.T.: Applicability of serverless computing in fog computing environments for IoT scenarios. In: Proceedings of the 12th IEEE/ACM International Conference on Utility and Cloud Computing Companion, UCC 2019, pp. 29–34. Companion, Association for Computing Machinery, New York (2019)
4. Kritikos, K., Skrzypek, P.: A review of serverless frameworks. In: 2018 IEEE/ACM International Conference on Utility and Cloud Computing Companion (UCC Companion), pp. 161–168 (2018)

Fighting Reluctance: Engagement, Participation, and Trust

A. M. Foley[1] and J.-Ch. Grégoire[2(✉)]

[1] Wilfrid Laurier University, Waterloo, ON, Canada
afoley@wlu.ca
[2] INRS-EMT, Montréal, QC, Canada
jean-charles.gregoire@inrs.ca

Abstract. We propose a multi-round competitive influence maximization model for overcoming vaccination reluctance.

Keywords: Trust · Multi-period threshold model · Multi-round diffusion

1 Introduction and Context

How do you build a model that deploys influence to increase trust and overcome reluctance when conditions and constraints are rapidly changing? This problem can be exemplified by the 2021 COVID-19 vaccination campaign. The reasons for an individual to be vaccine hesitant, or *reluctant*, are myriad, but many are issues of *trust*—of the vaccine itself, or in those administering it or advocating for it. Increased trust leads to increased *engagement* which in turn can lead to increased *participation*. This is related to a social network *influencer system* [4], and we propose a multi-round competitive influence maximization model.

Recent studies [6] indicate about 20% of the Canadian population aged 18+ are reluctant to be vaccinated[1]. Some of their reasons for reluctance are due to lack of trust: concerns over proper vaccine testing, historical abuse of a marginalized community by the medical profession, lack of endorsement by a community leader or family and friends, mixed messages from a regulation agency. Some of their reasons for reluctance are not trust-based, but are instead grounded in reality or convenience, e.g. time of day vaccination is offered, availability of time off work to recover, difficulty accessing clinic due to marginalized circumstances, contraindication due to an allergy or medical condition, fear of needles or side effects, procrastination. However, these factors tend to influence participation more than engagement, e.g. a wheelchair user may be very engaged, but if the vaccination clinic is not wheelchair accessible, they cannot participate.

Certainly engagement—or the lack thereof—comes from a variety of factors in addition to trust, e.g. a sense of duty, lived experience, belief system. And with

---

[1] Living in a rural area, or being female, are negatively correlated with willingness to be vaccinated, whereas having a higher income and/or more education, are positively correlated, and age is only weakly correlated [6].

K. Tserpes et al. (Eds.): GECON 2021, LNCS 13072, pp. 185–188, 2021.
https://doi.org/10.1007/978-3-030-92916-9_16

those who are anti-vaccine, it is essentially hopeless to try to create engagement. However, in general, to increase engagement, particularly in trust-based cases, *nudging*, often by influencers, is required. Furthermore the amount and type of nudging can vary through time[2].

Techniques for nudging vary. Advertisement campaigns can highlight a sense of loss or fear of missing out. Influencers, from community leaders to social icons, can remind their followers of the importance of participation. Other techniques include virtual town halls with public health authorities and scientific experts, clear messaging from government agencies, and recruitment of health professionals from marginalized communities to be the "face" of vaccination. Other, non-trust-based techniques could be considered, e.g. lotteries, or loosening of restrictions, although that is beyond the scope of this paper.

2   Model

Before we develop our model we outline the following assumptions: 1) throughout the pandemic health authorities maintain generic advertisement campaigns to sustain engagement; 2) the influence can be tailored to different segments of the population, based on a number of factors such as age, language spoken; 3) engagement is assessed through polls, participation is measured through the process itself, and overall success is measured through the number of vaccinations; 4) once someone is vaccinated no more influence is required; 5) there is a *counter-influence* from people who oppose the process and, combined with other factors, tends over time to bring down the level of engagement for some.

Now we isolate several constraints. First, the vaccination process is *supply*, *distribution*, and *time* constrained, and timely delivery of vaccine both to country and to arms are issues. Next, it is *participation* constrained. In particular, there is a minimum participation threshold to be crossed to be able to declare a success, but this threshold must also be met across various segments of the population, e.g. across age, gender, socio-economic, racialized groups. And, finally, it is *trust* constrained: trust in the outcome, in the process itself, in the people managing it, in individual, as well as societal, benefits. Building trust takes time, but also, conditions evolve. Techniques that worked at one point in time, with one community, may not work later as trust either builds or decays. As mentioned previously, trust drives engagement, which should in turn translate into increased rates of participation.

At a high level we have an optimization problem subject to these constraints whose purpose is to keep participation in line with supply at least until the threshold has been reached, while minimizing overall cost. That problem is

---

[2] The COVID-19 vaccination campaign has specific challenges: staggered vaccine deliveries, "vaccine shoppers" (or "vaccine sommeliers" in Brazil [7]) who are picky about which vaccine they take and additional trust issues [3], mixed messages from government agencies over "preferred" vaccines [2], and, of course, the fact that some vaccines require two doses, meaning some of the nudging may need to be repeated. We therefore consider the delivery of each dose as a different vaccination campaign for the sake of this work

periodic, the optimization is performed stepwise, and effects may only be measurable later[3]. Here we focus on the subproblem of selecting influencers to nudge participants, thereby reducing the cost related to reluctance.

Now we formalize these ideas. A campaign has a *participation level target*, $\mathcal{L}_{Pt}$, which is the percentage of the overall population that needs to be vaccinated to contribute to reaching *herd immunity*. The general population has an *engagement level* $\mathcal{L}_E$, which is the percentage of people eligible for vaccination who are in favour of receiving it. Further are *reluctance level* $\mathcal{L}_R$ and *opposition level* $\mathcal{L}_O$. Thus $\mathcal{L}_E + \mathcal{L}_R + \mathcal{L}_O = 100\%$. We also have a *participation level* $\mathcal{L}_{Pr}$ which reflects the percentage of the (eligible) population which has been vaccinated. We call $\mathcal{L}_{Pr} - \mathcal{L}_{Pt}$ the *participation gap*. Whereas $\mathcal{L}_{Pr}$ is a monotonic function, $\mathcal{L}_E$, $\mathcal{L}_R$ and $\mathcal{L}_O$ are functions of time and require periodic assessment. To reach our target we require $\mathcal{L}_E > \mathcal{L}_{Pr} > \mathcal{L}_{Pt}$. However, a shorter term objective is to try to use all available vaccine as it becomes available, for which we attempt to minimize the *vaccination gap*, through the use of *influence*.

We employ the following mathematical model, based on the idea of influence in a social network. Define a directed graph where every user is represented by a node and there are directed edges if there is potential for influence in that direction. Following [8] we can employ a variation on the *triggering model* [4]. Starting with a seed set of active nodes, then at each time step, according to a probabilistic distribution, active nodes will activate those they have edges pointing to.

The literature [1,4] introduced the problem of *influence maximization*: how to select key individuals who can exercise sufficient influence in the network to sway enough users to a given perspective. This can be characterized as a discrete optimization problem, and approximation algorithms can be derived for it [4]. Reference [8] explores the more general problem of a *multi-round influence maximization* problem and provides an adaptive algorithm that allows for multiple rounds of influence, and for feedback between the rounds. The algorithm in [8] achieves $1 - e^{-(1-1/e)} - \epsilon$ approximation to the adaptive optimal solution. Finally, there is also a *multi-round competitive influence maximization* problem [5] that deals with the issue of competing interests who may exert negative influence. This is relevant here as there may be anti-vaccination activists exerting influence. Thus we need to solve a *multi-round competitive influence maximization* problem, with a few twists: 1) we use a continuous scale from 0 to 1 rather than a binary assessment to quantify engagement for nodes, 2) there is a threshold of engagement to guarantee participation, and 3) nodes have a decay factor where, because of inertia, the level of engagement will diminish over time.

Based on supply predictions and a baseline distribution network, we set a time horizon Θ_h, which is divided in time intervals of fixed durations and where a total participation above the required threshold can be met. At the end of

---

[3] The objective function is intricate to establish, as there are material costs (supply, infrastructures, workers) as well as less tangible costs (e.g., morbidity and co-morbidity, public support, even political costs). We leave the specifics of such a function to future work since we are concerned here with a specific subproblem: engaging people and nudging them towards participation.

every period, the current levels of $\mathcal{L}_E$, $\mathcal{L}_R$ and $\mathcal{L}_O$ are assessed and the rate of progress of $\mathcal{L}_{Pr}$ is established across multiple categories. Based on these values, a decision is made on the actions in the next period. They must be long enough for effects to become noticeable, say, two weeks, but some actions are nevertheless multi-period as they can take time to establish and generate significant effect. Actions have costs of various types: expand the infrastructure, initiate a new background campaign, organize events, etc. At the same time, influence and the process itself must be synchronized sufficiently to mitigate engagement decay.

3   Next Steps

We have presented the problem of overcoming vaccine reluctance. The next steps are to specify the objective function and constraints in detail and solve the system. We could expand our inquiry to further include a cost benefit analysis, determine how the model results change based on the cost of influencing, and compute the social welfare maximization. We could also consider non-trust-based factors, and this leads to other issues influencing decay, e.g. potential backlash— if the distrustful are rewarded late in the game, does this decrease trust by those who engaged early? The dynamic nature of the problem is key, and reflecting it properly in the model is part of the challenge.

References

1. Domingos, P., Richardson, M.: Mining the network value of customers. In: ACM SIGKDD Knowledge Discovery and Data Mining, pp. 57–66 (2001)
2. Gollom, M.: Preferred vaccines message from federal health panel sparks concern, criticism from health experts, Canadian Broadcasting Corporation (CBC), May 5, (2021). https://www.cbc.ca/news/health/vaccine-hesitancy-naci-health-experts-1.6012961
3. Grant, K.: Why do Canadians think Pfizer is better than Moderna? A look at Covid-19 vaccine shopping, Globe and Mail, June 18 (2021). https://www.theglobeandmail.com/canada/articlewhy-do-canadians-think-pfizer-is-better-than-moderna-a-look-at-covid/
4. Kempe, D., Kleinberg, J., Tardos, E.: Maximizing the spread of influence through a social network. In: ACM SIGKDD Knowledge Discovery and Data Mining, pp. 137–146 (2003)
5. Lin, S.C., Lin, S.D., Chen, M.S.: A learning-based framework to handle multi-round multi-party influence maximization on social netowrks. In: ACM SIGKDD Knowledge Discovery and Data Mining (2015)
6. Loewen, P.: Reaching the vaccine hesitant, Report 5, Public Policy Forum, May 18 (2021). https://ppforum.ca/publications/report-5-reaching-the-vaccine-hesitant/
7. Phillips, T.: Crackdown on 'vaccine sommeliers' as Covid pandemic grips Brazil, Guardian, July 6, (2021). https://www.theguardian.com/world/2021/jul/06/crackdown-on-vaccine-sommeliers-as-covid-pandemic-grips-brazil
8. Sun, L., Huang, W., Yu, P.S., Chen, W.: Multi-round influence maximization. In: ACM SIGKDD Knowledge Discovery and Data Mining, pp. 2249–2258 (2018)

Workshop on Trustworthy Services, Information Exchange and Content Handling in the Context of Blockchain

Semantic Representation as a Key Enabler for Blockchain-Based Commerce

Giampaolo Bella[1], Domenico Cantone[1], Cristiano Longo[2],
Marianna Nicolosi Asmundo[1], and Daniele Francesco Santamaria[1(✉)]

[1] Department of Mathematics and Computer Science, University of Catania,
Viale Andrea Doria, 6, 95125 Catania, Italy
{giampaolo.bella,domenico.cantone}@unict.it,
{nicolosi,santamaria}@dmi.unict.it
[2] The Sicilian Wheat Bank S.p.A., Via Piazza Armerina, 30, 94100 Enna, Italy
longocristiano@bancadelgrano.it

Abstract. Decentralized applications (in short, DApps) built on blockchains are disrupting the digital commerce foundations by pursuing new business models based on trustless, decentralized transactions, where intermediaries and central authorities are discarded. One of those emerging means are the digital tokens, certificates emitted and exchanged on the blockchain to provide digital representations of assets, which grant to the owners specific rights that are publicly verifiable by smart automatic contractual types of arrangement called smart contracts. Due to the increasing complexity of commercial mechanisms, a clear unambiguous description of commercial participants and of their in and out of blockchain activities, on top of which trustworthy and affordable ecosystems are constructed, is demanded. To face the challenges that digital commerce nowadays poses on realizing such ecosystems, the ONTOCHAIN consortium has funded a third-party research and development project named *POC4COMMERCE*. In this paper, we discuss the advancements of the project, giving insights into the approach and the best practices adopted by the developing team, to build a suite of ontologies modelling representative entities of the digital commerce ecosystem such as commercial participants and assets traded leveraging the Ethereum blockchain.

Keywords: Semantic web · E-commerce · Blockchain

1 Introduction

Does today's e-commerce (that is, the technological support to commerce, including the surrounding ecosystem of assets, actors, supply chains, infrastructures, and blockchains) attain the goals of sustainability, resilience, and trustworthiness?

We contend that the present answer to this research question is not fully positive, hence the motivation that sparks off the ongoing experimental activities discussed in this paper.

© Springer Nature Switzerland AG 2021
K. Tserpes et al. (Eds.): GECON 2021, LNCS 13072, pp. 191–198, 2021.
https://doi.org/10.1007/978-3-030-92916-9_17

The overarching assumption supporting our research and developments is that the fundamental enabler for the goals outlined above is an expressive and disambiguating semantic representation. This motivates the scientific and technical methodology taken, of making available and exploiting a hierarchy of ontologies. While these ontologies should at least represent essential features such as mechanisms to determine price or produce individual trust values, they certainly ought to cope with blockchain technology, which is increasingly being leveraged to support commerce through its inherent immutability.

Taking the semantic approach to represent real-world uses of the blockchain lies precisely at the core of ONTOCHAIN [4], which has funded a third-party research and development project named "Making ONTOCHAIN practical for e-commerce" (POC4COMMERCE, in short). The core team executing the project also authors the present paper. POC4COMMERCE aims at making ONTOCHAIN practical and, at the same time, proof of concept—specifically for the e-commerce vertical domain, though with continuous attention at desirable generalisations on other domains. This paper outlines POC4COMMERCE, with its approach and objectives, and discusses the current status of the project.

In short, the project delivers three layers of ontological description, and the design of a search engine. The scientific and technical methodology entails leveraging an ontology of agents, *OASIS*, previously published by the team [2,3], in addition to other ontologies such as *BLONDiE* [8], for representing blockchain constitutional elements, and *GoodRelations* [5], for commercial offerings. Currently, the most two representative ontologies for blockchain, namely, the BLONDiE and Ethon [6] ontologies, provide very limited representation capabilities of blockchain smart contracts and tokens, thus preventing a deep and clear understanding of the operations carried on the blockchains. Indeed, the main progress beyond the state of the art is an ontological representation of ONTOCHAIN stakeholders up to Ethereum by the "mentalistic notion" of agent behavior [1], namely through their operational semantics, that is applied to smart contracts and tokens, delivering a clear description and, as consequence, indexing of blockchain activities, thus building a new generation of distributed applications (DApps).

The POC4COMMERCE ontological stack is populated and validated with real-world data, hence increasing overall confidence. The general impact of POC4COMMERCE on the various e-commerce stakeholders is expected to be huge thanks to the production of the foundational grounds for a marketplace and to the drastic enhancement of its interoperability, both internally, among its key components, and externally, with other marketplaces, supporting the coherent design of additional software agents in the future.

At the time of this writing, the ontological stack is completed at 95%, with the inclusion of Digital Identities, Supply Chains and Quality Valuation in the foundational level, of Auctions, Offerings and Price Determination at the commerce level, of Tokens and Smart Contract at the blockchain level. Of course, the hierarchy is mindful of the state of the art, hence appropriately leveraging the above mentioned foundational ontologies OASIS, GoodRelations, and BLONDiE, each at the appropriate level. Consistency check of the ontologies has been carried out by exploiting the most widespread reasoners. In addition, competency questions have been defined and implemented through SPARQL queries to verify whether the ontologies are truly being developed towards the project objectives and are reaching the stated representational goals.

The working use cases concern an apple producer who wants to publish their offer of a batch of apples. The use cases also include a potential buyer who is interested in finding an offer matching her personal needs, in deciding whether to purchase it and in understanding how to carry out the entire transaction. The project is on time and is not experiencing significant risks.

This paper is structured as follows. Section 2 reports the main concepts and goals behind POC4COMMERCE; Sect. 3 presents our solution and Sect. 4 discusses it over a real-world use case. Then, Sect. 5 outlines the impact that comes from the adoption of POC4COMMERCE, and Sect. 6 draws some concluding remarks.

2   Concept and Objectives of POC4COMMERCE

In order to promote a sustainable, resilient, and trustworthy e-commerce by defining it over the ONTOCHAIN ecosystem, the POC4COMMERCE project leverages an ontological approach consisting in a hierarchical semantic modelling towards the effective and efficient interoperability of blockchain technology with the e-commerce domain, enforcing the contribute of blockchain technology to a sustainable, resilient, and trustworthy e-commerce. The POC4COMMERCE project aims to address the challenge of developing a consistent, unambiguous, and shared semantic model supporting the interoperability of the heterogeneous stakeholders, ranging from the blockchain ledger elements to the relevant software agents and, ultimately, people. The project moves towards four main steps. The first step consists in deploying an ontology, namely the ontology "OC-Found", covering all relevant stakeholders in the ONTOCHAIN ecosystem and offering a base-level support to their interoperability. These comprise, but are not limited to, the blockchain ledger, including constitutive elements such as accounts, nodes, blocks, transactions, fungible, non-fungible, and semi-fungible tokens, smart contracts, services, and actual end-users, that is, people and organizations. The second step involves the construction of the ontology "OC-Commerce", specialising OC-Found on the e-commerce vertical domain. OC-Commerce exploits the OC-Found definitions to represent the specific stakeholders of the business and e-commerce activities carried out on the ONTOCHAIN ecosystem. Then, the ontology "OC-Ethereum", specialising OC-Commerce on the Ethereum blockchain environment, is defined. OC-Ethereum exploits the OC-Commerce definitions to represent the specific stakeholders of the Ethereum blockchain, in particular smart contracts and token representations compliant with standards ERC721, ERC20, and ERC1155. Finally, on top of the ontological stack, POC4COMMERCE designs a commercial software API, namely "OC-Commerce Search Engine" (OC-CSE, in brief) implementing a search service that enables end-users to conveniently find goods, products, and services in a semantic-enabled marketplace. It stands on the solid grounds provided by the full underlying ontology, thus leveraging the semantic interoperability of all involved stakeholders. During the developing of the ontological stack, the most widespread ontology metric criteria [7] have been adopted, which are necessary to evaluate ontologies both during the design and implementation phase, thus allowing for fast and simple assessment of ontologies while ensuring the suitability of the ontologies. Appropriate competency questions are defined and applied side by side with the development of the ontological stack: competency questions constitute questionnaires in natural language and are implemented in the SPARQL [9] query language, which helps to clarify the context and the scope of ontologies. Finally, OWL 2 compliant reasoners are executed on the ontologies, to verify their consistency, and real-world datasets provided by partners are used to validate them.

3   The POC4COMMERCE Solution

POC4COMMERCE describes an interconnected and interoperable digital commerce through three ontological layers modelling different degrees of knowledge. POC4COMMERCE is fully aware of the modern literature and embraces it in an ontological engineering process to promote an interoperable and sustainable shared e-commerce in the ONTOCHAIN ecosystem. The project takes a hierarchical ontology approach to deliver an ontological stack with three distinct building-blocks that practically port ONTOCHAIN to the e-commerce vertical domain. The first ontological layer provides a formal description of all ONTOCHAIN ecosystem stakeholders through the OWL 2 ontology OC-Found. Although ontologies for representing agents have been available since 2008, they are strictly focused on specific contexts, such as the Internet of Things, or tied to application domains, such as economy or health-care. OC-Found also provides a formal specification of how participants interact, exchange information, take decisions, and establish plans, provisions, and obligations. Therefore, OC-Found provides a high-level, consistent, broad representation of ONTOCHAIN stakeholders, in particular of ONTOCHAIN agents and their functionalities, which are described through the mentalistic notion of agent behavior implemented by the ontology OASIS. OC-Found provides a "semantic glue" for unifying the diversity of development technologies and communication standards, the large availability of architecture, hardware, software, and technologies of different types underlying the ONTOCHAIN ecosystem, hence favouring their interoperability.

The second ontological layer, that is, the OWL 2 ontology OC-Commerce, provides a full and comprehensive model of commercial agents and activities, goods, products, offerings, and services related with business and commerce. OC-Commerce describes how market activities are carried out by absorbing and extending the ontology for commerce GoodRelations by the general characterization of stakeholders introduced by OC-Found. OC-Commerce represents a unifying level for all the commercial activities carried out in the ONTOCHAIN ecosystem, regardless of the vendor and buyer sale channels.

The third ontological layer is the OWL 2 ontology OC-Ethereum specializing OC-Commerce and, hence, OC-Found. OC-Ethereum continues the mentalistic approach innovatively on Ethereum, thus it fully specifies the building blocks of the Ethereum blockchain such as accounts, nodes, blocks, transactions, fungible, non-fungible, and semi-fungible tokens compliant with standards ERC20, ERC721, ERC1155, respectively, as well as smart contracts, the latter being defined through the guidelines drawn by the conceptualization of agents in OC-Found. OC-Ethereum is exploited to share knowledge and services over Ethereum in a coherent, consistent, and fully interoperable way, thanks to the full definition of the semantics at ontological level.

This ontological core of POC4COMMERCE is exploited to design the OC-Commerce Search Engine (in short, OC-CSE), explaining how an ONTOCHAIN digital platform for commerce works by providing a shared and common semantic tool to profitably find goods, products, information, and services, meeting the end user requirements and published by the wide array of ONTOCHAIN commercial participants in the provided ontological knowledge base. OC-CSE enables the interoperability of commercial parties whose businesses would have been disconnected otherwise, favouring the spread of products and services through the ONTOCHAIN ecosystem and reducing economic inefficiencies.

4 Use Cases

A classical POC4COMMERCE use case is illustrated in Fig. 1, which depicts a green apples vendor, *AppleBay*, who wants to sell her assets by granting to the buyer *Bob* an Ethereum ERC721 compliant non-fungible token (NFT), which assigns ownership rights of the specific batch of apples purchased. A suitable Ethereum smart contract is published to mint and transfer ERC721 compliant tokens of apple batches. The user Bob would purchase apples using FIAT currency through a digital payment platform such as PayPal. To complete the purchase, the token corresponding to the apples batch bought by Bob is minted and transferred to the buyer's Ethereum wallet as a proof of quality and quantity of the product purchased and of the payment received by the seller. Then, the product shipment process is finalized through the shipment service chosen by the seller.

Initially, to join the commercial ecosystem, both the participants AppleBay and Bob publish the OC-Found-compliant ontological representation of their digital identities in the semantic knowledge base.

Next, AppleBay publishes the ontological representation of the service to be deployed by generating a fragment of OC-Found, representing the green apple selling service and a fragment of OC-Ethereum describing the smart contract releasing NFTs of apple batches. In this phase, specific APIs may assist AppleBay to semi-automatically build the required ontological representations. From now on, the supply chain of AppleBay is semantically described and publicly available through the ecosystem, and offerings concerning the marketable assets can be generated on request. The seller generates an ontological representation of the offering concerning the asset as a fragment of OC-Commerce, connecting it with the related supply chain constituted by the payment agent, the smart contract releasing the NFT, and the shipping courier. Such a representation depicts the distribution mechanisms provided by AppleBay, which are finally searchable by potential clients such as Bob. Above them, the apple seller manifests the promise that each time an offering is accepted and the related payment is completed, the seller mints and transfers to the buyer the related NFT.

Bob can rely on the OC-CSE search engine to find the desired product. For instance, Bob would search for a service realising NFTs, corresponding to apples batches as a proof of purchase. The search engine generates the SPARQL query describing Bob's requirements and submits it to one of the triple stores available so as to probe the repository for the desired results. Since AppleBay is a vendor corresponding to Bob's requirements, the available offerings produced by AppleBay are then presented to Bob by means of one of the standard RDF serializations. Bob now has the required information to complete the purchase or, alternatively, he may invoke a quality valuer to estimate the reputation of AppleBay, the number of NFTs already sold, or the age of the service. Once the purchase is completed, Bob can assess his experience by evaluating the offering, the asset, or the agents involved in the transaction, thus contributing to the trustworthiness of the ecosystem.

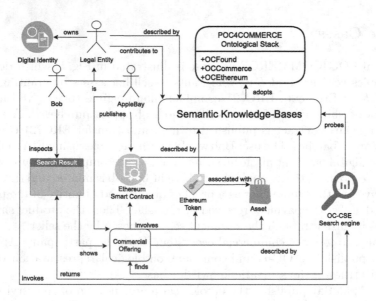

Fig. 1. A typical POC4COMMERCE use case.

5   POC4COMMERCE Impact

POC4COMMERCE contributes to many aspects of the ONTOCHAIN ecosystem. The POC4COMMERCE ontologies make the ONTOCHAIN ecosystem readily functioning to build a sustainable, interoperable, and trustworthy e-commerce environment for people and software to work together. The ontology OC-Found provides a unifying canvas for all ONTOCHAIN participants and relationships among them, a substrate describing and connecting what really exists, with the relevant stakeholders interoperating coherently in a heterogeneous context. OC-Found also lays the grounds for the semantic interoperability of potentially innumerable domain-specific ontologies for the ONTOCHAIN ecosystem, such as those for eScience, eEducation, eHealth, eGovernment, e-commerce, eTourism, and eInfrastructures. OC-Commerce impacts on how digital commerce is carried out in the Web 3.0 and beyond. Commerce on the digital representation of products requires affordable marketplaces, where sellers and buyers may freely choose the services associated with their business activities. There are significant costs to select the required features of goods, e.g., where they are produced and stored, and how they can be moved to the consumer: inevitably, such costs concur to the business costs, namely to the final price paid by consumers. Therefore, the results of POC4COMMERCE contribute to a shift towards a novel microeconomic model, where individuals and companies cooperate and coordinate, by deciding the allocation and utilization of resources, and the subsequent effect on price, demand, and supply merely upon the basis of personal choices and without the intermediation of third-parties. It opens up new business opportunities for companies of any size because the absence of price profiteers reinstates the equilibrium of the relation of demand and supply that determines the competitive capability of any organization—thus re-establishing their decision power in setting the price of goods and services. Such principle is strengthened by decentralized marketplaces that directly connect consumers and sellers. For this reason, OC-Ethereum promotes the concept of a semantic blockchain that conjoins the high level of trustworthiness and transparency of a decentralized public ledger, where economic parties interact with their own rules: no restrictions imposed by third parties and a machine interpretable representation of the knowledge is retrieved by meanings and not just by spellings. A semantic blockchain implies that smart contracts can be referenced without pre-existing knowledge of their deployment and of the underlying programming code: their functionalities are fully specified by formal and machine-understandable representations, thus realizing an interoperable environment, where off-chain services interact with applications lying potentially on any blockchains such as Hyperedger Fabric, NEO, ONTology. POC4COMMERCE is a success story about the application of ontologies to huge-scale business applications such as e-commerce, boosting the practical impact of the ONTOCHAIN ecosystem in this domain.

6   Conclusions

We presented the advancements and the general solution provided by the project POC4COMMERCE, funded by the ONTOCHAIN consortium, which was launched in 2020 by the European Commission's Next Generation Internet initiative. The POC4COMMERCE project leverages a hierarchical ontological stack in order to semantically represent and conjoin blockchain technologies with the e-commerce domain. The POC4COMMERCE stack is constituted by three ontologies, a) the ontology OC-Found, describing participants, digital identities, and valuation mechanisms that exploit the agent-behavior oriented representation mechanisms provided by the ontology OASIS; b) the ontology OC-Commerce, inheriting OC-Found and adopting and extending GoodRelations to provide supply chains associated with offerings, auctions, and price determination mechanisms; c) the ontology OC-Ethereum, inheriting OC-Commerce and hence OC-Found, and extending BLONDiE to define Ethereum tokens and smart contracts, in particular the ones associated with commercial transactions.

At the time of this writing, the ontological stack is almost fully implemented, whereas tests on real-word data are going to be developed. The next step will consist in designing on top of the ontological stack the search engine OC-CSE, a common semantic tool enabling ONTOCHAIN users to profitably find goods, products, information, and services, meeting their requirements.

Acknowledgements. The work of POC4Commerce has been supported by the ONTOCHAIN NGI European project grant agreement no. 957338. We are thankful to the ONTOCHAIN Consortium who mentored and assisted the research.

References

1. Bresciani, P., Perini, A., Giorgini, P., Giunchiglia, F., Mylopoulos, J.: Tropos: an agent-oriented software development methodology. Auton. Agent. Multi. Agent. Syst. **8**(3), 203–236 (2004)
2. Cantone, D., Longo, C.F., Nicolosi-Asmundo, M., Santamaria, D.F., Santoro, C.: Towards an ontology-based framework for a behavior-oriented integration of the IoT. In: Proceedings of the 20th Workshop From Objects to Agents, Parma, Italy, 26–28 June 2019, CEUR Workshop Proceeding, vol. 2404, pp. 119–126 (2019)
3. Cantone, D., Longo, C.F., Nicolosi-Asmundo, M., Santamaria, D.F., Santoro, C.: Ontological smart contracts in oasis: ontology for agents, systems, and integration of services. In: Proceedings of IDC 2021, The 14th International Symposium on Intelligent Distributed Computing, Scilla, Reggio Calabria, Italy, 16–18 September (2021)
4. ONTOCHAIN Consortium: ONTOCHAIN Project (2020). https://ontochain.ngi.eu/
5. Hepp, M.: GoodRelations: an ontology for describing products and services offers on the web. In: Gangemi, A., Euzenat, J. (eds.) EKAW 2008. LNCS (LNAI), vol. 5268, pp. 329–346. Springer, Heidelberg (2008). https://doi.org/10.1007/978-3-540-87696-0_29
6. Pfeffer, J., Beregszazi, A., Li, S.: EthOn - an Ethereum ontology (2016). https://ethon.consensys.net/index.html
7. Tartir, S., Budak Arpinar, I., Moore, M., Sheth, A.P., Aleman-Meza, B.: OntoQA: metric-based ontology quality analysis. In: Proceedings of IEEE Workshop on Knowledge Acquisition from Distributed, Autonomous, Semantically Heterogeneous Data and Knowledge Sources (2005)
8. Ugarte-Rojas, H., Chullo-Llave, B.: BLONDiE: blockchain ontology with dynamic extensibility. CoRR, abs/2008.09518 (2020)
9. World Wide Web Consortium. SPARQL 1.1 Query Language (2013)

CopyrightLY: Blockchain and Semantic Web for Decentralised Copyright Management

Roberto García(✉) ⓘ, Ana Cediel ⓘ, Mercè Teixidó ⓘ, and Rosa Gil ⓘ

Universitat de Lleida, 25001 Lleida, Spain
{roberto.garcia,anna.cs,merce.teixido,rosamaria.gil}@udl.cat

Abstract. CopyrightLY focuses on building an authorship and rights management layer for the ONTOCHAIN ecosystem. It provides a set of services to claim authorship, on both content and data. Moreover, it also makes it possible to attach reuse terms to these claims, which state the conditions to reuse the associated data or content. This authorship and rights management layer will constitute the foundation for future services built on top of the ONTOCHAIN ecosystem, like social media copyright management, media monetisation through Non-Fungible Tokens or specialised media and data marketplaces.

Keywords: Copyright · Blockchain · Distributed ledger · Ethereum · Smart contract · Oracle · Semantic web · Ontology · Tokenomics

1 Introduction

CopyrightLY is a decentralised application that leverages blockchain and semantic web technologies to facilitate copyright management. It is being developed as part of the ONTOCHAIN[1] Next Generation Internet software ecosystem to serve trusted knowledge and information needs and funded by the European.

CopyrightLY aims to provide ONTOCHAIN with a content ownership and copyright management layer. Its main use case is by being integrated into existing social media platforms and allows content creators to explore ways to exploit their media beyond those made possible by those platforms. It also provides potential re-users ways of checking authorship of the content they are willing to reuse and the conditions under which it is available.

To do so, content on social media platforms is linked by creators to on-chain authorship claims tied to their identities. Additional evidence can be provided combining off-chain data and on-chain transactions to sustain those claims. Thus, they can be used in case of a copyright complaint, even as evidence in court. This approach also discourages false claims, which cannot be retracted once on-chain.

Authorship claims are accompanied by default reuse conditions modelled using semantic technologies and based on a copyright ontology. They provide the necessary and unambiguous building blocks that also make the terms machine-actionable. Reusers

---

[1] http://ontochain.ngi.eu.

© Springer Nature Switzerland AG 2021
K. Tserpes et al. (Eds.): GECON 2021, LNCS 13072, pp. 199–206, 2021.
https://doi.org/10.1007/978-3-030-92916-9_18

can negotiate these terms and, after acceptance, on-chain transactions are generated to keep track of the agreed terms.

The rest of the paper is organised as follows. Section 2 presents the state of the art regarding blockchain technologies for copyright management. Then, Sect. 3 presents the proposed approach focusing on its architecture. Highlights about CopyrightLY's implementation are provided in Sect. 4, including token-based incentives to curate authorship claims, reuse offers negotiation and copyright reasoning based on semantic web technologies and the Copyright Ontology. Finally, Sect. 5 presents the conclusions and future work.

2   State of the Art

Distributed Ledger technologies are being applied to almost any conceivable domain, from logistics [1] to renewable energy production management [2]. In all cases, in addition to the technologies specific to the distributed ledger itself, developers face issues related to information management and integration similar to those faced by Web applications. In this regard, Semantic Web technologies are well-positioned to solve this kind of issues, and have been even used to model the key concepts in one of the main distributed ledgers, Ethereum's EthOn [3].

Efforts in this direction are quite recent and there is little literature regarding proposals similar to CopyrightLY's. One similar proposal [4], which also aims to facilitate copyright protection of social media content, proposes a blockchain framework with smart contracts to protect social media contents using IPFS, a decentralized file storage system [5]. Content uploaded to IPFS is securely stored using a secret sharing scheme. This is combined with a robust hash for images, a method of hashing images that is resistant to modification, rotation, colour alteration. The objective is to make it possible to detect near copies and block the registration of images that might be copies of previously registered ones.

Unfortunately, no further information is provided about the robustness of this algorithm and its implications from a legal standpoint when infringements are not properly detected or un-infringing content is considered otherwise. Moreover, though the use of smart contracts is mentioned as the way to ask permission to reuse registered images, no further details are provided about these smart contracts or the way reuse terms are negotiated and then stored on-chain to provide trust to those agreements.

Another similar proposal [6] is a system to fight intended or accidental image copyright infringement in social media platforms, mainly when professional images are used to increase the impact of posts. Photographers can use it to register their photos and re-users can use it to check if the image they want to use is copyright protected or not.

The main contribution of this paper is an algorithm that can extract a signature that is resistant to different levels of JPEG compression. The signature is stored on the blockchain along with the identification data of the copyright owner. It can be then used to detect copies when someone tries to register the same or a similar image, as determined by the algorithm. The algorithm can be also used by re-users to check if an image is already registered. In that case, the system allows the purchase of the right to use the photo.

However, the paper does not consider mechanisms to deal with situations when the registration considered a copy is in fact the original one, giving rise to potential complaints. Moreover, the paper focuses just on the detection mechanism and little details are provided about how registrations are stored on-chain, or how reuses are negotiated and managed using the smart contracts that are mentioned.

Regarding semantic technologies, CopyrightLY is based on previous work by some of the authors and applying Semantic Web technologies for the copyright management domain, the Copyright Ontology [7].

3 Approach

CopyrightLY is based on the combination of a set of Ethereum [8] blockchain smart contracts that manage authorship claim, complaints and reuse terms, including offering, negotiating and agreeing on these reuse conditions. These smart contracts are connected with decentralised storage and off-chain media and data through a set of oracles that connect it to the main social media and data-sharing platforms.

The proposed solution is also based on a web application providing frontend and backend components that interact with the previous smart contracts and oracles, including a wizard to assist users when defining reuse terms. A separate semantic application collects the semantic representation of all on-chain events to provide services like checking if intended content or data reuses are allowed by previously registered reuse agreements or offers.

Finally, to facilitate interoperability and dealing with a complex domain as copyright management, CopyrightLY is based on the use of semantic technologies and the formal conceptualisations provided by the Copyright Ontology.

3.1 Proposed Architecture

The central part of the CopyrightLY's architecture is on-chain and based on a set of smart contracts, as shown at the centre of Fig. 1. The smart contracts take care of registering Manifestations (i.e. authorship claims), Complaints (to denounce authorship claims potentially fraudulent) and Reuses (used to attach reuse terms to a manifestation, including the initial offer, the negotiation steps and the final reuse agreement, if reached).

Authorship claims and complaints are supported with evidence. The simplest kind of evidence is based on files uploaded to decentralised storage, managed by the Upload-Evidence smart contract that registers and links them to manifestations and the accounts triggering the transaction. All the previous smart contracts make use of decentralised storage based on IPFS to store manifestations, complaints or evidence content (data or media) plus the serialisation of the reuse terms, in the case of the Reuses smart contract.

The rest of the smart contracts are the on-chain part of oracles responsible for asserting on-chain off-chain information about social media platforms (YouTube, Twitter, Facebook...) or dataset marketplaces. For datasets, the oracle brings on-chain the watermark that identifies the dataset. For social media platforms, the oracles verify information about social media assets through the corresponding APIs, like YouTube's API to verify that a predefined identifier has been added to a video description. This allows checking

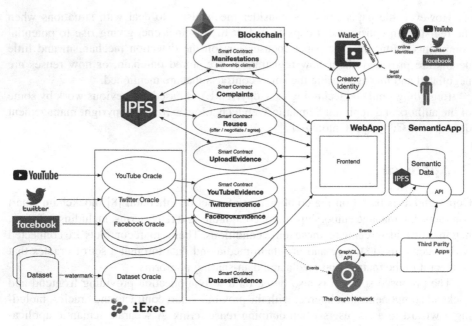

Fig. 1. Proposed architecture for CopyrightLY, including a layer of smart contracts operating on-chain (centre), a set of oracles based on iExec bringing off-chain data (left) and a front-end and API interfaces also managing user credentials (right).

that a certain on-chain account has control over the corresponding off-chain social media assets or datasets. The oracles infrastructure is based on iExec[2], a decentralized network giving applications access to trusted off-chain computation and data.

Consuming all this on-chain infrastructure, there are 3 main off-chain components. First of all, a creator identity based on a wallet that links the accounts used to interact with the blockchain with verifiable credentials[3]. This component takes care of storing in a private and self-sovereign way the credentials issued to the on-chain identities managed by the user. The user can request that third parties issue these credentials after some sort of verification process. In the case of CopyrightLY, the objective is to have both credentials about control of social media profiles (extensible to dataset repository platforms) and legal identities (required in case of litigation).

Additionally, there is an application backend that monitors blockchain events to keep track of the on-chain state without requiring connecting to the blockchain and also provides enhanced and more performant services. Currently, it is based on The Graph, an indexing protocol for querying networks like Ethereum and IPFS. It makes a model of the on-chain state for a set of smart contracts available through an API for third parties. For CopyrightLY, these are mainly other ONTOCHAIN projects but also initiatives outside the ecosystem. The API facilitates building vertical applications like social media, NFTs or data marketplaces.

---

[2] https://iex.ec.
[3] https://www.w3.org/TR/vc-data-model/.

Finally, there is a last component where semantic representations of on-chain state and reuse terms from IPFS are stored in a semantic repository. This component features the semantic querying and reasoning capabilities required to process reuse terms modelled using the Copyright Ontology. It provides an API that gives access to features like checking if an intended reuse is allowed by the current pool of agreements.

4 Implementation Highlights

The proposed architecture is being implemented following an agile methodology in the context of the ONTOCHAIN project. It is possible to follow the development process, get access to the source code and test the current version of the application from the project's dashboard[4]. The following subsection highlight some of the most relevant part of the project, including the incentives mechanisms to curate authorship claims, how reuse offers and modelled and negotiated and, finally, how semantic technologies and ontologies are applied to enable copyright reasoning.

4.1 Incentives to Curate Authorship Claims

One of the biggest issues detected in the state-of-the-art proposals analysed in Sect. 2 is that registering content on-chain does not provide any guarantee about its validity. It might be just the action of someone with access to a digital copy of a creation, but not necessarily the original creator. To deal with these false authorship claims, CopyrightLY leverages an incentive mechanism based on a token with economic value, the CLY token, and requires creators to stake an amount of this token together with their authorship claims, as shown in the upper left part of Fig. 2.

Authorship claimers risk losing their stake. Other creators can complain about existing claims. Like original claimers, they can also provide supporting evidence to convince other users to support their position with additional stake, as the side with more stake wins the other side stake and shares it proportionally to their stake. However, to avoid that players with big CLY token stakes dominate the play, an appeal mechanism based on an external arbitration court is also considered, especially a blockchain-based on like Kleros[5].

4.2 Reuse Offers, Negotiation and Agreements

Reuse agreements, and negotiations, are modelled on-chain by the Reuses smart contract, shown as part of the architecture in Fig. 1. This contract firsts models each reuse offer as a new entry of the Reuse structure, shown in Fig. 3, which initially just points to the address of the content owner making the offer and contain just one Negotiation Step. That Negotiation Step points to the reuse conditions of the initial offer, which are serialised as JSON-LD and stored on IPFS. The content hash is used on-chain and the content owner has signed the transaction generating this first step.

---

[4] https://github.com/rhizomik/copyrightly/wiki.
[5] https://kleros.io.

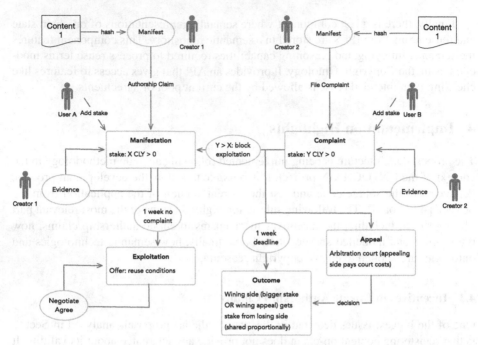

Fig. 2. Tokenomics of the CLY token to incentivise the curation of authorship claims.

If there is a negotiation, the proposed terms are serialised as JSON-LD[6], stored on IPFS and the hash pointed out from a new negotiation step. The steps counter corresponding to the Reuse is increased so it points to the last step. This process can continue as long as both parties do not agree on a common set of conditions. Every time a new step is added, the proposer has to sign the corresponding transaction introducing that new step and thus it is considered signed by that side of the negotiation process.

When one of the parties agrees on the conditions stated by the other party in the last negotiation step, an agreement is reached. This means that both parties have signed the terms linked to the agreed step through the corresponding transactions. Additionally, the time stamps for each transaction are also kept. Altogether, it is possible to retrieve all the components of the agreement (including the negotiation history) from the Reuses smart contract data structures.

4.3 Copyright Reasoning

CopyrightLY is based on semantic technologies and particularly ontologies, formal and explicit representations of shared conceptualisations. The main building block at the conceptual level is the Copyright Ontology[7], which includes:

---

[6] https://json-ld.org.

[7] https://rhizomik.net/ontologies/copyrightonto.

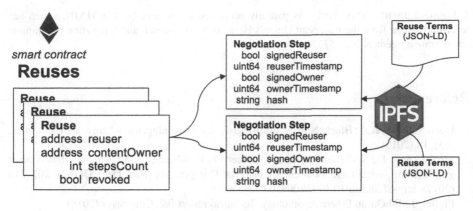

Fig. 3. Implementation of the Reuses smart contract to support reuse negotiation and agreements.

- **Creation Model:** the different shapes of copyright creations along their lifecycle (Manifestation, Performance, Recording…).
- **Rights Model:** the legal constructs regulating what actions are favoured or restricted. Different legal systems can be represented, from generic ones geared towards worldwide harmonisation like those proposed by the WIPO[8] to those in particular legal regimes.
- **Actions Model:** the finer level of modelling where copyright actions moving creations along their lifecycle are represented (manifest, perform, record, communicate…) together with actions' dimensions (who, what, when, where…).

The ontology defines the previous concepts so they can be used to represent specific content value chains. Based on them, license evaluation is implemented using SPARQL queries that check if the different dimensions of an intended reuse (like who, what, when, where…) do fit with existing agreements. Matches can be direct, like that the content or data to be reused has a particular identifier (or content hash). Matches can also be indirect, for instance, if the re-user (who) is a member of the organisation that is authorised to reuse.

5 Conclusions and Future Work

As shown in the previous sections, CopyrightLY provides an authorship and rights management layer to the ecosystem built as part of the ONTOCHAIN H2020 project. It will provide a set of services to claim authorship, on both content and data. Moreover, it will be also possible to attach reuse terms to these claims, which will state the conditions to reuse the associated data or content.

This authorship and rights management layer will constitute the foundation for future services built on top of the ONTOCHAIN ecosystem, like social media copyright management, media monetisation through Non-Fungible Tokens or specialised media and data marketplaces.

---

[8] World Intellectual Property Organization.

Acknowledgments. This work was partially supported by project ONTOCHAIN, which has received funding from the European Union's Horizon 2020 research and innovation programme under grant agreement No 957338.

References

1. Dobrovnik, M., et al.: Blockchain for and in logistics: what to adopt and where to start. Logistics. **2**(3), 18 (2018)
2. Mengelkamp, E., Notheisen, B., Beer, C., Dauer, D., Weinhardt, C.: A blockchain-based smart grid: towards sustainable local energy markets. Comput. Sci. Res. Dev. **33**(1–2), 207–214 (2017). https://doi.org/10.1007/s00450-017-0360-9
3. Pfeffer, J.: EthOn-an Ethereum ontology. Technical report 0.2. Consensys (2018)
4. Kripa, M., Nidhin Mahesh, A., Ramaguru, R., Amritha, P.P.: Blockchain framework for social media DRM based on secret sharing. In: Senjyu, T., Mahalle, P.N., Perumal, T., Joshi, A. (eds.) ICTIS 2020. SIST, vol. 195, pp. 451–458. Springer, Singapore (2021). https://doi.org/10.1007/978-981-15-7078-0_43
5. Benet, J.: IPFS - Content Addressed, Versioned, P2P File System. arXiv:1407.3561 [cs] (2014)
6. Dobre, R.A., Preda, R.O., Badea, R.A., Stanciu, M., Brumaru, A.: Blockchain-based image copyright protection system using JPEG resistant digital signature. In: Conference Proceedings of the IEEE 26th International Symposium for Design and Technology in Electronic Packaging (SIITME 2020), pp. 206–210 (2020)
7. García, R., Gil, R.: Social media copyright management using semantic web and blockchain. In: Proceedings of the 21st International Conference on Information Integration and Web-Based Applications & Services (iiWAS 2019), pp. 339–343. ACM, New York (2019)
8. Antonopoulos, A.M., Wood, G.: Mastering Ethereum: Building Smart Contracts and DApps. O'Reilly Media, Sebastopol (2018)

ISLAND: An Interlinked Semantically-Enriched Blockchain Data Framework

Alexandros Kalafatelis[1]([✉]), Konstantinos Panagos[2], Anastasios E. Giannopoulos[2],
Sotirios T. Spantideas[2], Nikolaos C. Kapsalis[2], Marios Touloupou[3],
Evgenia Kapassa[3], Leonidas Katelaris[3], Panayiotis Christodoulou[3],
Klitos Christodoulou[3], and Panagiotis Trakadas[1]

[1] Department of Port Management and Shipping, National and Kapodistrian
University of Athens, Sterea Ellada, 34400 Dirfies Messapies, Greece
ptrakadas@uoa.gr
[2] Four Dot Infinity, Athens, Greece
research@fourdotinfinity.com
[3] RedMullet Tech, Paphos, Cyprus

Abstract. Blockchain is currently one of the most popular technologies, providing privacy, transparency and trust. However, until now, it does not take into consideration the large amount of existing data and standards for decentralized data distribution and processing on the Web, that would leash new opportunities and business innovations for this emerging technology. Moreover, according to the vision of the Semantic Web, a key concept lies on data (semantic) annotations, querying and interlinking. Nevertheless, exporting knowledge resulting from different and possible interlinked blockchain networks, is still a major challenge. To address the aforementioned challenges, we propose ISLAND, a modular framework that is set to expose a unified abstraction layer to any data consumer that aims to infer meaningful knowledge from blockchain generated data, while at the same time enabling the semantic interoperability of them. In addition, a smart manufacturing use case scenario is presented as well as the potential business impacts are discussed.

Keywords: Semantic blockchain · Linked data · Machine learning

1 Introduction

Blockchain is one of the most innovative and popular technologies nowadays. After it was first introduced by Satoshi Nakamoto, it became known from the rise of cryptocurrencies [1], but soon the scientific community realized its value and started applying it in other fields, such as manufacturing [2], energy [3] and more [4], taking also care in security and privacy issues [5]. In particular, blockchain refers to a data structure, where various forms of data and smart contracts are stored, which are classified into a list of blocks [6, 7]. It is a decentralized network, managed by a peer-to-peer (P2P) network that complies with a protocol for communication between the nodes [8].

© Springer Nature Switzerland AG 2021
K. Tserpes et al. (Eds.): GECON 2021, LNCS 13072, pp. 207–214, 2021.
https://doi.org/10.1007/978-3-030-92916-9_19

Moreover, blockchain environments generate large volumes of distributed data that are publicly available due to their transparent and immutable properties. Even though blockchains are considered a fundamental building block in Web 3.0, they lack software standards that can lead to the emergence of a global, open, interoperable, and semantically rich data-space [9]. The creation of such an interoperable internet and knowledge exchange has been envisioned by Web 3.0, however, it does not yet have the appropriate tools for its pragmatic implementation and development [7, 10].

Furthermore, according to the current state-of-the-art, exporting knowledge resulting from different blockchain networks, is a major concern. In particular, the latter is not yet feasible since several challenges are present, such as: i) processing the data, ii) querying the data, (iii) inter-linking data; (iv) integrating the data under a uniform data model; (v) opening the data; (vi) annotating the data and finally in (vii) extracting knowledge [4, 10].

In this paper, we propose the ISLAND framework which aims to address major challenges such as the ones described above. The contributions of this paper include: i) the description of the proposed interlinked and interoperable semantically enriched blockchain data framework, ii) a smart manufacturing use case scenario, of how such a framework can be leveraged in complex real-world systems and iii) potential business impacts.

It is highlighted that the ISLAND architecture has been proposed and selected for funding during the open call of the European Commission project ONTOCHAIN, under the Horizon 2020 framework [11].

The paper is structured as follows: Sect. 2 gives an overview of the current state-of-the-art and how the ISLAND framework contributes beyond that. Section 3 describes the high-level architecture and the main functionalities of the ISLAND framework. Section 4 presents a use case scenario, while potential business impacts are also identified and discussed in Sect. 5. Finally, Sect. 6 summarizes and concludes the paper.

2   State of the Art and Beyond

Blockchain technology provides a decentralized architecture with privacy, transparency and trust but it should also take into consideration the large amount of existing data and standards for decentralized data distribution and processing on the Web. A key concept design of the Semantic Web vision is the semantic annotation of the data and that are easily queried and interlinked. According to Mikroyannidis et al., a Semantic Blockchain, which promotes interoperability between Blockchain networks and the Semantic Web, is needed to get the best out of both technologies [9]. Furthermore, Semantic Blockchain enables the mapping of smart contracts on the blockchain to contextual data about the corresponding data [9].

Towards that direction, Ugarte and Boris introduced a Blockchain Ontology with Dynamic Extensibility [12]. BLONDiE is an OWL ontology for defining the native structure of the blockchain and related data. It covers the two most currently used blockchain protocols (Bitcoin and Ethereum). An example of its abilities is that it is capable of connecting an individual to account data from Bitcoin and Ethereum. Moreover, English et al., demonstrated how blockchain technology can lead to the creation of a more stable Semantic Web, while also a context in which the Semantic Web is utilized to improve blockchain technology itself [13]. Furthermore, Baqa et al., highlighted the fact that although Smart Contracts (SC) are open to the public, it is challenging to discover and utilize such SCs for a wide range of usages since they are compiled in the form of byte-codes without any associated metadata [14]. The latter have motivated the authors to propose the idea of Semantic SC (SSC), a solution that incorporates semantic Web technologies in SCs, which are deployed on the Ethereum Blockchain network, for indexing, searching, and annotating the deployed SCs.

To address the aforementioned challenges and extend the current state-of-the-art, ISLAND focuses on enabling semantic interoperability services for the blockchain technology and beyond. More specifically, ISLAND capitalizes and enhances software blocks brought by enterprises, as background knowledge, to provide a set of tools that would facilitate users to extract pieces of unstructured data from blockchain networks, annotate them with semantic knowledge from Ontologies, and make them interoperable with the use of graph-based formats. Additionally, an innovative idea of the ISLAND framework, lies also in the introduction of the novel Reinforcement Learning algorithm which supports knowledge extraction from large graph sources, based on user requests.

3 Proposed Architecture

ISLAND's high level architecture, which is depicted in Fig. 1, consists of several components. Specifically, it incorporates the crawling and indexing services, the Semantic Annotation Module, the AI Knowledge Extraction Module and the Storage and Retrieval services. These components represent stages of heterogeneous data in the whole blockchain's lifecycle.

Raw data from various data sources are monitored by ISLAND's indexing and crawler services. Such data sources will be: (a) on-chain data (emit events from smart contracts or block data), (b) external data streams (IoT devices) and (c) external linked data (labeled property graphs). ISLANDs Crawling Service will be used in order to retrieve the required information that triggers a contractual agreement in a smart contract. However, because of the expected heterogeneity of the data sources, an extra layer which would act as the abstraction layer between those data sources and the ISLAND network is necessary. This component is depicted and referenced as Connectivity Manager in Fig. 1. The objective of the Connectivity Manager is to streamline the APIs of the heterogeneous data sources into one API for the Indexing Service to use, thus allowing the framework to be agnostic to the wide variety of data sources APIs.

The raw data from various data sources are streamed into the Semantic Annotation Module. These streams are likely to be poor in terms of their semantic annotations and data structure. Depending on the instantiation of the module, and the domain in hand, a Human Annotator "cherry-picks" terms from various vocabularies with different granularity or expressiveness to semantically annotate a sample of the data. In doing so, human annotations from the sample data are used to train a machine learning engine that can recommend future semantic annotations on similar data. At the same time, Human annotators can point ISLAND's Semantic Annotation Module to a set of open knowledge graphs for inferring semantic terms on entities and their attributes that potentially match to their domain of interest. By observing such annotations, the tool will improve its training thus recommending relevant semantic terms that are likely to be closer to the requirements of the user. The result of this process will be the generation of a final graph dataset that is semantically annotated, but not interlinked with external knowledge graphs and stored within the ISLAND's Distributed Database.

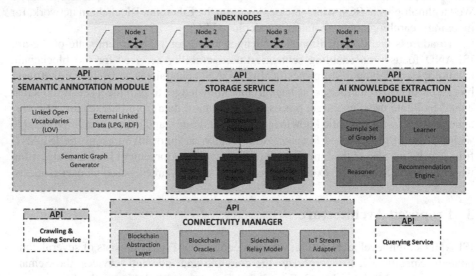

Fig. 1. A high-level view of the proposed architecture.

The ISLAND AI Knowledge Extraction Module (ISLAND AI KEM) uses as input the resulting graphs of the Semantic Annotation Module. Moreover, the objective of the AI KEM is to learn over reasoned, contextual knowledge. To achieve this goal, the AI KEM focuses on reasoning over the semantically annotated knowledge graphs using Reinforcement Learning (RL) and then, all the knowledge libraries and the outcome of these components are stored in the Distributed Databases.

We propose the use of RL, because in the first steps of the ISLAND framework, there will be no abundance of data. Moreover, contrary to current publications, we propose on conducting explicit multi-step path reasoning with knowledge of the decision-making stage. Furthermore, this approach combines recommendations with explainability, as it enables the provision of path data in a knowledge graph. The proposed method solves the great issue that most artificial intelligence algorithms face, which is the problem of explainability [15]. Additionally, because it is predicted that the size of the action area is going to be great in size for some nodes, we propose on using a user-conditional action pruning strategy to reduce this size. In several cases, pruning has shown to increase accuracy, a phenomenon which has been observed in a great number of publications [16, 17]. The selected paths are then sorted according to the reward value and are offered to the user.

Through the Indexing Service, the ISLAND platform is able to "scan" through the unstructured raw data and identify any relationships to better index these records for end-users' benefit. The retrieval of information is accomplished by physically matching keywords in documents with those in a query. Because there are several methods to convey a particular notion, the literal phrases in a users' query may differ from those in a related resource [18]. The Indexing Service, would allow users to retrieve information on the basis of a topic or meaning of the data. Additionally, it will allow to quickly retrieve records from the Storage Service.

The Storage Service of the ISLAND framework would use a stateless semantic graph database for storing the final produced graphs, while keeping data stored in a distributed manner. The final generated graphs should be stored and be available for future use either from the AI KEM or by the Querying Node in order to reply to an outside consumer request. Moreover, ISLAND's Storage service would be also responsible to store sample data (Graphs/Unstructured Data, etc.) in order to be used for learning processes from the AI Learner. Finally, knowledge libraries should also be generated storing the knowledge of the AI Recommendation Engine. Thus, on a future consumer request, the knowledge libraries should be searched in case of an already existing reply.

On top of the Storage Service lies the Querying Service, which provides a seamless way for executing queries over a distributed dataset held by different datastores that provide different interfaces. The connectivity for information retrieval can be facilitated via the use of SPARQL.

4 Smart Manufacturing Use Case Scenario

Nowadays, supply chain environments use IoT devices extensively to monitor the chain. However, in spite of the great variety of industries that they can be applied to, they come with certain challenges, due to their centralized structure [19]. Furthermore, because smart-manufacturing services need to exchange machine-readable properties during their end-to-end life-cycle, a semantic system is necessary.

Logistics interactions are supported by the use of electronic message exchanges, such as RosettaNet PIPs (Partner Interchange Processes) which uses XML Schema technologies, in which applications of Semantic Web technology have been repeatedly proposed [20].

This scenario assumes that a company has incorporated IoT (e.g. cameras, thermostats, etc.) devices to monitor its supply chain. In that case, while IoT manufacturing devices generate unstructured raw data, these will be imported in the ISLAND framework, using the crawling service, collecting data based on selected parameters defined by the Curator. Following, the Indexing Service would scan through the unstructured data to identify any relationships between terms collected and their context, to better index these records. The stored data should be provided to ISLAND Semantic Annotation Module, where using the tools included in this module, events are annotated using previously annotated data coming from the blockchain. Then, ISLAND's AI module is triggered by the new sample of data and is trained for future annotations. In the end, semantically enriched graph representations of the data are extracted (Fig. 2).

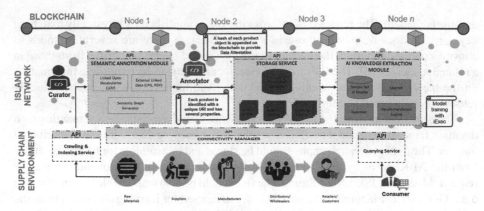

Fig. 2. Detailed view of the ISLAND framework applied in the use case scenario.

5 Potential Business Impact

The first business impact of the proposed approach is on the smart manufacturing domain. Namely, through the proposed framework, companies will be capable of having traceability and analytics for key logistics operations.

According to Gartner, semantic knowledge graphs and ML algorithms are necessary for Supply Chain operations. It is predicted that by 2024, half of the global enterprises will have invested in applications supporting artificial intelligence and analytics [21]. Additionally, blockchain technology is getting a great demand. One-way smart contracts can be used in Supply Chain, is for generating an invoice when a product delivery reaches the destination, thus resulting in an improved and faster process. The ISLAND framework touches on the heart of the problem and the evolution of the supply chain.

In addition, ISLAND aims to create a new real-world economy thus incentivizing users to participate in ISLAND'S ecosystem, to ensure its economic security and integrity of data being queried is a matter of significant importance. To achieve this, we propose the Island Token (ISL), the native token of ISLAND which will be used by all stakeholders, who participate in ISLAND. ISL is envisioned to be the catalyst for diverse new communities to access enriched semantic graph-based data benefiting real use-cases.

6 Conclusions

This paper proposes ISLAND, an interlinked and interoperable semantically-enriched blockchain data framework, that extends the current state-of-the-art, in the context of interoperability and semantically enriched data coming from blockchain networks. Moreover, the ISLAND framework exposes a human-centric interface to data consumers by generating semantically annotated graphs and enabling knowledge extraction operations on the data.

Furthermore, ISLAND offers numerous tangible advantages stemming from this innovative implementation, ranging from data and metadata validation, to straightforward interoperability, and the use of Ontologies and RDF graphs to extract knowledge over different blockchains combined with content external to the blockchain/DLT ecosystem. Additionally, the possible business impacts of such a solution as ISLAND, will offer a unique proposition of Semantic Blockchain with AI, currently in need for various industries and particularly supply chain.

In conclusion, the ISLAND framework envisions a layer of intermediation between the exposed APIs from the participating smart-contract-users and the data consumers. The framework aims to infer meaningful knowledge from smart contracts, while at the same time enabling the semantic interoperability of the data. Finally, this framework offers a fertile layer for marketable interoperable solutions for domains such as healthcare, economy, public services, energy and sustainability, media, entertainment and Industry 4.0.

Finally, the next step in our work is to complete the design and implementation of all the components of the proposed framework, while we aim to streamline and enhance the interfaces between the different components and the entities. What is more, we plan to implement a Proof of Concept which will be evaluated firstly against the presented manufacturing use case. Additionally, the authors envision to further extend and evaluate the presented approach and multiple heterogeneous use cases, towards the creation of a semantically enriched blockchain universe.

Acknowledgments. This work has been partially supported by the ONTOCHAIN project, funded by the European Commission under Grant Agreement H2020-ICT-2020-1, No. 957338 through the Horizon 2020 program (https://ontochain.ngi.eu/).

References

1. Nakamoto, S.: Bitcoin: a peer-to-peer electronic cash system. Decentralized Business Review (2008)
2. Lagutin, D., et al.: Secure open federation of IoT platforms through interledger technologies - the SOFIE approach. In: 2019 European Conference on Networks and Communications, pp. 518–522 (2019)
3. Kapassa, E., Themistocleous, M., Quintanilla, J.R., Touloupos, M., Papadaki, M.: Blockchain in smart energy grids: a market analysis. In: Themistocleous, M., Papadaki, M., Kamal, M.M. (eds.) EMCIS 2020. LNBIP, vol. 402, pp. 113–124. Springer, Cham (2020). https://doi.org/10.1007/978-3-030-63396-7_8
4. Makridakis, S., Christodoulou, K.: Blockchain: current challenges and future prospects/applications. Future Internet **11**, 258 (2019)
5. Lagutin, D., et al.: The SOFIE approach to address the security and privacy of the IoT using interledger technologies. Secur. Priv. Internet Things Challenges Solutions **27**, 76–93 (2020)
6. Ali Syed, T., Alzahrani, A., Jan, S., Siddiqui, M., Nadeem, A., Alghamdi, T.: A comparative analysis of blockchain architecture and its applications: problems and recommendations. IEEE Access **7**, 176838–176869 (2019)
7. Ugarte, H.: A more pragmatic Web 3.0: linked blockchain data, Bonn, Germany (2017)

8. Wu, H., et al.: Data management in supply chain using blockchain: challenges and a case study. In: 28th International Conference on Computer Communication and Networks, pp.1–8 (2019)
9. Mikroyannidis, A., Third, A., Domingue, J.: A case study on the decentralisation of lifelong learning using blockchain technology. J. Interact. Media Educ. **2020**(1), 23 (2020)
10. Belchior, R., Vasconcelos, A., Guerreiro, S., Correia, M.: A survey on blockchain interoperability: past, present, and future trends. ArXiv, abs/2005.14282 (2020)
11. ONTOCHAIN. https://ontochain.ngi.eu. Accessed 24 Mar 2021
12. Ugarte-Rojas, H., Boris, C.: BLONDiE: blockchain ontology with dynamic extensibility. ArXiv, abs/2008.09518 (2020)
13. English, M., Auer, S., Domingue, J.: Blockchain technologies and the semantic web: a framework for symbiotic development. In: Computer Science Conference for University of Bonn Students, pp. 47–61 (2016)
14. Baqa, H., Truong, N., Crespi, N., Lee, G., le Gall, F.: Semantic smart contracts for blockchain-based services in the Internet of Things. In: 2019 IEEE 18th International Symposium on Network Computing and Applications (NCA), pp. 1–5 (2019)
15. Makni, B., Abdelaziz, I., Hendler, J.: Explainable deep RDFS reasoner. ArXiv, abs/2002.03514 (2020)
16. Han, S., Pool, J., Tran, J., Dally, W.: Learning both weights and connections for efficient neural network. ArXiv, abs/1506.02626 (2015)
17. Suzuki, T., et al.: Spectral-pruning: compressing deep neural network via spectral analysis. ArXiv, abs/1808.08558 (2018)
18. Rosario, B.: Latent semantic indexing: an overview. In: INFOSYS, vol. 240, pp. 1–16 (2000)
19. Atlam, H., Alenezi, A., Alassafi, M., Wills, G.: Blockchain with Internet of Things: benefits, challenges, and future directions. Int. J. Intell. Syst. Appl. **10**, 40–48 (2018)
20. Cardoso, J., Bussler, C.: Mapping between heterogeneous XML and OWL transaction representations in B2B integration. Data Knowl. Eng. **70**, 1046–1069 (2011)
21. Gartner Predicts the Future of Supply Chain Technology. https://www.gartner.com/smarterwithgartner/gartner-predicts-the-future-of-supply-chain-technology/. Accessed 24 Mar 2021

Smart Contract for Cross-Border AI Model Management

Petar Kochovski[1], Seungwoo Kum[2], Jaewon Moon[2], Aleks Vujić[1],
and Vlado Stankovski[1(✉)]

[1] Faculty of Computer and Information Science, University of Ljubljana,
Ljubljana, Slovenia
{petar.kochovski,vlado.stankovski}@fri.uni-lj.si
[2] Korea Electronics Technology Institute, Seoul, Korea
{swkum,jwmoon}@keti.re.kr

Abstract. The new wave of Artificial Intelligence (AI) implementation
has made it possible to deploy and (re)use AI models seamlessly. Modern software engineering techniques make it possible to containerize and
orchestrate AI services globally, and across the whole computing continuum from the Cloud to the Edge. However, the data processed by AI
services may be subject to various privacy and governance constraints,
and thus subject to governmental regulations. In this work we present
an advanced Smart Contract that is built to achieve regulatory compliance in cross-border AI model sharing between the European Union and
the Republic of Korea. Key feature of the Smart Contract are specially
developed oracle adapters that are used to achieve fine-grained control
on AI model management.

Keywords: Artificial Intelligence · Cross-border · Data-management ·
Blockchain

1 Introduction

Nowadays, the huge influx of Big Data (variety, velocity, volume and other
aspects of data) requires the deployment and use of Artificial Intelligence (AI)
models at various geolocations in the Internet and across the Cloud to the Edge
computing continuum. The DECENTER project [2] has developed four use case
demonstrators where the Big Data pipeline starts from cameras that provide raw
video streams. The video streams are fed as input to AI methods, and the output
of the AI method takes the form of a structured file with specific information
derived from the video stream, for example, the identity of the person who is seen
in the video stream. By using DECENTER the AI processing models/methods
can be managed globally, so that they can be deployed in computing infrastructures close to the sources of the video streams, which improves the Quality of
Service (QoS) and Quality of Experience (QoE) for the end users.

The DECENTER project investigated a very specific cross-border AI model
and method management scenario which assumes that the described Big Data

K. Tserpes et al. (Eds.): GECON 2021, LNCS 13072, pp. 215–222, 2021.
https://doi.org/10.1007/978-3-030-92916-9_20

pipeline may start at one place (e.g. surveillance camera in Ljubljana, Slovenia), and can proceed through secure Internet channels towards the other processing application stages, which may be implemented in other administrative domains (e.g. private or public Cloud providers in Seoul, Korea). Here, the term "border" in context of our work refers to any administrative, organisational policy or government regulation in which the data stream, data or information file, should pass and under which conditions it must abide to specific policies and regulations, requirements for certification, permissions, including personal permissions and preferences.

The goal of this work is therefore to present our design and implementation of a cross-border data management mechanism that is implemented by using a Smart Contract that allows entities to control the AI model and method transport and management when it comes to their administrative domains. For example, a futuristic European regulation that may require certification from cloud providers when computing or storing sensitive private data. Another futuristic Korean regulation may require to process sensitive data of Korean citizens only on hardware resources that are capable of using hardware-based encryption (e.g. SGX). This paper presents a cross-border data management use case scenario that focuses on management of AI models that are initially stored in a repository, either in European or Korean side. The repository can be used to store sensitive (private) AI models and facilitates a selected AI model to be injected from the repository to a running Docker container. Hence, the cross-border management mechanism manages the movement of the sensitive AI model across regulatory and organisation borders.

The focus of this work is therefore to design mechanisms that can help the multiple parties, such as physical persons with their privacy and security concerns, different public and private organisations and countries impose their requirements for governance of data that moves across multiple borders.

2   Use Case Scenario

A cross-border data management scenario involves various types of data, which may be processed, stored and transported by using different protocols (e.g. TCP or UDP) and formats [6]. For instance, this includes: AI models consisting of biometric data, video streams' data that originates from surveillance cameras, owned by a private or public entity, video frames stored as files and used as evidence or other sensor streams.

Our cross-border data management scenario (see Fig. 1) assumes a use case when an EU citizen (e.g. person named John) travels to Korea. The biometric model to verify John is stored in a secure repository in the EU. To protect his privacy, he decides to use the model that is split into two parts. The inference done in the front part of the AI model is computationally less intense to compute and can be deployed in an edge near the site. The inference in the rear part of the AI model is computationally more intense and should be computed in a fog infrastructure. However, to avoid network high latency, both parts of the AI model will have to be deployed in Korea.

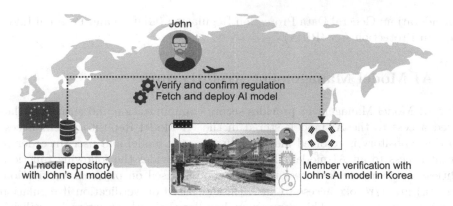

Fig. 1. Cross-border data management scenario.

At a construction site entrance in Korea, which John is visiting, a video camera will record John's face and perform member verification. Therefore, the construction site needs to deploy the AI method which uses John's biometric model for person identification. While doing so, John wants to make sure that the EU privacy regulations (i.e. GDPR) are respected. To further reduce the possibility of leaking private information, it is also necessary to deploy the model on certified infrastructure providers that use special-purpose hardware, such as Intel SGX, to process the data in a secure enclave.

In such scenario it is necessary to assure the ability to govern the data transported by all concerned participants and actors, such as: the owner of the AI models, owner of video stream data, the cloud and fog computing providers. Also it is necessary to meet the user preferences whose private data is being transported and processed from one place to another, and last, but, not the least, the laws and legislations of the states involved in the data pipeline. Though, this is a very challenging task, this paper will present a practical solution that was designed within the DECENTER project. For instance, physical persons, organisations and countries must establish trust that all data management and data movement can happen only if all requirements are fulfilled, including governmental legislations and regulations, organisational policies and personal permissions. From a technical viewpoint trust can be described with some probability, however, the trust management approach employed by the Fog Computing Platform should rely on binary decisions: trusted or not trusted. Therefore, it is a hard requirement that must be fulfilled in specific circumstances that makes it possible to manage data across administrative and country borders.

Nowadays, plethora of regulations and standards exist in the context of data collection, processing and storage. They propose rules related to: (i) data set collection, processing or generation, (ii) data management life cycle; (iii) methodology and standards in the context of the collected, processed or generated types of data; (iv) means and conditions for data sharing; and (v) means for data preservation. In the scope of our work, two main regulations were taken into consideration: General Data Protection Regulation (GDPR) and Personal Information Protection Act (PIPA).

3   AI Model Management Architecture

The AI Model Management provides secure communication and ensures authorised access to the AI models stored in the AI Model Repository. The access to the repository is resolved individually per each model and user. In order to grant access to an AI model, this component provides the following functionalities: (i) grant/revoke access to an AI model based on payment verification, and (ii) grant/revoke access to an AI model based on verification if regulation requirements are met. This component handles the authentication by utilising Smart Contracts, and it is able to intercept events emitted from the Smart Contracts that belong to the repository. The AI Model (Data) Management architecture (see Fig. 2) is composed of five components: Trusted Model Manager, Data Management, AI Model Repository, Blockchain Service and Smart Oracle. This component is a part of the DECENTER Fog and Brokerage Platform, hence it exploits the platform's resource orchestration mechanisms.

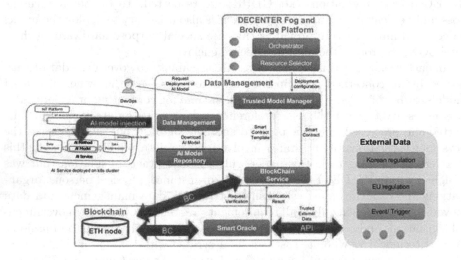

Fig. 2. Cross-border data management architecture.

Trusted Model Manager is the interface between the end user and the rest of the data management services. It collects input from the user that includes the URI of the target AI Model Repository and the query for a particular AI model. Moreover, it also can communicate with the user's digital wallet, meaning that the user is able to pay for the use of the model, pay the transaction fee and trigger other smart contract functions.

AI Model Repository is an off-chain storage, registry and API service that stores AI models and associated metadata. Typically, many independent AI Model Repositories could coexist, each containing their own set of AI models, which will require maintaining a list of the repositories. However, this version utilises only one repository, hence the sole responsibility of the user to provide a URI of an AI Model Repository to the Trusted Model Manager.

Blockchain Service facilitates the interaction between the Trusted Model Manager and the blockchain components (i.e. Smart Contracts and Smart Oracles), by providing an interface between the Ethereum blockchain network [3] and the data management modules. This service allows specific Smart Contract functions to be triggered and it also allows fetching trustworthy data through the Smart Oracles. Upon successful execution of the Smart Contract transactions, the fetching of the AI model from the AI model repository, as well as its deployment are initiated.

Smart Oracles are providers of external data to the Smart Contracts [4]. In a failure-tolerant setup, oracles form their own network and consist of the on-chain and the off-chain part. The on-chain part resides on the Blockchain and communicates with the user's Smart Contracts. In our data management scenario, the Smart Oracles, which are based on Chainlink [1], are used to: (i) ask for the conformance of the deployment configuration, (ii) ask for the conformance to use of AI model and the data flows with regulations of all the relevant regions, (iii) be asked to obtain end users' consent if a regulator requires so and if the list of the end users in question is known in advance.

External Data represents a collection of external data providers, which are in our context denoted as regulators that prescribe the use, processing and storage of private data, and the exchange of data across borders. While regulators do exist in reality, to the best of our knowledge they do not offer (yet) an API to be used for automated verification purposes; therefore, for our needs, regulators are implemented as simple standalone services.

4 AI Model Repository

Based on the DECENTER use cases' requirements, sensitive AI models represent an important part of the whole system. Hence, mechanisms for (i) storing AI models in repository, (ii) providing basis for data management operations (e.g. injection of AI models into running AI applications), (iii) injecting AI models at container runtime, are of highest importance [5]. This section will reveal details about the AI model repository design and implementation.

Instead of constantly building AI from scratch, with the AI model repository we focus on delivering AI from the cloud to the edge in an efficient manner. Furthermore, to maintain high level of security and safety, the access to the AI repository is managed through transparent and traceable blockchain operations. Hence, an AI model from the repository can be made available only upon successful execution of a smart contract transaction on the Blockchain. We propose to separate the AI model delivery from the AI microservice container. Hence, instead of storing AI model in a container for deployment, a container without AI model should be deployed onto the computing resources, whilst the AI model will be deployed later during runtime by fetching it from a AI model repository. Such separation of AI model delivery and container delivery gives the following benefits on resource utilization: (i) increase AI container reusability by enabling it to be used on the Edge with different AI models, (ii) optimize the network performance for the microservice by only delivering the container and specified model to the Edge. The proposed repository takes into account that a containerized AI method that is being deployed on the Edge does not include a static main AI model. The developers can register their model and the system can manage a variety of models based on the pre-defined structure. The AI application with partial AI model can be in conjunction with other edge's corresponding application. Therefore, this repository is designed to properly save and deliverer the AI model to the Edge. The repository structure is composed of information such as model name, version, whether it is partitioned or not, and the number of the partition. Figure 3 shows the stored structure of several variants of a modified AI model called VGG16.

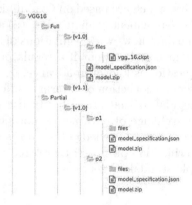

Fig. 3. Example of the AI model repository structure for VGG16 model.

5   Using the Cross-Border AI Model Management Application

The workflow of the cross-border data management is composed of 9 consecutive steps. The overall workflow is depicted in Fig. 1 and Fig. 2 and the graphical user interface of the cross-border AI model management application is shown in Fig. 4. The workflow steps are as follows: (i) Using application's GUI, the user gives consent for his personal data (i.e., AI model composed of his biometric data) to be used for a specific period by secure processing infrastructures after his arrival at the construction site in Korea; (ii) After the given consent, the application triggers a Smart Contract function that through the EU regulation Smart Oracle verifies

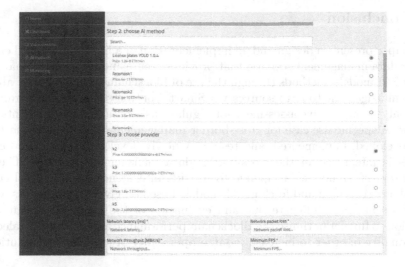

Fig. 4. Graphical user interface of the cross-border data management application.

the existence of the required data in the EU repositories; and registers the given consent on the Blockchain. The immutable consent log contains information about the data owner, data storage, data processor and the duration of the given consent; (iii) Upon arrival in Korea, John's data must be deployed on secure computing infrastructure in Korea. The construction company provides/sends John's wallet address to its application service provider to verify his consent on the Blockchain. (iv) The application service provider uses the DECENTER Fog platform to compose the application where the QoS parameters, provided by the construction company, are selected. The application requires specially crafted container for the AI model to be fetched from the AI repositories in EU at runtime; (v) DECENTER Fog and Brokerage platform components estimate a possible deployment from the pool of trusted Fog nodes in Korea, after which it passes over the deployment plan to the Data Management Module. (vi) Data Management Module grants access based on data accessed through the Smart Oracles: fulfilled EU regulations, fulfilled Korean regulations, permissions of the AI model owner – the physical person whose AI model is to be transferred; (vii) When selecting the target AI model, the application service provider has to pay the predetermined amount of tokens from its public wallet for the usage of the model; (viii) Once the transaction is confirmed, the Smart Contract locks the received tokens and allows access to the requested AI model and returns an API key for the retrieval of the AI model; (ix) The application manifest (in the form of an SLA) is handed to the infrastructure and John's biometric data will be available to the construction site throughout his stay in Korea. For the purposes of the implementation and evaluation, the application was containerized in Docker containers, whilst the blockchain transactions were executed on the Kovan testnet through 5 test nodes that were setup on our premises.

6 Conclusion

This paper presents a design and an implementation of a blockchain-based cross-border data management scenario that provides secure and trustworthy management of AI models/methods through the use of blockchain technologies. It allows access management to data sources via Smart Contracts that execute transactions only upon positive assessment for regulations' and users' requirements fulfilment. A specific use case for cross-border management of AI models/methods was developed, implemented, and tested. A newly developed repository for AI models is integrated in the cross-border data management scenario. The AI model repository acts as a pipeline to provide intelligence on individual edges that allows searching and fetching AI-models based on given requirements. Currently, we are performing testing and evaluation of the proposed design with intention to further optimise the Blockchain performance and provide intraledger functionality in order to increase the interoperability of the proposed solution.

Acknowledgements. The research and development reported in this paper have received funding from the European Union's Horizon 2020 Research and Innovation Programme under grant agreement no. 815141 (DECENTER: Decentralised technologies for orchestrated Cloud-to-Edge intelligence) and grant agreement no. 957338 (ONTOCHAIN: Trusted, traceable and transparent ontological knowledge on blockchain).

References

1. Blockchain oracles for hybrid smart contracts: Chainlink. https://chain.link/. Accessed 15 July 2021
2. Decentralised technologies for orchestrated cloud-to-edge intelligence: Decenter. https://www.decenter-project.eu/. Accessed 15 July 2021
3. Buterin, V., et al.: Ethereum white paper. GitHub Reposit. **1**, 22–23 (2013)
4. Kochovski, P., Gec, S., Stankovski, V., Bajec, M., Drobintsev, P.D.: Trust management in a blockchain based fog computing platform with trustless smart oracles. Future Gener. Comput. Syst. **101**, 747–759 (2019)
5. Moon, J., Kum, S., Kim, Y., Stankovski, V., Paśćinsk, U., Kochovski, P.: A decentralized AI data management system in federated learning. In: 2020 International Conference on Intelligent Systems and Computer Vision (ISCV), pp. 1–4. IEEE (2020)
6. Pepper, R., Garrity, J., LaSalle, C.: Cross-border data flows, digital innovation, and economic growth. Global Inf. Technol. Rep. **2016**, 39–47 (2016)

A Distributed Graph Data Storage in Ethereum Ecosystem

Dominik Tomaszuk[1,2], Dominik Kuziński[2], Mirek Sopek[2]([✉]),
and Bogusław Swiecicki[2]

[1] University of Bialystok, Institute of Computer Science, Bialystok, Poland
[2] MakoLab SA, Ogrodowa 8, 91-062 Lodz, Poland
sopek@makolab.com

Abstract. GraphChain – a framework for on-chain data management for Blockchains is presented. The framework forms the foundational technology for the Ontochain project offering the synergy between ontologies and the Blockchain mechanisms. The use of Ethereum based Layer-2 mechanisms helped create the idea of Ontospace, which designates an ecosystem for trusted ontologies and trusted processing of smart contracts that can directly use the semantic data.

Keywords: Blockchain · Graph data · Demantic data · RDF-star · Ontochain

1 Introduction

From the beginning of the Semantic Web, the awareness of the need for trust for data stored in the semantic data pools was strong. The original, famous Semantic Web Layer cake depicted a trust layer high on the stack. The birth of Blockchain technology enabled the addition of that layer in an entirely new way. However, there is a technological problem of storing data in formats typical for semantic technologies on the chain. This problem stems from the specific requirements for the structure of the Blockchain's blocks, so the only universal mechanism could be a kind of encapsulation. Such a solution, even if is theoretically possible, yields an inefficient storage system without any query mechanisms.

This paper describes our contribution to resolving that problem: GraphChain – a framework for on-chain data management for Blockchains. The framework forms the foundational technology for the Ontochain project by directly addressing the basic technological proposition of the project, i.e., the synergy between ontologies and the Blockchain mechanisms.

Supported by Ontochain (European Union's Horizon 2020 research and innovation programme under grant agreement No 957338), and its subprogramme *GraphChain – a framework for on-chain data management for Ontochain* under grant agreement No. 1477973.

K. Tserpes et al. (Eds.): GECON 2021, LNCS 13072, pp. 223–231, 2021.
https://doi.org/10.1007/978-3-030-92916-9_21

It allows to store the data in the native semantic formats. Thanks to its architecture, the fundamental features of data integrity, confirmability, non-repudiation, and high availability are guaranteed. Creating, storing, and working with ontologies, managing data related to digital identification, or data used by Knowledge Graphs is in demand in today's digital world. The data must be available across the entire network without the degradation of performance or universality of search. Our main contribution was to propose a radically different approach to achieve these goals – instead of encapsulating the semantic data into Blockchain blocks or using any external storage, GraphChain implements the Blockchain mechanisms on top of semantic data. GraphChain is usually delivered through an integrated installation of Blockchain nodes and a graph database. It was first delivered to the LEI.INFO portal[1] where the Blockchain nodes were based on Hyperledger Indy [1] and the graph database was Blazegraph[2]. In the most recent work, the Blockchain mechanisms used are those of Ethereum. This design choice allowed to creation of the concept of Ontospace, which designates an ecosystem of trusted semantic data pools with a smart-contract programming layer capable of using semantic data. As of the writing of this paper, the work is in progress. When finally delivered, it will be distributed using containerization technology, for example, as a Docker image[3].

The paper is organized as follows. In Sect. 2, we describe our approach. Section 3 presents a use case. In Sect. 4, we discuss related work. Finally, in Sect. 5, we summarize our findings and outline further research directions.

2   GraphChain 2.0 Architecture

In the big picture, we envision Ontochain as an ecosystem of several different blockchains all linked and pegged to the main chain of the system. We call that ecosystem *ontospace*. In our ecosystem, the core element is an *ontonode*, which is a single *ontoSidechain* node. The general idea of ontonode operation is similar to every blockchain network. The blockchain nodes process transactions and achieve consensus over data that represent them. The difference is that in parallel to the creation of new blocks in the Blockchains chain, the chain of named RDF-star graphs is created according to the GraphChain 1.0 specification [11]. More details are presented in Table 1 and Table 2. In the first table, we show terms from the Semantic Web area, while in the second table, we present terms from the Blockchain field and concepts that we use in the paper. The ontonode architecture is presented in Fig. 1.

2.1   Ontopod

Ontopod is one of the most important sub-elements of Ontonode. It is an RDF-star compliant graph database that stores all named graphs protected and distributed by blockchain network. GraphChain is neutral to the choice of a graph

---

[1] https://lei.info.
[2] https://blazegraph.com/.
[3] https://docs.docker.com/.

Table 1. Definitions of semantic web technology.

Concept	Description
RDF-star triple	An ordered set of subject, predicate, and object. In the subject and object position may be IRI, blank node, or nested triple. Only the IRI reference can be in the predicate position
RDF-star graph	An unordered set of RDF-star triples. Note that any RDF graph [13] is also an RDF-star graph, and any named RDF-star graph is also a named RDF graph
Named RDF-star graph	An RDF-star graph that is assigned a name in the form of an IRI

Table 2. Definitions of blockchain technology.

Concept	Description
Layer 2 protocol	It allows transactions between users through the exchange of authenticated messages via a medium that is outside of but tethered to, a layer-one Blockchain
Ontopod	It is a part of Ontonode responsible for handing semantic data chains of named RDF graphs
Ontoshell	A software module for external communication for Ontonode (API and Linked Data HTTP)
Ontonode	A single node of ontoSidechain. If the ontoSidechain is compliant with GraphChain concept, Ontonode contains Blockchain node, Ontopod and Ontoshell
OntoSidechain	A single Blockchain of Layer-2 sidechain type. It may have both Blockchain and semantic software modules but can also be a generic sidechain
Ontospace	An entire ecosystem of Blockchains and the semantic data pools

database engine. There is nothing in its architecture that requires a specific triplestore for its operations. The key cryptographic algorithms (Intervowen DotHash for RDF and Interwoven DotHash in the Stars for RDF-star) are, by design, independent from the choice of the triple store.

Our choice as an RDF-star triplestore is the Blazegraph database[4]. It is a high-performance graph database supporting Blueprints and RDF/SPARQL APIs that stands behind Wikidata[5], a knowledge base that acts as central storage for the structured data of its Wikimedia sister projects, including Wikipedia, Wikivoyage, Wiktionary, Wikisource, and others. Our decision to choose Blazegraph for the implementation of Ontopod is motivated by its features (RDF-star

---

[4] https://blazegraph.com/.
[5] https://www.wikidata.org/.

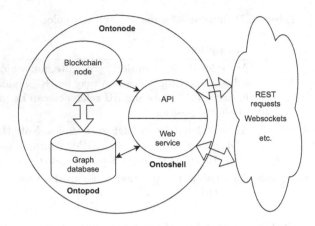

Fig. 1. GraphChain node architecture.

support, internal and external full-text search, and Linked Data support) and the open-source Java code, which is important from the perspective of the choice of Besu (also written in Java) as an Ethereum client.

Although Blazegraph can support up to 12.7B RDF/RDF-star triples on a single machine [10], as was stated earlier, Graphchain is triplestore agnostic; therefore, if in some production environment there was a need for a more powerful database, there are no obstacles in Graphchain infrastructure design to do so.

2.2 Ontoshell

Another important sub-element of ontonode is *Ontoshell* that is a set of endpoints and interfaces. It is a crucial component because all blockchain interactions, which are not internal, work on this layer. Ontoshell literally functions as a shell hiding both blockchain node and Ontopod from external access. It processes all requests and is responsible for dispatching queries to Ontopod and executing methods in deployed smart contracts.

The most standard way of interaction with Ontonode is through REST API. In this particular case, we decided to model our interface on SPARQL 1.1 Graph Store HTTP Protocol [8]. It is a list of HTTP verbs and the way they should be interpreted when interacting with a graph store. Since Graphchain's main piece of data is a named RDF-star graph, this standard is well suited for Graphchain basic operations like reading and writing graphs.

Besides REST, we provide another API standard, GraphQL [6]. GraphQL is a query language for APIs and a runtime for fulfilling those queries with existing data. GraphQL provides a complete and understandable description of the data in an API, gives clients the power to ask for exactly what they need and makes it easier to evolve APIs over time. GraphQL starts with building a schema, which is a description of all the queries one can possibly make in a GraphQL API, and all the types that they return. Schema-building is done in the strongly-typed Schema

Definition Language (SDL) [5]. Thanks to that, schema GraphQL publishes in advance what it can do, which improves its discoverability. By pointing a client at the GraphQL API, one can find out what queries are available.

GraphQL schema can also be used for describing RDF structures, even ontologies which make it almost perfect in Ontochain context where every project is dealing with semantic data one way or another. To further simplify this GraphQL and RDF synergy, there are projects like GraphQL-LD [12], which is a method for transforming GraphQL queries coupled with a JSON-LD context to SPARQL, and a method for converting SPARQL results to the GraphQL query-compatible response. GraphQL also offers subcribers real-time notifications from the server. This feature is of high importance in a distributed environment, where different nodes can be in a slightly different state due to the consensus mechanism. GraphQL subscriptions make it easy to notify users when a node is in a synchronized state and safe to consume data from it.

3   Ontohub as a Use Case

To present the proposed solution most clearly, we decided to describe the distributed ontology repository, called in the adopted nomenclature as OntoHub, that could be deployed in the ontospace ecosystem.

It is worth noting that our choice to use ontologies as a use case has nothing to do with the underlying technology of Graphchain. Graphchain is a distributed graph database and can handle instance data in the same way it handles ontologies.

While it is possible to store ontologies on any OntoSidechain of the project, there should exist a single, unique chain in the Ontospace ecosystem that is by design dedicated to the storage of the most important ontologies of the project. It is also important because the IRI schemes combined with Linked Data Principles [2] demand that dereferencing of the IRIs is based on the facts that they are proper URLs, that they must be resolved to some existing web server, and deliver useful responses.

OntoHub is a single point of access to a GraphChain platform serving as a distributed repository for ontologies. From the perspective of a regular user, it works just like a normal ontology publish platform. It has a SPARQL endpoint [4], a search, and an API service. On the backend, it is connected to multiple nodes in GraphChain sidechain and serves as a load balancer for queries and API calls. It is also connected to the main chain of Ontochain infrastructure.

However, the distinct feature of OntoHub architecture is related to the distributed storage for Ontologies. We assume that every Ontonode keeps the identical semantic graph in its Ontopods. The main web server of the OntoHub works as a load balancing reverse proxy server. For enhanced security, the main web server will check and compute the hash for every subgraph being served and compare it with the hash stored on the Blockchain. A diagram presented in Fig. 2 shows the design of an OntoHub, a unique chain in the ontospace ecosystem design to the storage of the most important project ontologies.

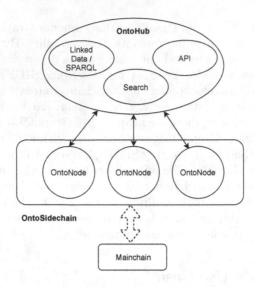

Fig. 2. Ontohub architecture.

OntoHub users can be divided into four general groups: (1) ontology creators/publishers, (2) ontology consumers/clients, (3) system administrators, and (4) node owners. Ontology creators can upload new ontologies, update existing ones (with versioning, previous versions could still be available), view and possibly delete their uploads. Consumers can search for ontologies by terms, dates, authors, etc. They can also verify their integrity. System administrators usually have tasks of creating users, groups, and roles. People or organizations that want to be a node owner in OntoHub may register as one, download a Docker image with node infrastructure, and become part of the OntoHub network. The use case diagram is presented in Fig. 3.

4   Related Work

Blockchain Technologies. Layer 2 is a collective term for solutions designed to help scale applications by handling transactions off the main chain (layer 1). Transaction speed suffers when the network is busy, which can make the user experience poor for certain types of distributed applications. And, as the network gets busier, prices increase as transaction senders aim to outbid each other. This can make using blockchain very expensive.

Most layer 2 solutions are centered around a server or cluster of servers, each of which may be referred to as a node, validator, operator, sequencer, block producer, or similar term. Depending on the implementation, these layer 2 nodes may be run by the businesses or entities that use them, by a 3rd party operator, or by a large group of individuals.

Ethereum platform [3] offers multiple types of Layer 2 implementations [9,14–16]. The first proposal is AZTEC [16], which defines a set of zero-knowledge

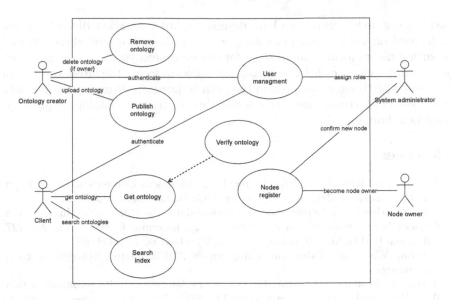

Fig. 3. Ontohub use cases.

proofs that determine a confidential transaction protocol, designed for use within blockchain protocols that support Turing-complete general-purpose computation. Another approach is Loopring [15] that runs as a public set of smart contracts responsible for trade and settlement, with an off-chain group of agents aggregating and communicating orders. Yet another proposal is Zecale [9] which is a general-purpose proof aggregator that uses a recursive composition of small arguments. Another one is Hermes [14], which is a platform for trading sensor data, using distributed ledgers as intermediaries to add safeguards against malicious behavior.

Graph Databases. We assume the use of graph databases at every blockchain node that participates in the semantic graph replication. There are several RDF-star databases (so called triplestore) that also support ontologies [7], i.e., AllegroGraph, AnzoGraph, Blazegraph, GraphDB, Stardog, etc.

RDF-star extends RDF to include edge annotations. This allows compatibility with the property graph model. A property graph is a type of graph model where edges (sometimes called relationships) not only are connections, but also carry a name and some properties. The property graph model is the most common data model in graph databases. This data model has a lot of implementations, e.g., Neo4j, Microsoft Cosmos DB, OrientDB, JanusGraph, etc.

5   Conclusions

We have presented the idea of a distributed graph data storage for the Ethereum ecosystem. By applying the GraphChain architecture in synergy with Ethereum based Layer-2 architectures, we have designed a 3rd generation Blockchain system focused on storing and processing semantic data. We have demonstrated how such a design forms a foundation for the entire ecosystem of trusted, intelligent data, which we called Ontospace. By allowing to use the latest variants of RDF format (RDF-star), we opened the path to integrate Property Graphs into the ecosystem. A crucial use case – a distributed, trusted Ontology repository, named Ontohub, has also been described.

References

1. Aggarwal, S., Kumar, N.: Hyperledger. In: Advances in Computers, vol. 121, pp. 323–343. Elsevier (2021). https://doi.org/10.1016/bs.adcom.2020.08.016
2. Bizer, C., Heath, T., Berners-Lee, T.: Linked data: the story so far. In: Semantic Services, Interoperability and Web Applications: Emerging Concepts, pp. 205–227. IGI global (2011). https://doi.org/10.4018/978-1-60960-593-3.ch008
3. Buterin, V., et al.: Ethereum white paper (2013). https://ethereum.org/en/whitepaper/
4. Harris, S., Seaborne, A.: SPARQL 1.1 query language. W3C recommendation, W3C (Mar 2013). https://www.w3.org/TR/2013/REC-sparql11-query-20130321/
5. Hartig, O., Hidders, J.: Defining schemas for property graphs by using the GraphQL schema definition language. In: Proceedings of the 2nd Joint Workshop on Graph Data Management Experiences and Systems and Network Data Analytics, pp. 1–11 (2019). https://doi.org/10.1145/3327964.3328495
6. Hartig, O., Pérez, J.: Semantics and complexity of GraphQL. In: Proceedings of the 2018 World Wide Web Conference, pp. 1155–1164 (2018). https://doi.org/10.1145/3178876.3186014
7. Kasenchak, B., Lehnert, A., Loh, G.: Use case: ontologies and RDF-star for knowledge management. In: European Semantic Web Conference, pp. 254–260. Springer (2021). https://doi.org/10.1007/978-3-030-80418-3_38
8. Ogbuji, C.: SPARQL 1.1 graph store HTTP protocol. W3C recommendation, W3C (Mar 2013). https://www.w3.org/TR/2013/REC-sparql11-http-rdf-update-20130321/
9. Rondelet, A.: Zecale: reconciling privacy and scalability on ethereum. arXiv preprint arXiv:2008.05958 (2020)
10. Salehpour, M., Davis, J.G.: A comparative analysis of knowledge graph query performance. arXiv preprint arXiv:2004.05648 (2020)
11. Sopek, M., Gradzki, P., Kosowski, W., Kuziski, D., Trójczak, R., Trypuz, R.: GraphChain: a distributed database with explicit semantics and chained RDF graphs. In: Companion Proceedings of the Web Conference 2018, pp. 1171–1178 (2018). https://doi.org/10.1145/3184558.3191554
12. Taelman, R., Vander Sande, M., Verborgh, R.: GraphQL-LD: linked data querying with GraphQL. In: ISWC2018, The 17th International Semantic Web Conference, pp. 1–4 (2018)
13. Tomaszuk, D., Hyland-Wood, D.: RDF 1.1: knowledge representation and data integration language for the web. Symmetry 12(1), 84 (2020). https://doi.org/10.3390/sym12010084
14. Tzianos, P., Pipelidis, G., Tsiamitros, N.: Hermes: an open and transparent marketplace for IoT sensor data over distributed ledgers. In: 2019 IEEE International Conference on Blockchain and Cryptocurrency (ICBC), pp. 167–170. IEEE (2019). https://doi.org/10.1109/BLOC.2019.8751331

15. Wang, D., Zhou, J., Wang, A., Finestone, M.: Loopring: a decentralized token exchange protocol (2018). https://github.com/Loopring/whitepaper/blob/master/en_whitepaper.pdf
16. Williamson, Z.J.: The aztec protocol (2018). https://github.com/AztecProtocol/AZTEC

Author Index

Printed in the United States
by Baker & Taylor Publisher Services

Printed in the United States
by Baker & Taylor Publisher Services